1866 - 1991

125th

ANNIVERSARY

RICE,

the Amazing Grain

RICE,
the Amazing Grain

Great Rice Dishes for Every Day

MARIE SIMMONS

Henry Holt and Company
New York

Published by Henry Holt and Company, Inc., 115 West 18th Street, New York, New York 10011.
Published in Canada by Fitzhenry & Whiteside Limited, 195 Allstate Parkway, Markham, Ontario L3R 4T8.

Library of Congress Cataloging-in-Publication Data
Simmons, Marie.
Rice, the amazing grain : great rice dishes for every day
Marie Simmons.— 1st ed.
p.   cm.
Includes bibliographical references and index.
1. Cookery (Rice)   2. Rice.   I. Title.
TX809.R5S47   1991

641.6'318—dc20   91-501
                                                                   CIP

ISBN 0-8050-1371-7 (alk. paper)

Henry Holt books are available at special discounts for bulk purchases for sales promotions,
premiums, fund-raising, or educational use. Special editions
or book excerpts can also be created to specification.
For details contact: Special Sales Director, Henry Holt and Company, Inc.,
115 West 18th Street, New York, New York 10011.

FIRST EDITION—1991

Book Design by Claire Naylon Vaccaro

Title page illustration by Ted Lewin
Interior illustrations by Madeline Sorel

Printed in the United States of America
Recognizing the importance of preserving the written word, Henry Holt and Company, Inc.,
by policy, prints all of its first editions on acid-free paper. ∞

1   3   5   7   9   10   8   6   4   2

The following recipes, some with adaptations and changes, are reprinted from "Wild
and Wonderful Rice" by Marie Simmons in the February 1, 1990, issue of Family Circle
magazine, copyright © 1990 THE FAMILY CIRCLE, INC.: Asparagus and Rice Salad
with Lemon Dressing; Mushroom, Beef, and Brown Rice Soup; Brown Rice and
Broccoli Salad with Lemon Dressing and Tamari Walnuts; Chicken Biryani; Creamy
Rice Pudding with Mangoes and Pistachios; Pilaf with Curry, Raisins, and Almonds;
Chinese Rice Soup with Egg Threads; Brown Rice with Onions, Garlic, and Walnuts.

Every effort has been made to locate and secure permission from the copyright holders
of the short poem on page xiii, which appeared in Food, by A. L. Simon, published by
Burke Publishing Company, 1949.

For the women in my life:
Nana, Mom, and Stephanie

CONTENTS

ACKNOWLEDGMENTS

I wish to thank Bill Goldsmith and Kristen O'Brien of the USA Rice Council, with an extra word of gratitude to Kris for patiently finding answers to my many questions and for being there every time I needed her. I am grateful to Gloria Spitz and Meghan Flynn of Burson-Marsteller for their help and advice. Special thanks to Dr. B. D. Webb, U. S. Department of Agriculture's Agricultural Research Center in Beaumont, Texas; David Kay, plant manager at American Rice, Inc., Freeport, Texas; Mark Denman at RiceTec, Inc., in Alvin, Texas; Darrow Gibbs, of Gibbs Wild Rice, for sharing his extensive knowledge of the wild rice industry with me; and Bill Dishman, Jr., of the Dishman Farms in China, Texas, for giving me a ride on his harvester.

Thank you to Harlan Lundberg and the Lundberg Family Farms in Richvale, California, for a memorable afternoon of rice talk enhanced by shimmering fields of rice and a brilliant blue sky, and for giving a city girl a chance to feel cool paddy mud between her toes and around her ankles; and to Dr. Kent McKenzie, plant breeder at the California Cooperative Rice Research Foundation, Inc., in Biggs, California, for graciously greeting my unannounced visit and sharing his experiences as a rice plant breeder.

I am delighted to finally say thank you in print to my friendly neighborhood grocer, Stewart Goldstein, who has managed to stock the rice section in his small Brooklyn store so that it is now stiff competition for the fanciest food shops across the bridge. Hearing the panic in my voice, he has delivered (to my doorstep) a box of rice—or a quart of olive oil—at a moment's notice.

And last, gratitude without measure goes to John, my husband and best friend, who managed to eat his way through hundreds of rice dishes and still ask for more; Stephanie, our daughter, who once told me I should write a rice cookbook; Susan Herner, for believing in me; and Elizabeth Crossman, an absolutely wonderful editor, for believing in this book.

PREFACE

Originally I imagined this as a book about rice, but along the way it became a rice cookbook. One could say that the research made me hungry for the subject, and in a way this is true. My real love is cooking.

Although I have included many recipes for classic rice dishes, they are here because they reflect the way I like to cook, not because they happen to be rice dishes. I decided early in this cookbook that it was presumptuous of me to attempt to mimic every rice dish in existence worldwide. It would also be slightly dishonest; I have a very well defined cooking style and am not capable of forcing my cooking into a mold that just doesn't fit. Being a child of a matriarchal family of Italian cooks, I often gravitate toward the Mediterranean when I cook. The subject of this book may be generic, but the recipes all come from the heart. I am now happy to emerge from behind a mountain of books, don my apron, and find comfort in my kitchen.

How nice
Is rice!

How gentle and how very free from vice
Are those whose fodder is mainly Rice.

Yes: Rice! Rice!
Beautiful Rice!
All the wrong in the world would be right in a trice
If everyone fed upon nothing but Rice.

INTRODUCTION

The Story of Rice

Rice Is More Than a Grain

In New York and Tokyo I have sat on a mat of woven rice straw called a tatami, drunk beer or sake, both brewed from rice, and eaten a dish of rice seasoned with rice vinegar and topped with strips of beef from cattle raised on a diet of rice bran.

In California I have seen rice hulls destined for the local power company where they will be burned to provide energy. I have worn leather shoes made supple with rice oil and a blouse cut from a synthetic fiber made from a rice hull product called furfural. At home I have walked in a flower garden growing in soil fertilized with rice hulls and started the day with spoonfuls of warm cooked rice cereal or a bowl of cold crispy rice cereal swimming in milk.

Rice, a staple food for more than half of the earth's population, is an amazing grain.

How Rice Grows

Little rice seedlings are reverently hand-planted in a small backyard paddy in Kyoto, Japan. Space-age technology computers, lasers, and airplanes are used to prepare the soil and sow the rice seeds on large farms in eastern Texas. Both ways, rice will still miraculously emerge from its meadowlike sea, transforming the dark glassy surface of the paddy into a shimmering chartreuse blanket. As the seedlings mature, they draw nutrients from the paddy water, the same water that keeps the weed population under control. Eventually small green flowers take shape and the wind pollinates the plants. The paddies of rice change from green to golden yellow to the familiar pale honey color of parched straw.

The levees are opened, the water is drained, and the soil is given time to set. In the United States, where the rice industry is thoroughly mechanized, a giant combine with an air-conditioned cab for the operator rolls across the field, cutting the plants and separating the rough or paddy rice from the straw. The rough rice is transported to enormous dryers where the moisture content is reduced. The rice is now ready for milling.

The milling process, although it can be extremely high-tech and efficient, is really very simple. Except for converted or parboiled rice, which is steam-pressure treated first, the milling process consists of simply removing the inedible hull from the rice. The hull is removed in a sheller, which is basically two rubber rollers that remove the hulls by friction. The result is brown rice, or rice with the bran layers still intact. The bran is removed from the brown rice by abrasion as the grains are forced to rub against one another. Broken grains are sorted out as the rice is sifted through a series of screens. In the most sophisticated of mills a laser scanner spots discolored kernels and almost simultaneously manages to blast them aside with a stream of pressurized air.

The rice is now ready for market.

Rice Facts and History

In Burma a person eats 500 pounds of rice a year, an astonishing figure when it is reduced to a daily consumption of 1¼ pounds per day, but perhaps not so astonishing when you consider that Burma is in the middle of land where rice cultivation most likely originated thousands of years ago. Radiocarbon dating of strata containing grains of rice found in south China indicate that rice was cultivated as far back as seven thousand years ago. Researchers claim that rice may have been indigenous to India and then moved eastward to Indochina and Southeast Asia.

There are literally thousands, perhaps as many as forty thousand, varieties of rice grown on every continent except Antarctica. China, India, Indonesia, Thailand, Vietnam, and Burma are the biggest rice producers in the world. Japan, also a large rice producer, consumes all the rice it grows and is unique because it is the only country that forbids importation of foreign grown rice. Brazil is the largest rice producer in South America; Australia grows rice and so does Nigeria.

In Europe rice is grown primarily in Portugal, Spain, and Italy with very minute quantities produced in France. But Europe grows very little rice compared to the rest of the world. Italy produces the most rice on the continent. The Italians' love of rice is evident from the variety of delicious and imaginative ways they prepare it. You will find Italian recipes in virtually every chapter in this cookbook.

The United States has always been more of a rice exporter than a rice consumer. In the early eighteenth century rice grown along the coastal plains of the Carolinas and Georgia was a major export. A labor-intensive crop, many of the wealthiest rice plantations had hundreds of slaves. Familiar with African rice cultivation, the slaves are credited with contributing significantly to the industry before it was destroyed by the Civil War. With the mechanization of agriculture, rice growing moved west to Louisiana. Today enough rice grows in Arkansas, California, Louisiana, Texas, Mississippi, and Missouri to rank the United States as the twelfth largest rice producer worldwide and the second largest exporter of rice (first is Thailand). The United States now exports about half of all the rice it grows.

The average American consumes only twenty pounds of rice per year, with about four pounds of that number attributed to the rice used for brewing American beer. But rice consumption is on the rise. In fact, Americans eat twice as much rice now as they did ten years ago. Marketing analysts attribute this phenomenon to the savvy consumer's awareness of rice as a healthy food, high in complex carbohydrates. Eating healthy is certainly a significant part of the picture, but the recent interest in the rice-based cuisines of Thailand, Vietnam, Indonesia, and Japan and the wide range of different types of rice now available, as many as twenty-five, have also contributed to this swing toward rice.

Rice Folklore

The Chinese word for rice is the same as the word for food; in Thailand when you call your family to a meal you say, "Eat rice"; in Japan the word for cooked rice is the same as the word for meal. Most of us have either thrown a handful of rice at newlyweds or personally experienced a prickly rice shower. This ancient rice-throwing ritual originally symbolized fertility and the blessing of many children; today it symbolizes prosperity and abundance. In India rice is the first food a new bride offers her husband; it is also the first food offered a newborn. In Japan where there is almost a mystical aura surrounding the planting, harvesting, and preparing of rice, it is believed that soaking rice before cooking releases the life energy and gives the eater a more peaceful soul. To encourage

Japanese children to eat all of their rice, the grains are affectionately called little Buddhas. In China young girls with finicky appetites are warned that every grain of rice they leave in their rice bowls represents a pockmark on the face of their future husband. In India it is said that the grains of rice should be like two brothers—close but not stuck together. Instead of "How are you?" in China a typical greeting is, "Have you had your rice today?" One is expected to reply, "Yes."

The Science of Rice

Rice is protected by a hull or rough outside layer when it is harvested. The bran layers are under the hull; under the bran is the starchy endosperm, easily recognized by the cook as a grain of white rice.

Ninety percent of the calories in rice come from complex carbohydrates or starch. Amylose and amylopectin are the two types of starch found in rice. Amylose is the starch in long-grain rice that makes the rice separate and fluffy. Amylopectin is the waxy starch found in medium- and short-grain rice that gives it a sticky consistency when cooked.

It is the amylose in cooked long-grain rice that causes it to seize up or harden when refrigerated. Called retrogradation, the starch cells collapse, squeeze the moisture out, cause the realignment of the starch molecules, and much to the chagrin of the cook, turns the rice hard. Retrogradation cannot be avoided, but it can be reversed when the rice is reheated. For details see the introduction to Salads, page 41.

The Good Grain

Rice is high in complex carbohydrates, contains almost no fat, is cholesterol free, and is low in sodium, unless you add salt to the cooking water. Generally, all rice—both brown and white—is considered a good source of vitamins and minerals. Although almost all the nutrients are stripped from white rice when the bran layer is removed during milling, ninety percent of all American-grown rice is enriched with thiamine, niacin, and iron, and in some instances riboflavin, vitamin D, and calcium. White rice, because it is enriched, has more iron and thiamine than brown rice. Brown rice has five times more vitamin E and three times more magnesium than white rice. Brown rice provides twice as much fiber as white rice, but it is not an especially rich source of fiber. On the other hand, rice bran alone is an excellent source of fiber (see page 7). Rice is a fair source of protein containing all eight essential amino acids. It is low in the amino acid lysine, which is found in beans, making the classic combination of rice and beans—popularly known as complementary proteins—a particularly healthful dish. Rice is gluten free and easily digestible, making it a good choice for infants and people with wheat allergies or digestive problems. A half cup of cooked white rice provides 82 calories; an equal amount of brown rice provides 89 calories.

Rice Vocabulary

As more and more types of rice appear in supermarkets and specialty shops the cook needs to develop a rice vocabulary. The following glossary is a useful guide to rice types and varieties.

Aromatic Rice The term given to numerous varieties of rice identified by a pronounced nutty aroma and flavor often compared to popping corn. This aroma is attributed to a much higher proportion of 2-acetyl-1-pyrroline, a naturally occurring compound found in all rice. Some popular brands of aromatic rices are Texmati, Konriko Wild Pecan Rice, Uncle Ben's Aromatica, Jasmine, and Ellis Stansel's Popcorn Rice.

Basmati Rice A type of aromatic rice. Many varieties of basmati are grown mostly in India and Pakistan. It is renowned for its long, slender shape that elongates rather than expands in width when it is cooked. The word *basmati* means "queen of fragrance," and the rice is distinguished by its aroma. Although the Indian people eat rice at least once a day, basmati rice is a high-quality luxury food eaten only on special occasions. Because India prefers its rice cooked separate and dry, the highest-quality rice has been aged up to two years.

Black Japonica A medium-grain rice with a black bran, grown on a limited basis at the Lundberg Farms in California and used by them in a mixed rice product called Gourmet Blend.

Brown Rice Rice with the hull removed and the bran layers left clinging to the grains. The color is tan, and the flavor is nutty with a slight chewy texture. Brown rice is slightly more nutritious than enriched white rice, with twice as much fiber, five times the vitamin E, and three times the magnesium. (Enriched white rice has more iron and thiamine.) Available as long-, medium-, and short-grain rice.

Glutinous Rice Also known as sticky, waxy, or sweet rice; most often used in desserts. The grains are either round or long and have a high percentage of amylopectin, the starch that makes the grains stick together when they are cooked. It is popular in East Asian cuisines.

Italian Rice Arborio, vialone nano, carnaroli, and padano are the most popular rices grown in the Piedmont and Lombardy regions of Italy. Technically they are medium-grain and have a high level of amylopectin and a large central core that cooks firm to the bite or *al dente*. These varieties are used to make risotto.

Jasmine Rice An aromatic long-grain rice originally grown only in Thailand. Distinguished by its fragrance and a water milling process that leaves the grains silken to the touch, jasmine rice is now being grown very successfully in the United States. The grains are similar in size to long-grain rice but cook moist and tender like a medium-grain rice.

Long-Grain Rice Considered long-grain if it is three or more times as long as it is wide. It is higher in the starch amylose; therefore, the grains cook separate and fluffy. Carolina, aromatic, basmati, and their brown counterparts are all in this broad category. Generally the growing regions for long-grain rice are closer to the equator.

Medium-Grain Rice Rice varieties that are less than two times as long as they are wide. This rice is high in the starch amylopectin, and the grains cook moist and tender and with a slight stickiness. The rices grown in Italy and Spain are medium-grain. Generally the growing regions for medium-grain rice are farther from the equator.

Parboiled or Converted Rice Rice that has been steam-pressure treated before milling, forcing all the nutrients from the bran layer into the endosperm. This process was perfected in the United States in response to the need for a stable and nutritious food to feed the armed forces during World War II, but research reveals that rice was being parboiled in Pakistan and northern India more than two thousand years ago. The rice is firm-textured and separate when cooked. Converted, which undergoes the same process as parboiled, is a trademark of Uncle Ben's rice.

Precooked, Quick, or Instant Rice Rice that has been milled, completely cooked, and dried. What is gained in cooking time for the consumer is lost in texture and flavor, but a new quick-cooking brown rice successfully retains some of the nutty flavor and chewiness of its unprocessed counterpart.

Rice Bran The tan nutrient-rich outer layer covering a rice kernel. When this bran is in place, the rice is brown; when this bran is removed by milling, the rice is white. Rice bran has a sweet nutty flavor and is an excellent source of nutrients, minerals, and fiber. Some studies suggest that the oil in rice bran may have cholesterol-reducing properties. Until recently rice bran was used exclusively as an animal feed supplement because an unstable enzyme caused rice bran to turn rancid quickly. Scientists have since discovered a way to stabilize rice bran so that it is now available on a limited basis in health-food stores and through mail order (see page 271). Make sure to buy from a busy store where the product is most likely to be fresh. To ensure freshness once the package is opened, store it in the refrigerator.

Rizcous The name of a product produced at the Lundberg Family Farms in California. They are broken grains of brown rice that have a similar appearance and texture to a popular semolina product called couscous.

Short-Grain Rice Considered short-grain if the length is less than two times its width. The cooked rice is softer and stickier than medium-grain rice when it is cooked. In Japan it is known as sushi rice.

Texmati Rice Called American basmati, texmati rice is a hybrid of aromatic rice and regular long-grain varieties. Its cooking properties are similar to basmati: light texture and nutty flavor and aroma. It is delicious in pilafs and other Indian dishes and is available as a white and a brown rice.

Valencia Rice A medium-grain rice grown in the province of Valencia, Spain, and available on a limited basis in specialty food shops. It is a soft rice, similar to Italian rices, that soaks up flavors but retains a partially firm central core when cooked. A favorite rice in paella.

Wehani Rice A brown rice with a rust-brown bran layer that partially splits when the rice is cooked, giving each kernel an appearance similar to that of a cooked kernel of wild rice but with an earth-red color. Considered an aromatic rice and related to basmati, Wehani is named for the four Lundberg brothers and their father (Wendell, Eldon, Harlan, Homer, and Albert) from the Lundberg Family Farms.

Methods of Cooking Rice

Methods of cooking rice vary not only with the different types of rice but with the expectations of the cook and the individual preferences of the rice eaters. For example, in Japan plain, sticky rice is eaten at every meal; in India rice is cooked dry and separate (not sticky) and is mixed with fat, nuts, and spices; in the American South rice is cooked dry and often topped with a spicy, saucy mix of red beans; while at a juice bar in southern California brown rice might be stir-fried with broccoli and drowned in soy sauce. Geography, agriculture, tradition, folklore, and history, even philosophy, all influence the way a person chooses to cook and eat rice.

I never soak or rinse rice before cooking. Many cooks, especially of Oriental and other Asian cuisines, rinse rice not just once but frequently, in an almost ritualistic way. This process is often dismissed as wasteful; it does rinse off some of the enrichment, but remember: this rinsing ritual is from a time when rice wasn't enriched. It is also called archaic, but before improved milling and storing, impurities could be found mixed in with the grains of rice—and in some parts of the world this is still a concern. Rice rinsed and in some instances soaked before cooking emerges extremely tender with a neutral flavor—the very texture and flavor preferred in many rice-based cuisines. The rice obviously absorbs some of the rinsing and soaking water; therefore, it is cooked in less water than rice that hasn't been rinsed and soaked.

WHITE RICE

Uncovered/Covered Method Standing at the airport in a small town in Texas one hot summer day, I struck up a conversation about rice with a fellow passenger. This is how the gentleman from Texas cooks rice: Spread the rice in the bottom of a wide pot and add just enough water to cover the rice by $^1/_2$ inch or the thickness of your hand. Heat to a gentle boil, stirring once, and cook, *uncovered,* for 5 minutes, or just until the water is almost all absorbed. Cover the rice and cook without lifting the lid for 15 or 20 minutes, or until the rice is tender and fluffy. Subsequently, cookbook author Jean Anderson told me she encountered this rice cooking technique consistently throughout Portugal.

Covered Method The following are the directions familiar to those of us in the United States who cook from the familiar red-and-white box: Heat the water, fat, and salt, if using, to a boil. Stir in the rice, cover, and cook over medium-low heat until the water is absorbed and the rice is tender, about 15 to 20 minutes. I prefer cooking for 15 minutes and then letting the rice stand, covered and off the heat, for 10 minutes before serving. The rule of thumb for long-grain rice is 1 cup of raw rice to 2 cups of water for moist, soft rice. For firm, more separate grains use 1 cup of raw rice to $1^3/_4$ cups of water. Medium- and short-grain rice require slightly less water or 1 cup of raw rice to $1^1/_2$ cups of water. Parboiled or converted long-grain rice has a much harder surface and requires slightly more water and a few minutes more cooking time.

Boiling Water Method Cooking rice in plenty of boiling water (like boiling pasta or potatoes) until it is cooked to the consistency desired and then draining in a strainer is an especially popular method among chefs. This method provides a certain amount of control, but because all the enrichment is drained away, some people consider it wasteful.

Rice Cookers Electric rice cookers are as common in most modern East Asian households as a kitchen sink. This convenient and efficient way to cook rice is becoming more popular in the United States, and has the added advantage of keeping the rice warm until needed. Follow the manufacturer's directions; rice cookers usually require $^1/_4$ to $^1/_2$ cup less water than conventional cooking methods. Also available are top-of-stove or nonautomatic rice cookers.

Microwave Although it doesn't save time, rice can be cooked in the microwave. Combine 1 cup of rice with 2 cups of water in a microwave-safe dish. Cover and microwave on high power for 5 minutes. Lower the power 50 percent and microwave 15 minutes more. Let stand for 5 minutes, covered, before serving.

BROWN RICE

Brown rice takes longer to cook and requires more time because the bran layer acts as a barrier to the heat and moisture. Texmati produces a light bran rice that cuts the cooking time by about half. One cup of regular brown rice cooks in $2^1/_4$ or $2^1/_2$ cups of liquid in 45 to 50 minutes. Parboiled or converted brown rice requires slightly more water. To reduce the cooking time of brown rice by about 20 minutes, soak 1 cup of rice in 2 cups of water overnight. Next day, drain the rice over a measuring cup and add enough fresh water to equal $2^1/_2$ cups. Heat to boiling. Add salt and cook, covered, until the liquid is absorbed and the rice is tender, about 25 minutes.

SOUPS

Vegetable

Milanese Vegetable Rice Soup

Broccoli and Rice Soup with Red Pepper Oil and Garlic

Broccoli and Rice Soup with Egg Threads and Parmigiano-Reggiano

Brown Rice, Onion, Mushroom, and Spinach Soup with Soy Sauce

Tomato

Cream of Tomato and Rice Soup

Tomato Soup with Rice and Spinach Meatballs

Tomato Soup with Porcini Mushrooms and Arborio Rice

Curried Tomato Soup with Brown Rice and Spinach

Dried Beans

Black Bean and Rice Soup with Cilantro Cream

Yellow Split Pea and Brown Rice Soup with Gremolata Sauce

Roasted Eggplant and Lentil Soup with Brown Rice and
Red Pepper Puree

Chowders

Corn and Rice Chowder with Smoked Prawns

Bacon, Clam, and Rice Chowder, Manhattan Style

Chicken and Meat

Chicken, Escarole, and Rice Soup

Chinese Rice Soup with Egg Threads

Mushroom, Beef, and Brown Rice Soup

Beautiful soup, beautiful soup! If you are a soup lover, as I am, a steaming pot of soup is an evocative dish. The Mock Turtle's words reverberate

Beautiful soup, so rich and green,
Waiting in a hot tureen!

I have a clear childhood memory of sticking my nose as close as possible to the surface of a steaming bowl of chicken soup and counting the grains of rice as I blow gently on the broth to quickly cool it. Soup with rice can be prepared simply by adding cooked rice to a simmering broth or by beginning with uncooked rice and cooking it until flavors of the other ingredients are absorbed. The variations on this theme are endless. In this chapter you will find homespun family favorites, contemporary hearty fare, and a version of a Chinese-style soup with egg threads that is traditionally eaten as a breakfast dish.

Milanese Vegetable Rice Soup

This soup is named for risotto alla Milanese, the classic risotto dish of Milan flavored and colored with threads of saffron. Here saffron (the name comes from the Arab word for yellow) adds its sophisticated flavor and golden color to an otherwise simple soup. This is also a delicate and lovely vegetable soup when prepared without the saffron.

8 cups unsalted chicken broth, preferably homemade
Pinch of saffron threads
2 cups packed, rinsed, trimmed, and torn (1-inch pieces) escarole
8 ounces slender green beans, trimmed and cut into $^1\!/_4$-inch pieces (about 2 cups)
1 cup pared and diced ($^1\!/_4$-inch) carrots
$^1\!/_3$ cup uncooked medium- or long-grain white rice *or* Italian arborio rice
1 cup trimmed and diced zucchini or yellow squash (about 1 small)
$^1\!/_2$ cup tiny peas, fresh or frozen, thawed
$^1\!/_2$ cup peeled, seeded, and diced fresh or canned tomato
Salt and freshly ground black pepper to taste
Freshly grated Parmigiano-Reggiano cheese (see Basics, page 267)

1. Combine $^1\!/_2$ cup of the broth and the saffron in a small saucepan. Heat to simmering, cover, and let stand off the heat for 15 minutes. Add the remaining broth to a large saucepan. Heat to boiling and stir in the saffron and broth mixture. Add the escarole, green beans, carrots, and rice. Cook, uncovered, stirring, until rice and vegetables are very tender, about 20 minutes.

2. Add the zucchini or yellow squash, peas, and tomato. Simmer, uncovered, until tender, about 10 minutes. Season with salt and freshly ground black pepper.

3. Ladle into bowls and sprinkle generously with grated cheese.

MAKES ABOUT 10 CUPS OR 6 SERVINGS

Broccoli and Rice Soup with Red Pepper Oil and Garlic

This robust, easy-to-make soup is the perfect quick supper when you are tired and hungry. Use ordinary broccoli, but if available, broccoli rape is excellent. Season with olive oil spiked with crushed red pepper and crunchy slivers of fried garlic, or add Parmigiano-Reggiano cheese. An egg beaten into cold water will enrich the soup with threads of cooked egg.

8 cups unsalted chicken broth, preferably homemade

1 medium carrot, pared and thinly sliced

1/2 cup uncooked medium- or long-grain white rice or Italian arborio rice

4 cups coarsely chopped fresh broccoli florets and tender stems *or* broccoli rape tops plus trimmed and peeled 1-inch lengths of broccoli rape stems

Salt and freshly ground black pepper to taste

Freshly grated Parmigiano-Reggiano cheese to taste (see Basics, page 267)

Red Pepper Oil and Garlic

2 tablespoons extra-virgin olive oil

¹/₄ cup thinly slivered (approximately ¹/₈ × ¹/₂ inch) red bell
    pepper

¹/₂ teaspoon crushed hot red pepper flakes, or more to taste

1 tablespoon thinly slivered garlic

1. In a large saucepan heat the broth, carrot, and rice to boiling, stirring well. Cover and cook over low heat for 10 minutes. Add the broccoli and cook until the broccoli is tender and the soup has thickened, about 10 minutes more. Season with salt and pepper.

2. Meanwhile, make the red pepper oil: Heat the oil in a small skillet. Add the red bell pepper slivers and the dried hot red pepper flakes. Sauté for 3 minutes or until the bell pepper begins to brown. Remove the skillet from the heat and transfer the bell pepper with a slotted spoon to the soup. Add the garlic to the hot oil and sauté over very low heat just until the garlic is golden, about 1 minute. Remove from the heat and immediately stir the hot oil and garlic mixture into the simmering soup.

3. Ladle into bowls and serve sprinkled with grated cheese.

MAKES ABOUT 8 CUPS OR 4 SERVINGS

BROCCOLI AND RICE SOUP WITH EGG THREADS
AND PARMIGIANO-REGGIANO

Omit the Red Pepper Oil and Garlic. Whisk one large egg with ¹/₂ cup of cold water. When the broccoli is tender and the soup has thickened, bring the soup to a full boil. Gradually pour the egg into the boiling soup in a slow, steady stream, stirring constantly, so that the mixture cooks into egg threads. Add ¹/₂ cup of grated cheese. Ladle into bowls and serve with more grated cheese if desired.

Brown Rice, Onion, Mushroom, and Spinach Soup with Soy Sauce

The flavors of soy sauce, mushrooms, and brown rice have a certain affinity for one another. Soy sauce is made from fermented soy beans, wheat, yeast, salt, and sugar.

4 tablespoons peanut oil
2 cups finely chopped sweet onions
10 ounces white button mushrooms, wiped clean, halved, and
   sliced crosswise
1 clove garlic, crushed
1 to 2 tablespoons chopped parsley
Salt and freshly ground black pepper to taste
4 cups unsalted chicken broth, preferably homemade, *or* half
   broth and half water
1 cup cooked short-grain brown rice
1 cup packed, washed, trimmed, and shredded spinach leaves
1 tablespoon soy sauce, or to taste
1 teaspoon Oriental sesame oil
2 teaspoons sesame seeds, toasted in a hot skillet until golden

1. Heat 2 tablespoons of the oil in a large heavy saucepan and add the onions. Cook, covered, over low heat, stirring frequently to prevent browning, until the onions are a pale straw color and very, very soft, about 25 minutes.

2. Heat the remaining 2 tablespoons of oil in a large nonstick skillet. Add the mushrooms and sauté, stirring, until the mushrooms are lightly browned, about 5 minutes. Stir in the garlic and sauté 1 minute more. Season with parsley, salt, and pepper.

3. Stir the mushrooms into the onions. Add the broth (or broth and water) and the cooked rice. Simmer, covered, over medium heat for 15 minutes, then stir in the spinach. Season with soy sauce and sesame oil.

4. Ladle into bowls and sprinkle with some toasted sesame seeds.

MAKES 6 CUPS OR 4 SERVINGS

Cream of Tomato and Rice Soup

Be forewarned: Cream of tomato soup is not red. It is a creamy shade of pink with flecks of tomato and a rib-sticking, soul-warming consistency. As a child I remember finding tiny cubes of half-melted cheddar cheese in the bottom of a steaming bowl of tomato soup. Here I suggest using pieces of Parmigiano-Reggiano cheese rinds. Simmer them along with the rice so they have a chance to soften to a nice chewy consistency.

2 tablespoons unsalted butter
1/2 cup finely chopped onion
1/4 cup uncooked long-grain white rice
2 cups unsalted chicken broth, preferably homemade
6 pieces (about 1/4 × 1 inch) Parmigiano-Reggiano cheese
    rinds (see Basics, page 267) (optional)
4 cups peeled and cored fresh ripe tomatoes *or* 2 cans (14 ounces
    each) good-quality Italian-style plum tomatoes with juice
2 cups half-and-half, at room temperature
Salt and freshly ground black pepper to taste
Shredded fresh basil or mint (optional)

1. Melt the butter in a large saucepan until the foam subsides. Stir in the onion and sauté over low heat, stirring, until the onion is tender but not browned, about 5 minutes. Stir in the rice and sauté for 1 minute. Add the chicken broth and cheese rinds,

if using, and heat to boiling. Cover and cook over low heat for 20 minutes, or until the rice is very tender.

2. Press the tomatoes through a food mill or strainer and discard the seeds. Add to the broth mixture. Stir in the half-and-half and cook over medium-low heat until very hot, stirring frequently. Do not boil or the mixture may curdle. Cover and cook over very low heat for 15 minutes before serving. Season with salt and pepper.

3. Ladle into bowls and garnish with fresh basil or mint, if desired.

MAKES ABOUT 8 CUPS OR 4 TO 6 SERVINGS

Tomato Soup with Rice and Spinach Meatballs

Use the best-quality canned Italian plum tomatoes available for this simple, homey soup. I am fortunate that my mother is a home-canning devotee and keeps me supplied with excellent home-canned tomatoes all winter.

Tomato Soup
2 tablespoons olive oil
$^{1}/_{2}$ cup thin, vertical slices from a small onion
8 cups canned Italian-style tomatoes with their juice
2 cups good-quality canned or homemade unsalted beef broth
Sprig of fresh basil

Meatballs

1 tablespoon olive oil

1 clove garlic, crushed

2 cups packed, shredded, trimmed, and rinsed spinach leaves

8 ounces ground lean meat mixture (usually beef, pork, and veal)

¹/₂ cup cooked long-grain white rice

1 large egg

Freshly grated Parmigiano-Reggiano cheese (see Basics, page 267)

Salt and freshly ground black pepper to taste

1. To make the tomato soup: Heat the oil in a large wide saucepan. Add the onion and sauté over low heat, stirring, until the onion is tender, about 5 minutes.

2. Set a food mill or strainer over the saucepan; add the tomatoes and puree them; discard the seeds. Add the broth and the basil sprig. Simmer the soup over low heat, stirring, for 15 minutes.

3. Meanwhile, make the meatballs: Heat the oil in a large skillet. Add the garlic and sauté, stirring, for 1 minute. Stir in the spinach to coat with oil. Cover and cook over low heat until the spinach is very wilted, about 5 minutes.

4. Combine the ground meat mixture, rice, egg, 2 tablespoons of grated cheese, salt, pepper, and the cooked spinach mixture in a large bowl. Stir until very well blended. Shape the mixture into about 32 tiny (about 1 inch diameter) meatballs, rinsing hands frequently with cold tap water to keep the meat from sticking.

5. Carefully lower a few meatballs at a time into the simmering tomato soup. Cover and cook for 15 minutes, or until the meatballs have risen to the surface of the soup. Season with salt and pepper.

6. Ladle into soup bowls, dividing the meatballs evenly. Serve sprinkled with additional grated cheese.

MAKES 8 CUPS OR 4 SERVINGS

Tomato Soup with Porcini Mushrooms and Arborio Rice

This is a rather elegant rendition of a simple tomato soup. We like it as a first course or as a light supper served with Italian whole wheat bread drizzled with extra-virgin olive oil.

1 ounce dried porcini mushrooms

2 cups unsalted beef or chicken broth, preferably homemade

2 tablespoons unsalted butter or flavorless vegetable oil

1/2 cup finely chopped onion

8 cups canned Italian-style tomatoes with their juice

1 cup cooked medium- or long-grain white rice or Italian
   arborio rice

Salt and freshly ground black pepper to taste

3 tablespoons heavy cream (optional)

1 tablespoon fresh thyme leaves stripped from stems *or* finely
   chopped parsley

1. Combine the dried mushrooms and broth in a small saucepan and heat to boiling. Remove from the heat, cover, and let stand for 30 minutes. Drain through a sieve lined with a dampened paper towel, setting aside the porcini-flavored broth. Pick over the mushrooms and rinse off or discard any hard or gritty parts. Finely chop the mushrooms and set aside the mushrooms and broth separately.

2. Meanwhile, heat the butter or oil in a large saucepan. Add the onion and sauté over low heat, stirring, until golden, about 10 minutes. Press the tomatoes through a sieve or food mill; discard the seeds. Add the strained tomatoes, porcini broth, and chopped mushrooms to the onions. Heat to boiling, then cover and simmer for 10 minutes.

3. Add the rice, cover, and simmer for 10 minutes, stirring occasionally. Season with salt and pepper.

4. To serve, ladle into bowls and drizzle with a half tablespoon of heavy cream, if using. Sprinkle with fresh thyme leaves or parsley. Serve at once.

MAKES 8 CUPS OR 6 SERVINGS

Curried Tomato Soup with Brown Rice and Spinach

Any type of rice is good stirred into this soup; it is a good place to use one of the interesting blends from the Lundberg Family Farm in California.

2 tablespoons unsalted butter
1 cup thin, vertically sliced sweet yellow onions
2 teaspoons curry powder, or to taste
1 teaspoon ground cumin
8 cups good-quality canned Italian-style plum tomatoes with
   their juice
2 cups packed, rinsed, trimmed, and torn spinach leaves
1 cup cooked long-grain brown rice or American basmati-type
   brown rice
1 cup unsalted chicken broth or water (optional, as needed)
Salt and freshly ground black pepper to taste
$\frac{1}{2}$ cup plain yogurt
2 tablespoons finely chopped cilantro leaves

1. Heat the butter in a large saucepan until melted. Stir in the onion and sauté over low heat, stirring, until the onion is golden, about 10 minutes. Stir in the curry powder and cumin, and sauté for 1 minute.

2. Press the tomatoes through a sieve or food mill and discard the seeds. Add the tomatoes to the onion. Cover and cook over low heat for 20 minutes.

3. Stir in the spinach and rice. Heat until very hot and the spinach is tender, about 10 minutes. Add broth or water as needed to thin the soup to the desired consistency.

4. Season with salt and pepper. Ladle into bowls. Stir the yogurt and cilantro together and place a spoonful in the center of each bowl.

MAKES 8 CUPS OR 6 SERVINGS

Black Bean and Rice Soup
with Cilantro Cream

The secret ingredient in this otherwise basic recipe for black bean soup is a bottle of Guinness stout. Inspired by a remarkable black bean salad created by Bradley Ogden, the talented chef at the Lark Creek Inn in Larkspur, California, the stout adds a delicious depth of flavor.

2 tablespoons olive oil

2 cups chopped onions

1 cup chopped sweet red bell peppers

1 poblano chili pepper, seeded and chopped (see Basics, page 263)

1/2 cup chopped celery

1/2 cup chopped carrot

2 tablespoons seeded and minced fresh jalapeño chili pepper (see Basics, page 263)

2 cloves garlic, minced

2 teaspoons ground cumin

1/2 teaspoon crushed red pepper flakes

1/2 teaspoon dried thyme

1 bottle (12 ounces) Guinness stout

1 cup peeled, chopped, and drained canned or fresh tomatoes

1 bay leaf

1 pound small black beans, rinsed and soaked (see Basics, page 264)

10 cups water

1 cup uncooked long-grain white rice

1 to 2 teaspoons salt, or to taste

Cilantro Cream

1 cup sour cream or half sour cream and half yogurt

1 cup loosely packed fresh cilantro leaves plus minced stems

1 jalapeño chili, seeded and chopped

1. In a large wide saucepan heat the oil. Add the onions, red bell peppers, poblano chili, celery, and carrot. Sauté over medium-low heat, stirring often, until the vegetables are golden, about 15 minutes. Add the jalapeño chili and garlic, and sauté for 1 minute. Add the cumin, red pepper flakes, and thyme, and sauté 1 minute more. Add the stout, tomatoes, and bay leaf. Heat to boiling, then simmer, uncovered, for 10 minutes.

2. Drain the soaked beans, then add to the saucepan along with the water. Cook at a gentle simmer for 2½ to 3 hours, or until the beans are very tender and the broth is thickened. With a slotted spoon transfer 1 cup of the beans to the bowl of a food processor; add about ½ cup of the broth. Process until smooth, then return to the saucepan. Add the rice and salt. Cook, covered, until the rice is tender, about 20 to 25 minutes.

3. Meanwhile, prepare the cilantro cream: Process the sour cream, cilantro leaves, and jalapeño chili in a food processor until smooth. Transfer to a bowl, cover, and refrigerate until ready to serve. The cream will thicken while standing.

4. To serve, ladle the soup into bowls and spoon some of the cilantro cream into the center of each. Serve the remaining cream on the side.

MAKES ABOUT 8 CUPS OR 6 SERVINGS

Yellow Split Pea and Brown Rice Soup with Gremolata Sauce

In Italian cooking a gremolata (also spelled gremolada) is a finely chopped mixture of Italian parsley, lemon zest, and raw garlic that is added to soups and stews just before serving. I first tasted it sprinkled on osso buco. Here I blend the classic mixture of parsley, lemon, and garlic with extra-virgin olive oil and gently swirl a spoonful into each serving of soup. It gives a pleasant jolt of fresh flavor to every bite.

2 tablespoons olive oil
1 cup chopped onions
$\frac{1}{2}$ cup diced ($\frac{1}{4}$ inch) celery
$\frac{1}{2}$ cup slivered baked or cured ham (optional)
1 clove garlic, chopped
10 cups unsalted chicken broth, preferably homemade
1 cup dried yellow split peas, sorted, rinsed, and drained
1 cup uncooked short-grain brown rice
1 bay leaf
1 cup pared and cubed ($\frac{1}{2}$-inch chunks) carrots
1 teaspoon salt, or to taste
Freshly ground black pepper to taste

Gremolata
$\frac{1}{2}$ cup packed, coarsely chopped Italian (flat leaf) parsley,
   tender stems included
2 cloves garlic
2 strips (about $\frac{1}{2}$ × 1 inch) lemon zest (removed with a
   vegetable parer)
$\frac{1}{2}$ cup extra-virgin olive oil

1. Heat the olive oil in a large heavy saucepan. Stir in the onions and celery, and sauté until golden, about 10 minutes. Add the ham, if using, and garlic, and sauté for 2 minutes.

2. Add the broth, dried peas, rice, and bay leaf. Heat to boiling, stirring occasionally. Lower the heat and cook, uncovered, over medium-low heat, stirring occasionally, for 1 1/2 to 2 hours, or until the split peas are almost tender. Stir in the carrots and cook until the carrots and peas are very tender, about 30 minutes. Season with salt and pepper.

3. To make the gremolata sauce: Finely chop the parsley, garlic, and lemon zest in the food processor. With the motor running add the olive oil in a slow, steady stream until thoroughly blended. Spoon into a small bowl.

4. Ladle the soup into bowls. Swirl a spoonful of the sauce in the center of each bowl. Serve the remaining sauce on the side.

MAKES ABOUT 10 CUPS OR 6 SERVINGS

Roasted Eggplant and Lentil Soup with Brown Rice and Red Pepper Puree

Roasted eggplant and vegetables make a delicious side dish served solo or cut into chunks and tossed with hot cooked pasta. Here the roasted vegetables mingle with the lentils and brown rice to make a satisfying soup. Lentils are among my favorite legumes; this quote from Pliny sums it up nicely: "I . . . consider the eating of lentils promotes an even temper. Even temper and satiated appetite—need we ask for anything more?"

1 medium eggplant (about 1 pound), trimmed and quartered lengthwise

1 large sweet yellow onion (8 to 10 ounces), quartered

1 large tomato, quartered

1 jalapeño or other hot chili pepper, halved and with stem and seeds removed (see Basics, page 263)

$1/2$ large green bell pepper, with stem and seeds removed

$1/2$ large red bell pepper, with stem and seeds removed

3 cloves garlic, peeled

3 tablespoons olive oil, preferably extra-virgin

6 cups water, or half water and half unsalted chicken broth

1 cup dried lentils, sorted, rinsed, and drained

$1/2$ cup uncooked long-grain brown rice

2 teaspoons ground cumin

1 bay leaf

$1 1/2$ to 2 cups half-and-half, at room temperature

2 teaspoons salt, or to taste

$1/4$ teaspoon freshly ground black pepper, or less to taste

Red Pepper Puree

3 tablespoons extra-virgin olive oil

1/4 cup chopped onion

1/2 clove garlic, chopped

2 roasted red peppers (see Basics, page 267–268) *or* 1 jar (7
 ounces) roasted red peppers, drained and rinsed

Freshly ground black pepper to taste

1. Heat the oven to 400°F. Place the eggplant, onion, tomato, jalapeño chili, green and red bell peppers, and garlic in a single layer in a large roasting pan. Drizzle with the oil. Roast the vegetables about 45 minutes, turning every 15 minutes so that the edges brown evenly. Remove from the oven and let stand until cool enough to handle.

2. Carefully scoop the eggplant from the skin and discard the skin. Cut all the roasted vegetables into 1-inch pieces and combine in a bowl. Add about 1 cup of the water (or water and broth) to the roasting pan. Set over low heat and scrape any charred bits from the bottom and sides of the pan. Add this deglazing liquid to the roasted vegetables.

3. Set a food mill over a large saucepan. Puree the vegetables and the liquid through a food mill; discard the solids. Stir the remaining water (or water and broth), lentils, brown rice, cumin, and bay leaf into the puree.

4. Cook the mixture, uncovered, for 1 1/2 hours, or until the lentils and rice are very tender. Stir occasionally and add up to 1 cup of additional liquid if the soup thickens too much. But remember the soup will be thinned with half-and-half.

5. Stir the half-and-half into the soup until blended. Add salt and pepper. Reheat gently—do not boil—about 10 minutes before serving.

6. To make the roasted red pepper puree: Heat 1 tablespoon of the oil in a small skillet. Add the onion and sauté, stirring, until tender. Stir in the garlic and sauté for 30 seconds. Combine the red peppers, sautéed onion mixture, and remaining 2 tablespoons of olive oil in the bowl of a food processor and process until very smooth. Transfer to a small bowl and add black pepper.

7. Ladle the soup into bowls. Stir a spoonful of the red pepper puree into each bowl.

MAKES ABOUT 8 CUPS OR 6 SERVINGS

Corn and Rice Chowder with Smoked Prawns

This chowder was inspired by the summer corn season and an experimental batch of smoked Sweetwater prawns—freshwater farm-raised prawns from Texas, available to the consumer on a limited basis. The chowder is equally delicious made with smoked oysters or mussels—or for a nonsmoky flavor, use fresh shrimp, scallops, and/or pieces of salmon. To remove the corn kernels from the cobs easily, break the ears in half before cutting down through the base of the kernels with a sharp paring knife.

3 ears fresh corn, husked
1 tablespoon unsalted butter
1/3 cup chopped shallots
2 cups unsalted chicken broth, preferably homemade
1/2 bay leaf
1 sprig fresh thyme *or* 1/4 teaspoon dried thyme
1/3 cup uncooked long-grain white rice
Salt
2 cups half-and-half, or more as needed
6 ounces smoked prawns, shrimp, mussels, or oysters
Tabasco sauce
1 tablespoon very finely minced red bell pepper
Fresh thyme leaves, stripped from stems, if available

1. Cut the kernels from the corn with a small, sharp knife. Set aside the kernels (about 1 1/2 cups) and cobs separately.

2. Heat the butter in a large heavy saucepan. Add the shallots and sauté, stirring, until tender. Add the broth, bay leaf, thyme, and reserved corn cobs.

3. Heat to boiling over medium heat. Cover and simmer over low heat for 20 minutes. Remove the corn cobs and discard. Stir in the rice and 1 teaspoon of salt. Cover and cook over low heat until the rice is very soft, about 20 minutes.

4. Stir in the half-and-half and the reserved corn kernels. Heat, uncovered, over medium heat until very hot. Do not boil. Simmer for 10 minutes, stirring occasionally.

5. Stir in the smoked seafood of choice and just heat through. If using raw seafood, cover and cook over very low heat for 5 minutes, just until the seafood is cooked through. Thin with more half-and-half if necessary.

6. Remove the bay leaf. Add additional salt and the Tabasco to taste. Ladle into bowls and sprinkle each serving with minced bell pepper and a few fresh thyme leaves, if available.

MAKES 5 CUPS OR 4 SERVINGS

Bacon, Clam, and Rice Chowder, Manhattan Style

Clam chowder was one of my mother's signature dishes. I can still recall the smoky aroma of chopped vegetables slowly cooking with the bacon. Although not exactly like Mom's recipe, this chowder comes pretty close.

2 cups water
1 bay leaf
1 clove garlic, bruised with the side of a knife
1 slice onion
Salt
2 pounds small cherrystone or Manila clams (see Basics, page 265), scrubbed and rinsed
6 slices thickly cut bacon, diced ($1/4$ inch)
1 cup diced ($1/4$ inch) onion
$1/2$ cup diced ($1/4$ inch) celery
$1/2$ cup diced ($1/4$ inch) carrot
2 cans (14 ounces each) Italian-style plum tomatoes with juice
$1/3$ cup uncooked long-grain white rice or Italian arborio rice
Freshly ground black pepper
2 tablespoons torn fresh basil leaves or chopped Italian (flat leaf) parsley

1. In a medium-sized saucepan heat the water, bay leaf, garlic, onion slice, and $1/2$ teaspoon of salt to boiling. Stir in the clams, cover, and cook over medium heat until all the clams are opened, about 5 minutes. Drain into a large sieve set over a bowl, setting aside the broth. Let the clams cool. Retrieve the bruised garlic clove from the sieve and press through a garlic press into the clam broth.

2. Meanwhile, sauté the bacon in a large wide saucepan until browned. Stir in the onion, celery, and carrot. Sauté, stirring occasionally, until the vegetables are tender,

about 10 minutes. Set a food mill over the saucepan and puree the tomatoes into the bacon mixture; discard the seeds left in the food mill. Simmer the tomato and vegetable mixture, covered, for 15 minutes.

3. Rinse out the medium-sized saucepan and add the strained broth. Heat to boiling, then stir in the rice. Cook, uncovered, over medium heat, stirring occasionally, until the rice is tender, about 12 minutes. Set aside.

4. Separate the clams from the shells; discard the shells. Stir the clams and the rice and clam broth mixture into the tomato mixture. Cook over medium heat for 5 minutes, stirring occasionally. Season with salt and pepper to taste. Sprinkle with the basil or parsley just before serving.

MAKES 8 CUPS OR 4 TO 6 SERVINGS

Chicken, Escarole, and Rice Soup

When I was growing up, the tender inside leaves of escarole were set aside for a mixed green salad and the outside leaves were cooked and served as a vegetable or in soups. I disliked the slightly bitter flavor of the raw leaves in salad but loved the sweet flavor and almost velvety texture of the cooked darker outside leaves. Now that I'm the cook, the whole head of escarole goes into the soup.

1 whole chicken (about 3 pounds), thoroughly rinsed
3 quarts water
1 large carrot, trimmed and pared (left whole)
1 clove garlic, bruised with the side of a knife
1 bay leaf
$\frac{1}{2}$ cup uncooked medium- or long-grain white rice or Italian
  arborio rice
Salt and freshly ground black pepper
1 small head escarole (about $1\frac{1}{4}$ pounds), trimmed, rinsed,
  and with leaves torn in bite-sized pieces
$\frac{1}{2}$ cup drained, peeled, seeded, and chopped fresh or canned
  tomatoes (optional)
Freshly grated Parmigiano-Reggiano cheese (see Basics, page
  267)

1. Remove any clumps of fat from the rinsed chicken. Place in a large saucepan and add the water, carrot, garlic, and bay leaf. Cook, uncovered, over medium heat—do not boil. Skim any foam from the surface. Simmer for 1 hour and 15 minutes. Remove the chicken and carrot, and set aside to cool. Discard the bay leaf and garlic clove. Skim the fat or blot with a paper towel.

2. Heat $1\frac{1}{2}$ cups of the broth to boiling. Stir in the rice and $\frac{1}{2}$ teaspoon of salt. Cover and cook for 15 minutes, or until the rice is tender. Let stand, uncovered, off the heat. The broth will not be completely absorbed.

3. While the rice is cooking, discard the skin and bones of the chicken. Tear the chicken into thin shreds and set aside. Cut the carrot into thin slices or small dice.

4. Season the remaining broth with salt and pepper to taste, then heat to boiling. Add the escarole, cover, and cook until tender, about 15 minutes.

5. Just before serving add the chicken, carrot, and cooked rice to the escarole and broth. Add the tomatoes if using. Heat until very hot. To serve, ladle into bowls, distributing the ingredients evenly. Sprinkle each serving generously with grated cheese.

MAKES 6 TO 8 SERVINGS

Chinese Rice Soup with Egg Threads

This pretty, flavorful soup is a long way from its original inspiration, a thick Chinese soup called congee *that is traditionally served as a breakfast dish.*

6 cups water
1 large carrot, pared and halved lengthwise
1 thick slice (about ¼ inch) fresh ginger
¼ cup uncooked long-, medium-, or short-grain white rice
¼ cup chopped (about 2 scallions) white part of scallion,
    trimmed (set aside 1 tablespoon of slivered green scallion
    tops for garnish)
Salt
8 ounces boneless and skinless chicken breast, trimmed and
    cut into ¼-inch crosswise slices
1 teaspoon seeded and minced fresh jalapeño chili pepper
1 large egg
1 teaspoon sesame oil
½ cup packed, washed, and thinly sliced fresh spinach leaves
1 tablespoon finely chopped red bell pepper
½ cup chicken broth, as needed to thin the soup (optional)

1. In a large saucepan heat the water, carrot, ginger, rice, chopped scallion, and 1 teaspoon of salt to boiling, stirring well. Cover and cook over low heat, stirring occasionally, for 45 minutes, or until the rice is swollen and the soup has thickened.

2. Stir in the chicken pieces and jalapeño chili. Cover and cook over low heat for 15 minutes—do not boil. Lift the carrot halves from the saucepan and cool slightly. Cut into thin slices and return to the saucepan. Discard the ginger.

3. Whisk the egg and sesame oil together in a small bowl. Heat the soup to a rolling boil. Gently stir in the egg in a slow, steady stream while the soup is boiling. The egg will become short threads.

4. Stir the spinach and red pepper into the soup. Remove from the heat, cover, and let stand for 2 minutes. Add broth, if desired, to thin the soup. Season to taste with more salt. Stir in 1 tablespoon of the reserved scallion tops just before serving.

MAKES 6 CUPS OR 4 SERVINGS

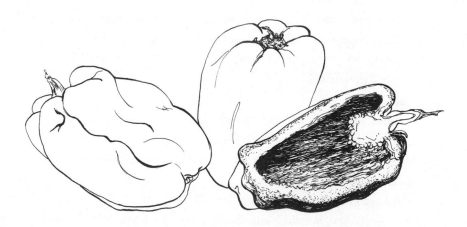

Mushroom, Beef, and Brown Rice Soup

This soup is a classic in our house. I usually make it in two easy stages by preparing the broth one day (steps 1 and 2) and then refrigerating the strained broth overnight. The next day I lift off and discard the fat on the surface of the broth, add the remaining ingredients, and finish cooking the soup just before serving.

2 tablespoons olive oil
1 piece (1 to 1½ pounds) meaty beef shin, about 1 inch thick
½ onion, with skin left on, plus 1 cup finely chopped onions
1 clove garlic, with skin left on, bruised with the side of a
   knife
3 quarts water
1 large carrot, trimmed and pared
1 bay leaf
2 cups coarsely chopped mushrooms (white button, cremini,
   or shiitake caps)
½ cup uncooked long-grain brown rice
1 tablespoon tomato paste
1½ teaspoons salt, or to taste
Freshly ground black pepper
¼ cup finely chopped parsley

1. Heat 1 tablespoon of the olive oil in a large heavy saucepan. Add the beef, onion half, and garlic and brown over medium-low heat, turning once. Add the water, carrot, and bay leaf. Cook over low heat (for a clear broth, try to keep just below the boiling point) for 3 hours, or until the broth has been reduced to 2 quarts and the meat is falling off the bone.

2. Lift the beef shin from the broth and set aside to cool. Strain the broth and reserve; remove the carrot, reserve, and discard the other solids. Pull the meat from the bone and shred or finely chop; save the bone and discard the gristle and fat. Set aside the meat separately. Push the marrow from the center of the bone and dice. Reserve

separately from the meat. Dice the carrot and add to the marrow. Carefully blot any fat from the surface of the broth with a double thickness of paper towels. (If preparing steps 1 and 2 a day ahead, cover and refrigerate the meat, carrot, and marrow separately. Place the broth in a separate bowl, cover, and refrigerate. Next day remove the fat from the surface before using.)

3. In a large saucepan heat the remaining tablespoon of oil. Add the cup of chopped onions and sauté over low heat, stirring, until tender, about 5 minutes. Stir in the mushrooms. Sauté over low heat, stirring, until the mushrooms are tender and lightly browned, about 10 minutes. Add the reserved broth, shredded meat, rice, tomato paste, and salt, and heat to boiling. Cook, uncovered, over low heat for 50 minutes, or until the rice is tender. Add the reserved carrot and marrow. Add more salt if needed and pepper to taste.

4. Ladle into bowls and sprinkle with chopped parsley.

MAKES ABOUT 8 CUPS OR 6 SERVINGS

SALADS

Main Dish Salads

Curried Chicken and Brown Rice Salad with Currants and Walnuts
Brown Rice, Shrimp, and Corn Salad
Brown Rice, Lentil, and Sausage Salad with Roasted Red Peppers
Wehani Salad with Spinach, Bacon, and Toasted Almonds
Mussel and Saffron Rice Salad
Tuscan Rice Salad
Black Bean and Yellow Rice Salad with Cilantro, Chili, and Lime Dressing
Arborio Rice and Poached Salmon Salad with Lemon, Mint, and Dill
Rice Salad with Chick-peas, Feta, and Black Olives

Side Dish Salads

Brown Rice Salad with Two Sesame Flavors
Brown Rice Salad with Fresh and Dried Apricots
Brown Rice and Mango Salad with Jalapeño-spiked Cilantro Yogurt
Brown Rice and Broccoli Salad with Lemon Dressing and Tamari Walnuts

Quick Rice Salad
Tomato and Black Olive Salad
Cucumber, Shrimp, and Dill Salad
Chicken, Basil, and Green Pea Salad
Curried Rice Salad with Raisins and Toasted Almonds
Asparagus and Rice Salad with Lemon Dressing
Rice Salad Provençal
Green Olives and Rice Salad, Sicilian Style
Summer Rice Salad
Tabbouleh-style Basmati Rice Salad
Jasmine Tea Rice Salad with Snow Peas and Ginger
Hoppin' John with Vinaigrette

The first rice salad I remember eating was a Tuscan rice salad. Now, dozens of salads later, it is just one of many favorite rice salad recipes I make and serve from spring right into fall. I find rice—like pasta—a perfect canvas when I am feeling creative in the kitchen. At some time or other vegetables, meats, nuts, fruits, herbs, and spices all find their way into the rice salad bowl. Add meat, fish, or legumes, and it becomes a delicious main dish; add just vegetables, and you have a tasty, convenient, and healthy side dish.

I prefer making a rice salad from scratch with a batch of freshly cooked rice. Rice that has been refrigerated tightens and becomes firm and waxy. This is called retrogradation and is explained in some detail on page 4. Heating the rice to room temperature by steaming in a foil packet at a low temperature in the oven or heating in a microwavable container for about 2 minutes in the microwave will soften the rice slightly. But the grains are never as moist and tender as when the rice is freshly cooked and served at room temperature.

This becomes a problem when you want to make rice salad ahead of time. Rice salad that doesn't contain meats or dairy products that might spoil can be stored safely in a cool dark place (a kitchen cabinet is good) for several hours and even overnight. You can refrigerate the perishable portions separately and then add them to the room-temperature rice before serving. Rice, like pasta, absorbs flavors as it stands, so don't be shy about tasting and adding more seasoning before serving.

Curried Chicken and Brown Rice Salad with Currants and Walnuts

I am partial to the nutty flavor and chewy consistency of short-grain brown rice, but this salad is also good with long-grain white or brown rice. There are some interesting flavors at play here. The sweetness of the dried currants tempers the heat of the curry powder, while the walnuts complement the nutlike flavor of the rice. The flavor of the chicken is best when it is freshly cooked, cooled at room temperature, and then used without refrigerating. Serve as a main course on a generous bed of assorted dark green lettuce leaves and garnish with tomato wedges and small clusters of green or red seedless grapes.

2 tablespoons water or chicken broth

2 teaspoons good-quality curry powder

3/4 cup mayonnaise or half mayonnaise and half low-fat yogurt

1/2 teaspoon salt

1/8 teaspoon freshly ground black pepper

3 1/2 cups cooked short-grain brown rice or long-grain brown
   or white rice

1 cup small red or green seedless grapes, rinsed and with stems
   removed, plus 4 small clusters for garnish

1/2 cup sliced celery

1/2 cup slivered (about 1-inch lengths) red or green bell pepper

2 tablespoons finely chopped sweet red onion

2 tablespoons dried currants or raisins

2 to 2 1/2 cups diced cooked chicken (preferably white and dark
   meat from a cooked 3-pound chicken; see Basics, page 263)

1/2 cup broken walnuts

Assorted dark green lettuce leaves, rinsed and dried

1 tomato, cored and cut into wedges

1. Combine the water or broth and curry powder in a small saucepan. Stir over very low heat for 2 minutes, or until the water is very hot and the curry dissolves. Remove the saucepan from the heat and stir in the mayonnaise and yogurt, if using, until blended.

2. In a large bowl combine the mayonnaise mixture, salt, pepper, rice, grapes, celery, red or green pepper, onion, and currants or raisins until well blended. Add the chicken and gently fold just until blended.

3. Gently toast the walnuts in a dry skillet over medium-low heat until fragrant, stirring constantly, about 3 minutes.

4. Line a large platter or individual serving plates with a generous bed of lettuce. Spoon the rice salad in the center. Sprinkle with the toasted walnuts and garnish with tomato wedges and clusters of grapes. This salad is best served at room temperature.

MAKES 4 TO 6 SERVINGS

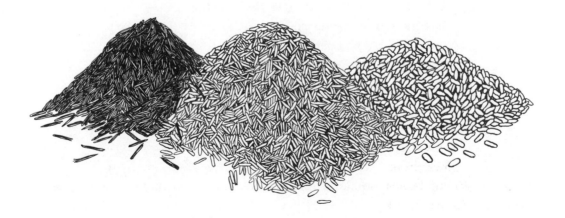

Brown Rice, Shrimp, and Corn Salad

Heating spices in a warm dry skillet before adding them to other ingredients helps bring out their flavor. You can substitute shredded cooked chicken for the shrimp in this versatile salad or omit the shrimp and serve it as a side dish. Fresh corn in season is best, but in a pinch good-quality canned corn can be used.

1 cup uncooked short-grain brown rice
1 pound medium-sized shrimp, peeled and deveined
$\frac{1}{2}$ cup olive oil
$\frac{1}{4}$ cup fresh lime juice
$\frac{1}{2}$ teaspoon grated lime zest
1 small clove garlic, crushed
1 teaspoon fresh thyme leaves, stripped from stems
$\frac{1}{2}$ teaspoon salt
Freshly ground black pepper to taste
1 teaspoon ground cumin
4 ears fresh corn, husked and corn kernels cut from the cob
    with a small sharp knife (about 2 cups kernels)
$\frac{1}{2}$ cup thinly sliced scallions (about 1 bunch)
$\frac{1}{2}$ cup diced green bell pepper
$\frac{1}{2}$ cup diced red bell pepper
2 teaspoons seeded and minced fresh jalapeño chili pepper, or
    more to taste (see Basics, page 263)
Curly or red leaf lettuce leaves
1 lime, cut into wedges
Sprigs of cilantro (optional)

1. Cook the rice according to package directions, then cool, uncovered, before using.

2. Cook the shrimp in plenty of boiling salted water until they turn pink, about 3 to 5 minutes. Drain immediately, rinse with cold water, and set aside.

3. Combine the oil, lime juice, lime zest, garlic, thyme, salt, and pepper in a large bowl. Sprinkle the cumin in the bottom of a small dry skillet and heat over low heat, shaking the pan until the cumin is fragrant, about 1 minute. Add to the dressing and whisk to blend.

4. Add the rice, half of the shrimp, corn, scallions, green and red peppers, and jalapeño chili to the bowl, and toss to blend.

5. Line a large shallow bowl with lettuce leaves and spoon the rice mixture into the center. Garnish with the remaining shrimp and the lime wedges. Add a few sprigs of cilantro, if desired.

MAKES 4 SERVINGS AS A MAIN DISH SALAD

Brown Rice, Lentil, and Sausage Salad with Roasted Red Peppers

The intense flavors in this salad are best when it is served warm or at room temperature. You can take the chill off any refrigerated leftovers with a zap in the microwave.

1 cup uncooked long-grain brown rice
2 large red bell peppers, roasted and peeled, plus additional
    marinated roasted red peppers for garnish, if desired (see
    Basics, pages 267–268)
1 cup dried lentils, rinsed and sorted
6 cups water
12 to 16 ounces well-seasoned sweet and/or hot Italian pork or
    turkey sausage
1/2 cup diced (1/4 inch) green bell pepper
1/2 cup diced (1/4 inch) celery, including some leaves
1/2 cup trimmed and thinly sliced scallions (about 1 bunch)
1/2 cup finely chopped Italian (flat leaf) parsley
Romaine lettuce leaves

Red Wine Vinaigrette
³/₄ cup olive oil
¹/₂ cup red wine vinegar
1 tablespoon fresh thyme leaves stripped from stems *or* ¹/₂
   teaspoon dried thyme chopped with parsley (see Basics,
   pages 264–265)
1 clove garlic, crushed
¹/₂ teaspoon salt
¹/₄ teaspoon freshly ground black pepper

1. Cook the rice according to package directions, then let it stand, uncovered, until cooled. Cut the red peppers into thin (¹/₄ inch) strips and then crosswise into ¹/₄-inch dice. There should be about 1 cup of diced roasted peppers.

2. Combine the lentils and water in a large saucepan. Heat to boiling, then simmer, uncovered, until the lentils are tender, about 15 to 30 minutes, and drain. Be careful not to overcook. Some lentils cook in as little as 15 minutes.

3. Remove the casings from the sausage. Heat a large skillet over medium-high heat and crumble the sausage into the skillet. Cook the sausage until well browned, stirring and breaking up the pieces with the side of a spatula. Drain off any fat (not necessary if using turkey sausage) and set the sausage aside.

4. Combine the rice, lentils, diced roasted red peppers, browned sausage, green bell pepper, celery, scallions, and parsley in a large bowl. In a measuring cup make the red wine vinaigrette: Whisk together the oil, vinegar, thyme, garlic, salt, and pepper. Pour over the salad ingredients and toss to blend.

5. Line a large shallow bowl with a bed of Romaine lettuce leaves. Spoon the salad in the center. Garnish with marinated roasted red peppers, if using.

MAKES 6 SERVINGS AS A MAIN COURSE OR 8 TO 10 SERVINGS AS A SIDE DISH

Wehani Salad with Spinach, Bacon, and Toasted Almonds

The crunch of Wehani rice is perfect in this hearty main dish salad. Read all about Wehani on page 8.

1 cup uncooked Wehani rice
2$\frac{1}{2}$ cups water
8 ounces thickly sliced bacon
$\frac{1}{2}$ cup sliced natural (unblanched) almonds
10 ounces fresh spinach leaves, washed, stems trimmed, and
    cut into $\frac{1}{4}$-inch-wide strips
$\frac{1}{2}$ cup trimmed and thinly sliced celery
$\frac{1}{2}$ cup thinly slivered (1-inch lengths) sweet red onion
$\frac{1}{2}$ cup thinly slivered (1-inch lengths) red bell pepper
2 hard-boiled eggs, peeled and quartered
1 cup small cherry tomatoes, rinsed and with stems removed

Vinaigrette
$\frac{1}{3}$ cup olive oil
3 tablespoons red wine vinegar
$\frac{1}{2}$ clove garlic, crushed
$\frac{1}{2}$ teaspoon salt
$\frac{1}{8}$ teaspoon freshly ground black pepper

1. Combine the rice and water in a medium saucepan. Heat to boiling, stirring well. Cover and cook over low heat until the liquid is absorbed and the rice is tender, about 40 minutes. Uncover and let cool off the heat until lukewarm.

2. Meanwhile, cook the bacon until it is crisp. Drain, cut into $\frac{1}{2}$-inch pieces, and set aside.

3. Heat the oven to 350°F. Spread the almonds on a baking pan. Bake until toasted, about 5 minutes, stirring once, then set aside.

4. Make the vinaigrette: Whisk the oil, vinegar, garlic, salt, and pepper in a large bowl. Add the rice, spinach, celery, red onion, red pepper, and half of both the bacon pieces and the almonds. Toss to blend.

5. Spoon into a shallow bowl. Garnish the edge of the bowl with the egg quarters and cherry tomatoes. Sprinkle the top with the remaining bacon pieces and almonds. Serve at once.

MAKES 4 SERVINGS

Mussel and Saffron Rice Salad

The colors in this salad—striking blue-black mussel shells and golden yellow rice kernels—are almost as dramatic as the flavors. The mussels are cooked in a white wine–based broth, which is then used to cook the rice. Leave at least two dozen of the mussels in their shells and use as a stunning edible garnish.

Mussels
4 pounds mussels, preferably farm-raised (see Basics, page 265)
1 cup water
1 cup dry white wine
1 small onion, thinly sliced
1 stem fresh basil
1 stem fresh parsley
1 stem fresh thyme
1 clove garlic, bruised with the side of a knife
1/2 teaspoon salt

Saffron Rice
Generous pinch of saffron threads
1 cup uncooked long-grain white rice
$1/2$ cup seeded and diced plum tomato
$1/2$ cup diced (about $1/8$ inch) red bell pepper
$1/4$ cup minced sweet red onion
$1/4$ cup minced green bell pepper
$1/4$ cup minced tender inside of celery stalk
$1/4$ cup finely chopped parsley
2 tablespoons chopped fresh basil leaves
1 tablespoon minced tender pale-green celery leaves
$1/3$ cup extra-virgin olive oil
3 tablespoons fresh lemon juice
1 small clove garlic, crushed
Freshly ground black pepper to taste
Sprigs of fresh basil, parsley, and thyme

1. Prepare the mussels (see Basics, page 265).

2. Combine the water, wine, onion, basil, parsley, thyme, garlic, and salt in a very large saucepan or deep skillet with a tight-fitting lid. Heat to boiling, then simmer over low heat for 5 minutes. Drain the mussels and add to the simmering broth. Cover and cook over very high heat for 5 minutes, without lifting the cover. Remove the open mussels with a slotted spoon and continue to cook the remaining mussels until they open; discard any mussels that refuse to open. Cool the mussels and broth separately.

3. Strain the reserved mussel broth through a fine sieve into a 2-cup measure. Add enough water to equal 2 cups. Set aside in a bowl 2 dozen of the mussels in their shells. Remove the remaining mussels from their shells and set aside for the salad. Discard the shells.

4. To make the saffron rice: Heat the broth and water mixture and the saffron threads in a medium-sized saucepan until boiling, then stir in the rice. Cover and cook over medium-low heat until the broth is absorbed and the rice is tender, about 15 minutes. Let stand, uncovered, until cooled.

5. Meanwhile, combine the tomato, red bell pepper, red onion, green bell pepper, celery, parsley, basil, and celery leaves in a large bowl. Add the reserved shelled mussels,

cooled saffron rice, olive oil, lemon juice, garlic, and a grinding of black pepper. Toss gently to combine.

6. Spoon the salad into a large shallow bowl. Garnish the edges with the reserved mussels in their shells and the fresh basil, parsley, and thyme.

SERVES 6 AS A FIRST COURSE OR 4 AS A MAIN COURSE

Tuscan Rice Salad

This is pretty, fresh tasting, and presents a canvas for endless variations.

1 cup uncooked medium- or long-grain white rice or Italian
    arborio rice

3 large eggs, beaten

1 teaspoon olive oil

1 small clove garlic, crushed

1 tablespoon torn fresh basil leaves

Salt and freshly ground black pepper

1/3 cup fresh lemon juice

1/4 cup extra-virgin olive oil

1/2 cup peeled and diced carrot

1/2 cup frozen baby green peas, thawed, or fresh peas, cooked

1/4 cup diced red onion

2 tablespoons finely chopped Italian (flat leaf) parsley

2 ounces prosciutto or other flavorful baked or cured ham, cut
    into thin slivers

Ruby or oak leaf lettuce leaves

1 large ripe tomato, cut into wedges

Small chunks of Parmigiano-Reggiano cheese (see Basics, page
    267)

Sprigs of fresh basil

1. Stir the rice into 2 cups of boiling salted water. Cover and cook over medium-low heat until the liquid is absorbed and the rice is tender, about 15 minutes. Let stand, uncovered, until cooled.

2. Meanwhile, whisk together the eggs, olive oil, and garlic. Heat a small, preferably nonstick, skillet over medium-low heat. Add the eggs and cook, stirring, until scrambled into large clumps. Stir in the tablespoon of torn basil leaves, remove from the heat, and sprinkle lightly with salt and pepper to taste. Set aside.

3. In a large serving bowl whisk together the lemon juice, extra-virgin olive oil, ¼ teaspoon of salt, and ⅛ teaspoon of pepper. Add the rice, scrambled eggs, carrot, peas, red onion, parsley, and prosciutto or ham. Gently toss to blend.

4. Line a platter with the lettuce leaves. Spoon the rice in the center. Garnish the dish with wedges of tomato, small chunks of cheese, and sprigs of fresh basil.

SERVES 6 AS A FIRST COURSE OR SIDE DISH OR 4 AS A MAIN COURSE

Black Bean and Yellow Rice Salad with Cilantro, Chili, and Lime Dressing

Turmeric gives the rice a brilliant yellow color and a slightly nutty flavor that complements the distinctive and assertive flavors of cumin. Both spices are popular in Indian cooking, turmeric being the spice that gives curry its yellow color. This salad is pretty when served straight from a serving bowl or when stuffed into hollowed-out tomatoes.

1 cup dried black beans, rinsed, sorted, and soaked (see Basics, page 264)
1 onion, halved
1 clove garlic, bruised with the side of a knife
1 bay leaf
1¾ cups water
1 cup uncooked long-grain white rice
1 tablespoon vegetable oil
Salt
1 teaspoon turmeric
½ teaspoon ground cumin
½ cup diced (¼ inch) sweet red onion
½ cup seeded and diced (¼ inch) fresh tomato
½ cup diced (¼ inch) green bell pepper
¼ cup torn cilantro leaves
Ground red pepper (cayenne)
Sprigs of fresh cilantro (garnish)

Chili and Lime Dressing
⅓ cup mild-flavored olive oil
3 tablespoons fresh lime juice
1 to 2 teaspoons seeded and finely chopped serrano, jalapeño, or other hot chili pepper, or to taste (see Basics, page 263)
Salt to taste

1. Drain the black beans into a large saucepan and combine with 8 cups of water, onion, garlic, and bay leaf. Heat to boiling, then lower the heat and simmer until the beans are tender, about 1½ hours depending on the beans. Drain and discard the onion, garlic, and bay leaf.

2. Meanwhile, combine the water, rice, vegetable oil, 1 teaspoon of salt, turmeric, and cumin in a medium-sized saucepan. Heat to boiling, stirring occasionally. Cover and cook over medium-low heat until the liquid is absorbed and the rice is tender, about 15 minutes. Let stand, uncovered, until cooled. Fluff with a fork.

3. To make the dressing: In a large bowl whisk together the oil, lime juice, chili pepper, and salt.

4. Mix together the room-temperature rice, red onion, tomato, green pepper, and torn cilantro leaves. Toss to coat with the dressing. Add the black beans and gently toss until blended. Season to taste with salt and cayenne and garnish with cilantro sprigs.

MAKES 4 TO 6 SERVINGS

Arborio Rice and Poached Salmon Salad with Lemon, Mint, and Dill

Serve this sophisticated salad for a light supper with crusty sourdough rolls and a dry California sauvignon blanc.

1 cup uncooked medium- or long-grain white rice or Italian arborio rice
2 salmon steaks, about 6 ounces each, *or* 12 ounces leftover grilled, broiled, or poached salmon
1/2 cup frozen green peas, thawed, or fresh peas, cooked
1/2 cup pared and diced (about 1/8 inch) seedless or Kirby cucumber
1/4 cup thinly sliced scallions
3 tablespoons chopped fresh dill
1 tablespoon finely chopped fresh mint
1 teaspoon grated lemon zest
Sprigs of fresh dill

Lemon and Dill Dressing
1/3 cup mild-flavored olive oil
1/4 cup fresh lemon juice
1/2 clove garlic, crushed
1/2 teaspoon salt
1/8 teaspoon freshly ground black pepper
1 tablespoon chopped fresh dill

1. Stir the rice into 2 cups of boiling salted water. Cover and cook over low heat for 12 to 15 minutes, or until the water is absorbed and the rice is tender. Let stand, uncovered, until the rice has cooled.

2. To cook the fresh salmon steaks, boil 1 inch of water in a medium-sized skillet with a tight-fitting lid and add the salmon. Cover and simmer over low heat for 5

minutes, or until the salmon is almost cooked through. Cool in the broth. Carefully remove the skins, bones, and any dark pieces of fat, leaving the salmon in 1-inch chunks. Arrange on a plate. If using leftover salmon, remove the skin and bones as above and place on a plate.

3. Make the lemon and dill dressing: In a cup whisk together the oil, lemon juice, garlic, salt, pepper, and dill. Spoon about 2 tablespoons over the salmon, cover, and refrigerate until ready to serve.

4. Combine the rice, peas, cucumber, scallions, dill, mint, and lemon zest in a serving bowl. Add the remaining lemon and dill dressing and toss to coat.

5. Add the pieces of salmon and gently mix in, but don't toss or the salmon will break into small pieces. Garnish with sprigs of fresh dill. Serve at once.

MAKES 4 SERVINGS

Rice Salad with Chick-peas, Feta, and Black Olives

Inspiration for this salad comes from the tastes most often associated with the foods of Greece: feta cheese, oregano, mint, lemon, chick-peas, and olives. Fresh feta is preferable, but if unavailable, rinse, drain, and store prepackaged supermarket feta cheese in milk overnight to tame the saltiness.

1 cup uncooked long- or medium-grain white rice or Italian arborio rice

2 cups cooked chick-peas; if using canned chick-peas, rinse well

6 ounces feta cheese, drained, patted dry, diced or chopped (about 1 cup)

1/2 cup chopped celery including leaves

1/2 cup diced (1/4 inch) red onion

1/4 cup pitted and coarsely cut Kalamata or other black brine-cured olives

Salt and freshly ground black pepper to taste

Romaine lettuce leaves

Lemon wedges

Sprigs of parsley, mint, and oregano

Dressing

1/3 cup extra-virgin olive oil

1/4 cup fresh lemon juice

1/4 cup finely chopped Italian (flat leaf) parsley

1 tablespoon finely chopped fresh mint leaves

1 tablespoon finely chopped fresh oregano leaves

1 clove garlic, crushed

1. Stir the rice into 2 cups of boiling salted water. Cover and cook over medium-low heat until it is tender and the liquid is absorbed, about 15 minutes. Let stand, off the heat, uncovered, until cooled.

2. Combine the cooled rice, chick-peas, feta cheese, celery, onion, and olives in a large bowl.

3. To make the dressing: In a separate bowl whisk together the oil, lemon juice, parsley, mint, oregano, and garlic until blended. Add the dressing to the salad and toss to blend. Season with salt and pepper.

4. Line a shallow bowl with Romaine lettuce leaves. Spoon the salad in the center of the bowl and garnish with lemon wedges and herb sprigs.

MAKES 4 TO 6 SERVINGS

Brown Rice Salad with Two Sesame Flavors

1 cup uncooked long- or short-grain brown rice

2 tablespoons flavorless vegetable oil

2 tablespoons fresh lemon juice

2 teaspoons Oriental-style sesame oil

1 cup pared and coarsely shredded carrots

1/2 cup thinly sliced trimmed scallions

1/2 cup chopped dry-roasted peanuts

2 teaspoons sesame seeds, toasted in a dry skillet over low heat

1. Cook the rice according to package directions. Let stand, uncovered, until cooled.

2. Whisk the oil, lemon juice, and sesame oil in a large bowl. Add the cooled rice, carrots, and scallions. Toss to blend. Sprinkle with the peanuts and sesame seeds, toss once, and serve.

MAKES 4 TO 6 SERVINGS

Brown Rice Salad with Fresh and Dried Apricots

Intensely flavored fresh apricots from California are available midsummer for a very short time. To get my fill I eat them out of hand, cut them up and stir them into yogurt, bake at least one apricot tart, make some jam— and then one day, feeling quite desperate because the season was waning and my appetite was not, I devised this salad. It was such a great success that I adapted it slightly for peach season by substituting dried and fresh peaches for the apricots.

1 cup uncooked short-grain brown rice

1/2 cup coarsely chopped natural (unblanched) whole almonds

3 tablespoons flavorless vegetable oil

2 tablespoons fresh lemon juice

1 tablespoon honey

Pinch of salt

Freshly ground black pepper

1/2 cup diced (about 1/4 inch) dried apricots

1/2 cup trimmed and thinly sliced scallions (about 1 bunch)

1/2 cup finely chopped celery

2 tablespoons finely chopped tender pale-green celery leaves

2 cups pitted and cut up (about 1/2-inch pieces) fresh apricots
   (about 1 pound)

1. Cook the rice according to package directions. Let stand, uncovered, until cooled before using.

2. Heat the oven to 350°F. Spread the almonds on a baking sheet and toast until golden, about 10 minutes. Let cool.

3. Combine the oil, lemon juice, honey, salt, and a grinding of black pepper in a large bowl. Add the cooled rice, dried apricots, scallions, celery, and celery leaves. Toss to coat.

4. Just before serving add the fresh apricots. Gently toss to blend. Sprinkle with the toasted almonds and serve.

MAKES 4 TO 6 SERVINGS

Brown Rice and Mango Salad with
Jalapeño-spiked Cilantro Yogurt

The largest and most delicious mangoes are grown in India, but by midsummer there are usually plenty of mangoes in our markets from Mexico, Florida, and the West Indies. Or substitute papaya if you cannot find mangoes. Serve this salad as a side dish with broiled chicken breast.

1 cup uncooked short-grain brown rice
1 cup peeled, seeded, and diced ripe mango or papaya
$\frac{1}{4}$ cup diced ($\frac{1}{8}$ inch) sweet red onion
2 tablespoons finely chopped parsley
3 tablespoons mild-flavored olive oil
2 tablespoons fresh lime juice
$\frac{1}{8}$ teaspoon salt
$\frac{3}{4}$ cup plain low-fat yogurt
1 tablespoon minced cilantro leaves
2 teaspoons seeded and minced fresh jalapeño chili pepper, or
    more to taste (see Basics, page 263)
6 sprigs of cilantro

1. Cook the rice according to package directions. Let stand, uncovered, until cooled.

2. Combine the mango or papaya, red onion, parsley, olive oil, lime juice, and salt in a large bowl. Add the rice and toss to blend.

3. In a small bowl stir together the yogurt, cilantro, and jalapeño chili. Spoon a mound of rice salad on a salad plate. Top with a spoonful of the yogurt. Garnish with a cilantro sprig.

MAKES 6 SERVINGS

Brown Rice and Broccoli Salad with Lemon Dressing and Tamari Walnuts

I like the flavor of tamari in this particular salad, although soy sauce can be used. Serve with thin slices of grilled soy- or tamari-marinated flank steak, or with a platter of freshly cooked corn on the cob and thick slices of ripe tomato. The tamari-coated walnuts are also good sprinkled over green bean or tossed salad, or served as a snack.

1 cup uncooked short-grain brown rice
1 teaspoon olive or other vegetable oil
1/2 cup walnut halves
2 tablespoons tamari or soy sauce
1 bunch broccoli, with tough stems trimmed, stems sliced into
   1/4-inch-thick rounds, and flowers separated into 1-inch
   clusters
3 scallions, trimmed and cut diagonally into thin slices (about
   1/2 cup)

Lemon Dressing
1/4 cup olive or other vegetable oil
2 tablespoons fresh lemon juice
1 tablespoon tamari or soy sauce
1 teaspoon grated fresh ginger
1/2 teaspoon grated lemon zest
1 small clove garlic, crushed

1. Cook the rice according to package directions. Let stand, uncovered, until cooled.

2. Meanwhile, heat the oil in a medium-sized heavy skillet over medium heat and add the walnuts. Stir-fry just until fragrant, about 20 seconds. Sprinkle with the tamari

or soy sauce and stir-fry, adjusting the heat so that the tamari does not burn, until the walnuts are coated with the thickened tamari, about 1 minute. Turn out onto a double thickness of paper toweling to blot and then transfer to a small bowl. (Do not cool the walnuts on paper towels; they will stick to the paper.)

3. Place the broccoli in a vegetable steamer set over gently boiling water and steam, covered, until tender, about 4 minutes. Lift the steamer from the saucepan, and then rinse the broccoli with cool water. Drain and cool.

4. To make the dressing: In a large bowl whisk together the oil, lemon juice, tamari or soy sauce, ginger, lemon zest, and garlic.

5. Just before serving add the cooked rice, tamari walnuts, broccoli, and scallions. Toss to blend. (Note: If making the salad ahead, set aside the broccoli and tamari walnuts and add just before serving.)

MAKES 4 SERVINGS

Quick Rice Salad

Cooked rice becomes a flavorful salad by adding a simple dressing and just a few fresh vegetables or bits of seafood or meat. These variations use a basic dressing to make flavorful combinations.

Dressing
3 to 4 tablespoons olive oil (use extra-virgin when an assertive
    olive flavor is preferred)
2 tablespoons fresh lemon juice or wine or cider vinegar
1/2 teaspoon salt, or more to taste
Freshly ground black pepper to taste

Seasonings (optional)
1 clove garlic, crushed
1 teaspoon prepared mustard
1 teaspoon grated fresh lemon zest

TOMATO AND BLACK OLIVE SALAD

2 to 3 cups cooked white or brown rice
1 cup seeded and diced fresh tomato
1/4 cup pitted and coarsely chopped brine-cured black olives
1 teaspoon fresh thyme leaves stripped from stems

CUCUMBER, SHRIMP, AND DILL SALAD

2 to 3 cups cooked white or brown rice
1 cup diced seedless cucumber
1 cup diced cooked shrimp
1/4 cup trimmed and sliced scallions
1 to 2 tablespoons chopped fresh dill

CHICKEN, BASIL, AND GREEN PEA SALAD

2 to 3 cups cooked white or brown rice
1 cup diced or shredded fresh cooked chicken
1 cup tiny frozen peas, thawed
1/4 cup finely chopped sweet red onion
2 tablespoons torn fresh basil leaves

Whisk the olive oil, lemon juice or vinegar, salt, and pepper and the seasonings of choice until blended. Add the rice and the ingredients from one of the three salads suggested above. Toss to blend and serve at once.

MAKES 2 TO 3 SERVINGS

Curried Rice Salad with Raisins
and Toasted Almonds

4 tablespoons olive or other vegetable oil

1 cup uncooked long-grain white rice

1¾ cups water

2 tablespoons dried raisins or currants

1 teaspoon curry powder

½ teaspoon turmeric

Salt

1 bay leaf

1 small piece (about ¼ × 1 inch) cinnamon stick

1 whole clove

¼ cup slivered blanched almonds

1 cup chopped tart green apple (Granny Smith)

½ cup trimmed and thinly sliced scallions

½ cup chopped celery

¼ cup chopped green or red bell pepper

2 tablespoons lime or lemon juice

Freshly ground black pepper to taste

1. Heat 1 tablespoon of the oil over low heat in a heavy saucepan. Stir in the rice and sauté, stirring constantly, for 1 minute or until the rice is coated with oil. Add the water, currants, curry powder, turmeric, ½ teaspoon of salt, bay leaf, cinnamon stick, and whole clove. Heat to boiling over high heat, stirring once. Cover and cook over medium-low heat until all the water is absorbed, about 15 minutes. Let stand, uncovered, until cool. Remove and discard the bay leaf, cinnamon stick, and clove.

2. Heat the oven to 350°F. Spread the almonds in a small baking pan and place in the oven for 5 minutes, or until lightly toasted. Set aside to cool.

3. Add the apple, scallions, celery, and green or red pepper to the cooled rice. Whisk the remaining 3 tablespoons of oil, the lemon juice, ¼ teaspoon of salt, and pepper until blended. Add to the salad and toss to coat. Sprinkle with the toasted almonds and serve at room temperature.

MAKES 4 SERVINGS

Asparagus and Rice Salad
with Lemon Dressing

Serve this simple, springlike salad of rice and fresh asparagus crowned with thick curls of Parmigiano-Reggiano cheese. It is a perfect dish for a buffet-type supper or my favorite menu of cucina fresca *dishes, which loosely translated means foods served at room temperature.*

1 cup uncooked long-grain white rice
1 pound asparagus, trimmed, soaked, drained, peeled, and cut diagonally into 1-inch pieces
¼ cup pignoli (pine nuts)
¼ cup mild-flavored extra-virgin olive oil
3 tablespoons fresh lemon juice
1 teaspoon grated lemon zest
½ teaspoon salt
Freshly ground black pepper to taste
½ cup trimmed and thin, diagonally sliced scallions
6 thick curls Parmigiano-Reggiano cheese (see Basics, page 267)

1. Stir the rice into 2 cups of boiling salted water. Cover and cook over medium-low heat until the water is absorbed and the rice is tender, about 15 minutes. Let stand, uncovered, until slightly cooled. Fluff with a fork.

2. Meanwhile, place the asparagus in a vegetable steamer set over simmering water. Steam, covered, until crisp-tender, about 3 minutes. Lift the steamer from the saucepan, and then rinse the asparagus with cool water. Drain and cool.

3. Toast the pignoli in a small skillet over low heat about 2 minutes, stirring constantly until golden.

4. Whisk together the oil, lemon juice, lemon zest, salt, and pepper until blended in a large bowl. Add the rice, asparagus, and scallions, and toss to blend. Spoon into a large deep platter or shallow bowl. Sprinkle with the toasted pignoli and curls of cheese that you have shaved off the cheese wedge with a vegetable parer.

MAKES 4 TO 6 SERVINGS

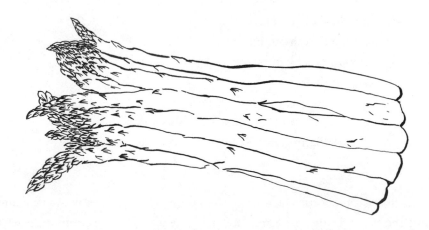

Rice Salad Provençal

Serve this salad as a side dish with grilled tuna or chicken. Add chunks of good-quality canned tuna or leftover grilled tuna to make this side dish salad a substantial main dish.

1 cup uncooked long-grain white rice or imported basmati or
    basmati-type white rice
8 ounces slender fresh green beans, with stem ends trimmed
$1/2$ cup finely chopped Italian (flat leaf) parsley
$1/2$ cup chopped celery
$1/2$ cup chopped sweet red onion
$1/2$ cup roasted and diced red pepper (see Basics, pages 267–268)
$1/4$ cup pitted and chopped brine-cured black olives
1 tablespoon capers, rinsed and drained
6 to 8 leaves red leaf lettuce, rinsed and dried
1 large tomato, cut into wedges
Brine-cured black olives
Sprigs of Italian (flat leaf) parsley
Sprigs of fresh thyme
2 hard-boiled eggs, with shells removed and cut into $1/2$-inch
    pieces

Dressing
$1/2$ cup olive oil
$1/4$ cup fresh lemon juice
1 teaspoon fresh thyme leaves, stripped from stems
$1/2$ clove garlic, crushed
$1/2$ teaspoon salt
Freshly ground black pepper to taste

1. Stir the rice into 1¾ cups of boiling salted water. Cover and cook over medium-low heat until the liquid is absorbed and the rice is tender, about 15 minutes. Let stand, uncovered, until slightly cool. Fluff with a fork.

2. Cook the beans in boiling salted water until crisp-tender, about 5 minutes. Drain, rinse with cold running water, and set aside.

3. To make the dressing: Whisk together the olive oil, lemon juice, thyme, garlic, salt, and pepper in a small bowl, then set aside.

4. Spoon about 1 tablespoon of the dressing over the green beans, stir to coat, then set aside.

5. In a large bowl combine the cooled rice, parsley, celery, red onion, roasted pepper, chopped black olives, and capers. Add the remaining dressing and toss to blend.

6. Line a large platter with the lettuce leaves. Spoon the rice in the center. Surround the rice with bundles of the green beans. Garnish with tomato wedges, whole black olives, and sprigs of parsley and thyme. Sprinkle the pieces of hard-boiled eggs over the rice salad. Serve at once.

MAKES 6 SERVINGS

Green Olives and Rice Salad, Sicilian Style

The ingredients in a Sicilian olive salad can vary, but the basic mixture is usually brine-cured green olives, thick slices of celery, sweet red onion, and capers. In my version I have added diced roasted red pepper and folded in freshly cooked white rice. The wider grains of Italian arborio or domestic medium-grain rice add a nice chewiness to the texture of the finished dish.

1 cup uncooked long- or medium-grain white rice or Italian arborio rice

1 cup pitted and coarsely chopped brine-cured green olives

1 cup sliced (¼ inch) dark green outside celery ribs

¼ cup roasted and coarsely chopped red pepper (see Basics, pages 267–268)

¼ cup coarsely chopped Italian (flat leaf) parsley

¼ cup diced sweet red onion

1 tablespoon finely chopped tender green celery leaves

1 tablespoon capers, rinsed and drained

3 tablespoons extra-virgin olive oil

1 tablespoon fresh lemon juice

1 clove garlic, bruised with the side of a knife

Pinch of crushed red pepper flakes (optional)

1. Stir the rice into 2 cups of boiling salted water. Cover and cook over medium-low heat until the liquid is absorbed and the rice is tender, about 15 minutes. Let stand off the heat, uncovered, until slightly cooled. Fluff with a fork.

2. In a large bowl combine the olives, celery ribs, roasted red pepper, parsley, red onion, celery leaves, capers, olive oil, lemon juice, garlic, and crushed red pepper, if using. Toss to blend. Add the rice and gently fold until blended.

3. Serve at room temperature.

MAKES 4 TO 6 SERVINGS

Summer Rice Salad

This is wonderful served with grilled chicken, seafood, or meat.

1 cup uncooked long-grain white rice
3 tablespoons extra-virgin olive oil
2 tablespoons red wine vinegar
1 clove garlic, crushed
Salt and freshly ground black pepper to taste
2 ears fresh corn, husked and corn kernels cut from the cobs with
    a small sharp knife (about 1 1/4 cups)
1 large tomato, cored and diced (about 1/3 inch)
1/4 cup diced (1/4 inch) sweet red onion
1/4 cup packed, coarsely chopped basil leaves
6 large lettuce leaves (optional)

1. Stir the rice into 1 3/4 cups of boiling salted water. Cover and cook over medium-low heat until the liquid is absorbed and the rice is tender, about 15 minutes. Let stand, uncovered, until slightly cooled. Fluff with a fork.

2. In a large bowl whisk together the olive oil, vinegar, garlic, salt, and a grinding of black pepper. Add the rice, corn, tomato, red onion, and basil, and toss to blend.

3. Spoon into a shallow bowl lined with lettuce leaves, if desired. Serve at once.

MAKES 4 TO 6 SERVINGS

Tabbouleh-style Basmati Rice Salad

Basmati rice or Rizcous gives this dish the flavors of tabbouleh. Finely chop the parsley and mint efficiently and quickly by using the food processor, but the other chopped ingredients should be chopped with a sharp knife.

1 cup uncooked imported basmati or American basmati-type
    white or brown rice or 1 cup Rizcous
¼ cup extra-virgin olive oil
3 tablespoons fresh lemon juice
1 clove garlic, crushed
½ teaspoon salt
Freshly ground black pepper to taste
2 cups seeded and diced (¼ inch) fresh tomatoes
1 cup diced seedless (English) unpared cucumber
½ cup trimmed and finely sliced scallions (about 1 bunch)
1 cup finely chopped curly leaf parsley, including stems
¼ cup finely chopped mint leaves, preferably spearmint, stripped
    from stems

1. Stir the rice into 1¾ cups boiling salted water. Cover and cook over medium-low heat until the liquid is absorbed and the rice is tender, about 15 minutes. Let stand, uncovered, until slightly cooled. Fluff with a fork. Prepare the Rizcous, if using, according to package directions.

2. In a large bowl combine the olive oil, lemon juice, garlic, salt, and pepper, and whisk to blend. Add the cooked rice, tomatoes, cucumber, scallions, parsley, and mint. Toss to blend.

MAKES 6 SERVINGS

Jasmine Tea Rice Salad
with Snow Peas and Ginger

Jasmine rice, a fragrant rice reminiscent of the tea, is a popular rice in Southeast Asia. Its delicate flavor blends successfully with jasmine tea, fresh snow peas, and ginger.

2 teaspoons loose jasmine tea or 1 jasmine tea bag

1³/₄ cups boiling water

1 cup uncooked delicately grained white rice, such as Jasmine or imported basmati or American basmati-type rice

¹/₂ teaspoon salt

4 ounces fresh snow peas, washed and trimmed

¹/₄ cup thinly sliced scallions (set aside 2 tablespoons of diagonally sliced green scallion tops for garnish)

¹/₄ cup pared and minced carrot

1 teaspoon sesame seeds, toasted in a warm skillet

Ginger and Rice Vinegar Dressing

¹/₃ cup flavorless vegetable oil

3 tablespoons rice vinegar

1 teaspoon grated fresh ginger

¹/₂ teaspoon salt

1. In a 2-cup glass measure combine the jasmine tea and boiling water. Cover with a saucer and steep for 5 minutes. Discard the tea bag or strain out the tea leaves, and transfer to a medium-sized saucepan. Add the rice and salt, and heat to boiling, stirring once. Cover and cook over low heat for 12 to 15 minutes, or until the liquid is absorbed and the rice is tender. Uncover and let stand until cooled.

2. Steam the snow peas in a vegetable steamer set over gently boiling water until crisp-tender, about 3 minutes. Lift the steamer from the saucepan, and then rinse the

snow peas with cold water to refresh. Set aside until cooled. Cut the peas into ¼-inch-wide diagonal slices.

3. To make the dressing: Whisk together the oil, rice vinegar, ginger, and salt until blended.

4. Just before serving combine the cooled rice, snow peas, ¼ cup of scallions, and carrot. Add the dressing and toss to coat. Spoon into a serving bowl and sprinkle with sesame seeds. Garnish with green scallion tops.

MAKES 4 SERVINGS

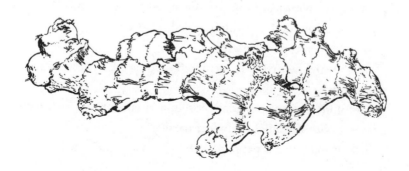

Hoppin' John with Vinaigrette

South of the Mason-Dixon line it is considered good luck to start the New Year with a dish of black-eyed peas and rice. The following recipe from Richard Sax, a friend and culinary colleague, is a pleasant variation on the traditional theme. The recipe borrows the basic ingredients from the hot dish—bacon, black-eyed peas, rice, green pepper, and spices—and transforms them into a terrific salad. Use frozen black-eyed peas if available; they are better than the canned.

5 strips bacon
2 packages (10 ounces each) frozen black-eyed peas *or* 2 or 3 cans
    black-eyed peas, rinsed and drained, *or* 1¼ pounds dried peas,
    soaked, cooked until tender, and rinsed and drained (see Basics,
    page 264)
3 cups boiling water
2 cloves garlic, crushed
Pinch of dried thyme
1 bay leaf
Salt
1 cup uncooked long-grain white rice
3 slender carrots, halved lengthwise and thinly sliced (about 2
    cups)
3 celery ribs with leafy tops, thinly sliced (about 2 cups)
4 scallions, trimmed and thinly sliced (reserve some of the
    sliced green tops for garnish)
1 medium red bell pepper, stemmed, with seeds removed, and
    cut into ½-inch dice
3 ripe plum tomatoes, seeded, cored, and cut into ½-inch dice
3 tablespoons chopped curly leaf parsley
Freshly ground black pepper to taste

Dressing
2 tablespoons Dijon mustard, plus more to taste
$^1/_2$ cup red wine vinegar, plus more to taste
$^1/_4$ teaspoon Tabasco sauce, or more to taste
Salt and freshly ground black pepper to taste
$^1/_2$ cup mild-flavored olive or other vegetable oil

1. Cook the bacon in a skillet until crisp. Drain on a paper towel and set aside. Crumble 1 piece of the bacon into a saucepan and add the frozen black-eyed peas, boiling water, garlic, thyme, and bay leaf. Return to a boil and separate the peas with a fork. Simmer over low heat, covered, until the peas are tender but not mushy, 30 to 40 minutes. Drain and discard the seasonings. Place the warm beans in a large bowl.

2. While the peas are cooking, heat a large saucepan of water to boiling. Add salt and rice. Boil the rice, uncovered, stirring occasionally, until the rice is *al dente,* about 12 minutes. Add the carrots during the last 30 seconds of cooking. Drain the rice and carrots in a large strainer. Rinse with hot water and drain. Add to the black-eyed peas. Add the celery, scallions, red bell pepper, tomatoes, and parsley. Season with salt and pepper.

3. To make the dressing: In a bowl whisk together the mustard, vinegar, Tabasco, salt, and pepper until blended. Gradually whisk in the oil. Pour $^2/_3$ of the dressing over the salad ingredients while they are still warm. Toss gently. Let stand at room temperature at least 1 hour before serving.

4. Before serving whisk the remaining dressing and add to the salad. Toss gently and taste. Add additional mustard, Tabasco, and vinegar if needed. The salad should be spicy. Spoon the salad into a serving bowl. Crumble the remaining reserved bacon and sprinkle over the top. Garnish with the reserved sliced scallions. Serve at room temperature.

MAKES 6 TO 8 SERVINGS

LITTLE RICE DISHES

Appetizers and Snacks

Mushroom, Cheese, and Rice Pancakes
Risotto Pancakes, *Risotto al Salto*
Spinach and Rice Croquettes with Tomato and Mushroom Sauce
Parmesan and Rice Timbales with Sautéed Roasted Red Peppers
Rice Dumplings, *Arancini*
Prosciutto-and-Cheese-filled *Arancini*
Rice Croquettes with Melted Cheese, *Suppli al Telefono*
Stuffed Grape Leaves, *Dolmades*

Vegetable and Rice Side Dishes

Stirred Rice with Spinach
Buttered Rice with Slowly Cooked Leeks
Crunchy Buttered Rice with Zucchini and Carrots
Fresh Tomato Sauce with Rice
Brown Rice and Wheat Berries with Crisp-cooked Eggplant
Rice Primavera
Baked Stuffed Tomatoes, Sicilian Style
Broccoli Rape with Arborio Rice, Hot Red Pepper Oil, and Garlic

Rice Side Dishes

Brown Rice with Onions, Garlic, and Walnuts
Brown Rice with Garlic and Cashews
Brown Rice with Chanterelles, Dried Apricots, and Almonds
Brown Basmati Rice with Crisp Onions and Cumin Seed Butter
Sonia's Crusty Basmati Rice

Rice Stuffings

Apricot and Brown Rice Stuffing for Cornish Hens
Rice, Sausage, and Raisin Stuffing for Turkey

Quick Hits with Rice

Gloria's Parmesan Rice
Garlic Rice
Pecan, Almond, or Walnut Rice
Lemon Rice
Double Sesame Rice
Rice with Peas and Mint
Curried Rice
Rice with Toasted Pignoli
Orange Rice with Dried Currants
Anna Lisa's Brown Rice with Raisins and Sunflower Seeds
Mushroom Rice
Indian-style Rice with or without Coconut
Raisin and Peanut Rice
Saffron Rice
Summer Garden Rice

I call these little dishes not because they are tiny servings, but because they are all appropriate for snacking or grazing, as appetizers or side dishes, or are so simple—as in the section called Quick Hits with Rice—that they barely require a recipe.

A fair number of the following dishes are Italian inspired. This is because the Italians like rice and have many interesting and creative ways to cook and serve it, and also because of my insatiable interest in and enjoyment of Italian food.

To cook rice in any form is to jaunt around the world. From the exotic and scrumptious Sonia's Crusty Basmati Rice to Parmesan and Rice Timbales with Sautéed Roasted Red Peppers we can traverse the flavors of the globe without leaving our kitchens.

Mushroom, Cheese, and Rice Pancakes

Make these as small individual patties or as a large thick skillet-sized cake. Here I use only white button mushrooms, but shiitake or cremini—a cultivated Italian brown mushroom with an intense flavor (see Basics, page 266)—is also a good choice. Serve as a first course, as a vegetable side dish, or as a snack.

2 tablespoons unsalted butter or vegetable oil
1 cup finely chopped white button mushrooms
$\frac{1}{2}$ cup chopped onion
1 clove garlic, crushed
Salt and freshly ground black pepper to taste
3 cups cooked long-grain white rice
3 large eggs *or* 1 large egg and 2 egg whites, beaten
$\frac{1}{2}$ cup freshly grated Parmigiano-Reggiano cheese (see Basics,
    page 267)
$\frac{1}{2}$ cup shredded mozzarella cheese
2 tablespoons finely chopped parsley (optional)
1 teaspoon fresh thyme leaves, stripped from stems, *or* $\frac{1}{4}$
    teaspoon dried thyme (optional)
1 tablespoon unsalted butter, cut into small pieces

1. Heat 1 tablespoon of the butter or oil in a large, preferably nonstick, skillet. Add the mushrooms and onion and sauté, stirring, until the onion is tender and the mushrooms are browned, about 10 minutes. Add the garlic and sauté for 1 minute. Season with salt and pepper.

2. In a large bowl stir the sautéed mushroom mixture and the rice together. Add the beaten eggs and stir until thoroughly blended. Add the Parmigiano-Reggiano and mozzarella cheeses, parsley, and thyme, if using. Stir until blended.

3. Heat the remaining butter and the olive oil in the skillet until very hot. Rinse hands with cold water and, working with about $\frac{1}{2}$ cup of the rice mixture at a time, form patties (the mixture will be loose) and drop onto the hot skillet. Continue until the

pan is filled. Sauté the pancakes until they are well browned and set. Carefully turn and brown the other side.

4. Keep the cooked pancakes warm in the oven set at the lowest temperature while cooking the remaining pancakes. Serve warm.

5. If you wish to make one big pancake, add all the rice mixture to the hot skillet, spread it out with a spatula, and press down. Cover and cook until the bottom is well browned and crisp, about 12 minutes. Turn out, crisp side up.

MAKES 12 PANCAKES APPROXIMATELY 4 INCHES IN DIAMETER

Risotto Pancakes, Risotto al Salto

Risotto al salto *are pancakes made with leftover cooked risotto. In Milan—where risotto reigns supreme—risotto al salto is made into one large pancake. I rarely have enough risotto left over to make a large pancake so I usually make smaller ones, which I find easier to handle and also fun to serve as a snack, appetizer, or even a side dish. Here is the simple formula (the recipe can be doubled).*

1 large egg, well beaten
1 to 2 cups leftover cold risotto (see pages 183–184)
1 to 2 tablespoons unsalted butter
Freshly grated Parmigiano-Reggiano cheese (see Basics, page
   267)

1. Add 1 tablespoon of the beaten egg at a time to the risotto. If the mixture is soft, do not add all of the egg.

2. Rinsing your hands frequently with cold water, shape the risotto into patties about 2 inches in diameter. Set aside on waxed paper. (This can be done ahead of time, and the patties can be covered and refrigerated until ready to sauté.)

3. Just before serving melt the butter in a large heavy, preferably nonstick, skillet over medium heat until the foam subsides. Add the risotto pancakes and sauté until browned and crusty on one side. Carefully turn and sauté the other side.

4. Serve warm or arrange on a heat-proof platter and keep warm in an oven set on the lowest temperature. Sprinkle with grated cheese before serving.

MAKES 4 TO 8 PANCAKES

Spinach and Rice Croquettes with Tomato and Mushroom Sauce

I like croquettes because they are old-fashioned, comforting, and not considered chic. Hard-boiled eggs, spinach, cheese, and rice—all pretty basic ingredients—make this dish as nourishing and homespun as food can get.

2 hard-boiled eggs, peeled and cut into chunks
5 ounces rinsed and trimmed fresh spinach (about 4 cups packed)
2 tablespoons butter
2 tablespoons plus $1/2$ cup (approximately) all-purpose flour
1 cup milk
Salt
1 cup cooked long-grain white rice
$1/4$ cup freshly grated Parmigiano-Reggiano cheese (see Basics, page 267)
Freshly ground black pepper to taste
1 cup (approximately) fine dry bread crumbs
1 extra-large egg
Oil for frying

Tomato and Mushroom Sauce
3 tablespoons olive oil
1 cup coarsely chopped mushrooms
1/4 cup chopped onion
1 clove garlic, minced
1 can (28 ounces) Italian-style plum tomatoes with juice
1 tablespoon chopped Italian (flat leaf) parsley and/or fresh
   basil
Salt and freshly ground black pepper to taste

1. Prepare the hard-boiled eggs and set aside. In a vegetable steamer set over simmering water in a covered saucepan, steam the spinach until wilted and tender, about 5 minutes. Drain in a sieve, squeezing out the excess moisture. Pat dry between paper towels and set aside.

2. Melt the butter in a small saucepan. Stir in 2 tablespoons of flour until blended. Cook over low heat, stirring, for 2 minutes. Gradually whisk in the milk and heat to boiling. Add 1/2 teaspoon of salt and cook over medium-low heat, stirring, for 5 minutes.

3. Fold the eggs, spinach, and rice into the sauce. Season with the cheese, salt to taste, and pepper. Refrigerate the mixture until it is very thick and cold enough to shape. (The mixture can be made up to 1 day ahead at this point.)

4. To prepare the tomato and mushroom sauce: Heat the oil in a large skillet. Add the mushrooms and onion, and sauté, stirring, until golden, about 5 minutes. Add the garlic and sauté 1 minute more. Add the tomatoes and heat to boiling, stirring and breaking up the tomatoes with the side of a spoon. Lower the heat and simmer the sauce, uncovered, stirring often until thickened, about 20 minutes. Add the parsley and/ or basil, salt, and pepper. Keep warm until ready to serve. Makes about 2 cups of sauce. (It can be made 1 to 2 days before serving.)

5. To shape the croquettes: Spread the remaining 1/2 cup of flour and bread crumbs on separate sheets of waxed paper. Beat the egg in a shallow soup bowl. Scoop up the rice mixture with a tablespoon, and with hands frequently rinsed with cold water, form the mixture into croquettes about 3 inches long and 1 inch in diameter. After the croquettes have been shaped, roll in the flour to lightly coat, then roll in the beaten egg and the bread crumbs to coat. Set aside and let the crumbs set before frying. (The croquettes can be assembled and refrigerated up to 1 hour before cooking.)

6. Heat 1 to 2 inches of oil in a large skillet until hot enough to sizzle and brown a

crust of bread. Add the croquettes a few at a time and fry until golden, about 3 to 5 minutes per side. Drain on paper towels. Serve hot with the tomato and mushroom sauce.

MAKES 16 CROQUETTES OR 4 SERVINGS

Parmesan and Rice Timbales
with Sautéed Roasted Red Peppers

Serve the rice mixture as individual timbales or press into a 3- to 4-cup ring mold and make an impressive presentation on a large platter surrounded by a wreath of red peppers.

Sautéed Roasted Red Peppers

6 to 8 large red bell peppers, roasted and peeled (see Basics, pages 267–268)

¼ cup extra-virgin olive oil

1 clove garlic, halved

1 tablespoon fresh thyme leaves, stripped from stems

1 teaspoon minced fresh oregano leaves, stripped from stems

Salt and freshly ground black pepper to taste

Sprigs of fresh thyme and oregano (optional)

Rice Timbales

4 cups water

2 tablespoons olive oil, plus additional for oiling timbales

1 teaspoon salt

2 cups uncooked medium- or long-grain rice or Italian arborio rice

1 cup freshly grated Parmigiano-Reggiano cheese (see Basics, page 267)

1. To make the sautéed roasted red peppers: Cut the roasted and peeled peppers into 1-inch-wide strips. Strain ¼ cup of the roasted pepper juice into a small bowl and set aside. Heat the oil in a large skillet over low heat. Add the garlic and sauté just until golden. Remove and discard. Add the roasted peppers, thyme, oregano, and reserved pepper juice. Sauté just until heated through, turning the peppers. Season with salt and pepper. Keep warm until ready to serve.

2. To make the rice timbales: Combine the water, 2 tablespoons of olive oil, and salt in a medium-sized saucepan. Heat to boiling, then stir in the rice. Cover and cook over medium-low heat for 15 minutes, or until the liquid is absorbed. Stir in the cheese.

3. Meanwhile, lightly oil six 8-ounce custard cups or timbales with olive oil. Spoon the hot rice into the molds, dividing it evenly. Press firmly in place with the back of a spoon and immediately invert on serving plates.

4. To serve, spoon the peppers around the rice timbales and drizzle some of the juice on top of the rice. Garnish with sprigs of the fresh thyme and oregano, if desired.

MAKES 6 SERVINGS

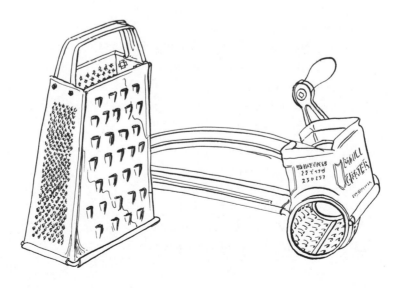

Rice Dumplings,
Arancini

Arancini *means little oranges. Often as big as a softball, these popular rice dumplings are sold throughout Sicily by street vendors who fry them right before your eyes. The dumplings are usually flavored with saffron, but the size and filling can vary. Sometimes they are stuffed with mozzarella and prosciutto, sometimes with a mixture of pork, liver, beef, or even lamb. These are stuffed with slowly simmered pork or beef seasoned with raisins and ground cinnamon. The rice is golden from the saffron and rich with the flavor of Parmigiano-Reggiano. For a more authentic and sharper flavor, use grated Pecorino-Romano, a popular sheep's milk cheese. This is a fairly labor-intensive recipe, but the components can be made a day or two ahead. Serve as a snack, appetizer, or light lunch with a big green salad. They can also be fried ahead and reheated in a hot oven. Leftovers freeze well.*

Meat Filling
1 tablespoon olive oil
1 2-ounce-piece boneless pork shoulder or beef round or
    chuck, cut into 1 1/2-inch cubes
1/2 cup finely chopped onion
1/2 cup pared and finely chopped carrot
1 clove garlic, minced
2 cups beef broth, preferably unsalted
2 tablespoons tomato paste
2 tablespoons dried currants
1/4 teaspoon ground cinnamon
1/4 cup tiny frozen peas, thawed
Salt and freshly ground black pepper to taste

Rice

Generous pinch of saffron threads

2 cups unsalted chicken broth, preferably homemade

2 tablespoons olive oil

⅓ cup finely chopped onion

1 clove garlic, minced

1 cup uncooked American medium-grain white rice or Italian
  arborio rice

½ cup freshly grated Parmigiano-Reggiano cheese (see Basics,
  page 267)

1 extra-large egg, beaten

2 egg whites

2 cups (approximately) fine dry bread crumbs

1 to 2 quarts olive or other vegetable oil for deep-frying

1. To make the meat filling: Heat the oil in a Dutch oven or deep heavy skillet with a tight-fitting lid. Add the meat cubes and brown on all sides. Stir in the onion and carrot. Sauté over medium-low heat, stirring, until tender, about 10 minutes. Add the garlic and sauté for 1 minute. Add the beef broth and tomato paste, and heat to boiling. Cover and cook over medium-low heat for 1½ to 2 hours, or until the meat is very tender. Check the broth level occasionally and add more broth or water if needed.

2. Transfer the meat to a platter and let stand until cool. Set aside the juice in the pan. Cut the meat into thin slices and then shred or chop into small pieces. Return the meat to the cooking juice and add the currants and cinnamon. Cook, uncovered, over medium heat until the broth is almost completely reduced. Add the peas and cook, stirring, until the mixture is very dry and thick. Remove from the heat and season with salt and pepper. (This can be made up to 2 days ahead.)

3. To make the rice: Steep the saffron in ¼ cup of the boiling broth for 10 minutes. Meanwhile, heat the oil in a medium-sized saucepan. Add the onion and sauté over medium-low heat, stirring, until tender, about 5 minutes. Add the garlic and sauté for 1 minute. Add the rice and stir to coat with oil. Stir in the saffron mixture and the remaining 1¾ cups of chicken broth. Heat to boiling, stirring to keep the rice from sticking.

4. Cover and cook over medium-low heat for 20 minutes, or until the water is absorbed and the rice is very tender. Uncover and stir in the cheese while the rice is still

hot. Cool to room temperature. Stir the beaten egg into the rice mixture until well blended.

5. Whisk the whites in a shallow bowl until foamy. Place the bread crumbs on a large sheet of waxed paper. Have ready a waxed paper–lined tray or baking sheet.

6. Divide the rice mixture evenly into 16 portions (see Note below). Constantly rinse hands with water while working to prevent sticking. Flatten the rice mound in the palm of your hand and spoon a rounded tablespoonful of the meat mixture in the center. Gently close your hand so that the meat is surrounded by the rice. Dip in the beaten egg white, letting the excess egg white drip off. Roll the dumpling in bread crumbs, shaking off the excess. Place the dumplings on the waxed paper–lined tray as they are prepared. (They can be prepared up to 2 hours ahead and refrigerated until ready to fry.)

7. Heat the oil in a deep-fat fryer to 365°F. or in a deep frying pan until hot enough to turn a crust of bread golden. Fry the dumplings, a few at a time, turning gently, until they are dark golden brown. Remove with a fry basket or slotted spoon and drain on paper towels. Serve warm or at room temperature.

MAKES ABOUT 16 DUMPLINGS OR 4 TO 6 SERVINGS

Note: This amount of rice (1 cup raw) will make 18 small dumplings (approximately 1½ inches in diameter) or 12 to 16 larger dumplings. An easy way to divide the rice evenly is to spread it in a thick even layer in a foil-lined 13 × 9-inch baking pan. Divide the rice mixture into 12, 16, or 18 even portions. Use a wide spatula to transfer each "square" of rice mixture to the palm of your hand and follow the directions in the recipe for shaping the *arancini*.

PROSCIUTTO-AND-CHEESE-FILLED ARANCINI

This simple version of arancini *has a filling of diced prosciutto and cheese instead of the more traditional filling of cooked meats. You can also omit the saffron if you wish. Just make the following changes to the preceding recipe.*

1. Substitute about 4 ounces of prosciutto and 4 ounces of mozzarella, Italian Fontina, or Gorgonzola for the meat filling. Cut them into small dice and use a few pieces in the center of each *arancini*.

2. Follow the recipe above for the rest of the directions.

Rice Croquettes with Melted Cheese,
Suppli al Telefono

Suppli al telefono—*rice croquettes with melted cheese in the center—*
uses leftover risi e bisi. Suppli al telefono *means telephone wires, which*
is exactly what the melted cheese looks like when you take a bite out of one
end of the croquette. In our family we call this an embarrassing food—as
we wipe the "telephone wires" of melted cheese off our chins. Serve as a
snack or light meal with a piece of fruit and a few walnuts or almonds.
Serve with Italian red wine—a Chianti Classico or a Dolcetto d'Alba.

1 1/2 cups leftover *Risi e Bisi* (recipe page 195)
1/4 cup slivered (about 1 × 1/8 inch) prosciutto (optional)
2 tablespoons freshly grated Parmigiano-Reggiano cheese (see
    Basics, page 267)
2 eggs, lightly beaten separately
2 tablespoons milk
1/2 cup all-purpose flour
1/2 cup fine dry bread crumbs
4 ounces mozzarella cheese
Olive oil for frying

1. In a bowl stir the *risi e bisi,* prosciutto, Parmigiano-Reggiano cheese, and 1 of the
eggs until well blended. Spread in a 13 × 9-inch baking pan. Cover with plastic wrap
and refrigerate until very cold, about 1 hour.

2. When ready to prepare, beat the remaining egg with the milk in a shallow bowl,
then set aside. Place the flour on a large sheet of waxed paper and the bread crumbs on
another large sheet of waxed paper. Line them up on the counter in order of use. Have
ready a wire rack set over a sheet of waxed paper or a baking sheet.

3. Cut the mozzarella cheese into twelve 1/2-inch cubes. Using a knife divide the
rice mixture into 12 evenly sized pieces. Rinse hands with cold water to prevent

sticking. Place the rice in the palm of your hand and make an indentation in the center. Place the cube of mozzarella in the indentation and with wet hands shape the rice over the mozzarella and into a smooth ball.

4. Lightly coat the balls by rolling in the flour, shaking off the excess. Using tongs dip the balls in the egg mixture, letting the excess drip off. Roll in the bread crumbs and shake off the excess. Line up on the wire rack and let stand for 30 minutes before frying. (You can make these ahead and let stand in a cool kitchen or refrigerate for an hour or more before frying.)

5. Heat 2 inches of olive oil in a large skillet or a deep-fat fryer until hot enough to quickly brown a crust of bread, or 365°F. on a deep-fat frying thermometer.

6. Fry a few at a time, turning until they are evenly golden, about 3 minutes. Drain on paper towels as they brown. Serve at once.

MAKES 10 TO 12 CROQUETTES OR 4 SERVINGS

Stuffed Grape Leaves,
Dolmades

Stuffed grape leaves, or dolmades *as they are called in Greek cuisine, are stuffed with rice, meat, lentils, or any combination of the three, plus herbs, most conspicuously fresh mint. This recipe is from a good friend and fellow cook, Barbara Chernetz, who has traveled extensively throughout Greece, where she sharpened her appetite for its foods.*

1 jar (8 ounces) grape leaves
3 tablespoons olive oil
1 cup finely chopped onions
2 garlic cloves, minced
1/3 cup uncooked long-grain white rice or imported basmati or
   American basmati-type white rice
1/2 teaspoon ground allspice
1 cinnamon stick
2/3 cup water
1/2 teaspoon salt
1/4 teaspoon freshly ground black pepper
2 tablespoons pignoli (pine nuts), toasted
2 tablespoons dried currants
1 tablespoon chopped fresh mint
1 tablespoon chopped fresh Italian (flat leaf) parsley
2 tablespoons fresh lemon juice
Lemon wedges

1. Rinse the grape leaves under cold water and drain. Blot dry with paper towels. Using a sharp knife cut the stems off all the leaves. Set aside any torn or small leaves separately.

2. In a medium-sized saucepan heat 1 tablespoon of the oil over medium heat. Add

the onion and garlic, and sauté, stirring, until tender, about 5 minutes. Add the rice, allspice, and cinnamon stick, and sauté for 1 minute. Add the water, salt, and pepper, and heat to boiling. Lower the heat and simmer, covered, until all the liquid is absorbed, about 15 minutes. Remove from the heat and discard the cinnamon stick. Stir in the pignoli, currants, mint, and parsley.

3. Place one grape leaf, smooth or shiny side down, on a work surface. Place about 1 tablespoon of the rice mixture in the center of the leaf. Fold the sides of the leaf in and then roll the leaf up firmly, jelly-roll style. Repeat with the remaining leaves until 24 rolled grape leaves are completed.

4. Use the remaining grape leaves (including the reserved torn or small ones) to line a large skillet with a tight-fitting lid. Place the stuffed grape leaves in the skillet in a single layer, seam side down and lining them up side by side.

5. In a small bowl combine the remaining 2 tablespoons of olive oil and the lemon juice. Sprinkle over the grape leaves. Heat the skillet over medium-high heat until the juice is simmering. Cover and cook over medium-low heat for 30 minutes. Serve cold or at room temperature with lemon wedges.

MAKES 24 STUFFED GRAPE LEAVES OR 4 SERVINGS

Stirred Rice with Spinach

It is surprising how just 3 ingredients—spinach, grated Parmigiano-Reggiano cheese, and toasted pignoli—can transform a pot of rice into a delicious side dish. Utilize the time it takes to cook the rice to rinse and trim the spinach. Toast the pignoli in a small dry skillet, stirring constantly over low heat. Don't take your eyes off them—I've learned the hard way that they will burn the moment you are distracted.

1 tablespoon olive oil

$^1\!/_2$ cup chopped onion

1 small clove garlic, minced

1 cup uncooked long-grain white rice

$1^3\!/_4$ cups water or half water and half chicken broth

Salt to taste (optional)

1 package (10 ounces) fresh spinach, rinsed, trimmed, and torn
   into 1-inch pieces

$^1\!/_4$ cup freshly grated Parmigiano-Reggiano cheese (see Basics,
   page 267)

2 tablespoons pignoli (pine nuts), lightly toasted in a skillet

1. Heat the oil over low heat in a large heavy saucepan. Add the onion and garlic, and sauté, stirring occasionally, until golden, about 10 minutes. Stir in the rice and turn the heat to medium-low. Sauté, stirring constantly, about 2 minutes.

2. Stir in the water (or broth and water) and salt, if using, and heat to simmering. Cook, covered, over low heat for 12 minutes. Add the spinach and cheese to the saucepan, stirring once or twice just to blend. Cover and cook over medium-low heat for 3 minutes, or until the spinach is wilted.

3. Spoon into a serving dish and sprinkle with toasted pignoli. Serve at once.

MAKES 4 SERVINGS

Buttered Rice with Slowly Cooked Leeks

The robust, assertive flavor of leeks becomes sweet and mellow when they are slowly sautéed with butter. This is a good accompaniment to grilled or broiled fish. Use a squirt of lemon juice and a dusting of finely chopped fresh chives or dill for an interesting counterpoint to the sweet onion flavor.

3 to 4 medium-sized leeks
1 cup uncooked long-grain white rice
4 tablespoons unsalted butter
Salt and freshly ground black pepper to taste
1 tablespoon fresh lemon juice
2 tablespoons minced fresh chives and/or dill

1. Trim the dark green tops and the roots from the leeks and halve lengthwise. Wash in lukewarm water to remove sand from between the layers and rinse well. Soak in a bowl of cold water for 5 minutes, then drain and dry. Chop into 1/4-inch pieces. There should be 2½ to 3 cups of chopped leeks.

2. Cook the rice in a medium-sized saucepan, covered, over low heat in 1¾ cups of boiling salted water until the water is absorbed and the rice is tender. Let stand, uncovered, for 5 minutes before using.

3. While the rice is cooking melt the butter in a medium-sized skillet over low heat. Add the leeks and stir to coat. Cover and cook, uncovering to stir and check often (do not brown or allow the butter to sizzle) until the leeks are tender, about 10 to 15 minutes. Season with salt and pepper.

4. Add the cooked rice to the skillet and toss to blend thoroughly. Sprinkle with the lemon and herbs, and toss gently. Serve immediately.

MAKES 4 SERVINGS

Crunchy Buttered Rice with Zucchini and Carrots

I am so crazy about those pieces of sizzling crispy rice often served floating in soup in Chinese restaurants that I decided to create a whole dish of crunch. The flavor and textural contrasts of the pieces of crisp and crunchy rice on the outside, the soft buttery rice on the inside, and the tender carrots and zucchini are a pleasant surprise.

4 tablespoons unsalted butter

¹/₂ cup chopped onion

2 cups unsalted chicken broth, preferably homemade, or half broth and half water

1 cup uncooked long-grain white rice

1 medium carrot, pared and diced (about ¹/₃ cup)

1 pound zucchini, trimmed and very thinly sliced (preferably in a food processor)

Salt and freshly ground black pepper to taste

1. Melt 1 tablespoon of butter in a large nonstick skillet. Add the onion and sauté, stirring, until tender, about 5 minutes. Stir in the broth, cover, and heat to boiling.

2. Stir in the rice and carrot. Cover tightly and cook over medium-low heat for 15 minutes, or until all the liquid is absorbed.

3. Meanwhile, melt the remaining 3 tablespoons of butter. When the rice has cooked for 15 minutes, uncover and drizzle 2 tablespoons of the melted butter evenly over the rice. Turn the heat to moderately high and press down on the rice with a spatula. Spread an even layer of the zucchini slices on top of the rice. Drizzle with the remaining tablespoon of butter and sprinkle with salt and pepper.

4. Cover tightly and cook over moderately high heat for 10 to 15 minutes, or until the layer of rice on the bottom of the pan is toasted a rich golden brown. (You will be

able to smell the aroma, or you can lift the lid and the edge of the rice to check the progress.)

5. Serve a little of the crunchy toasted rice layer with every spoonful.

MAKES 4 TO 6 SERVINGS

Fresh Tomato Sauce with Rice

Come summer—and the height of the tomato and basil season—I chop tomatoes with basil and with a liberal addition of a robustly flavored olive oil create a basic raw tomato sauce that I serve on everything from hot fresh-cooked pasta to rice. Serve as a separate course or as a side dish with grilled chicken or seafood.

1 tablespoon extra-virgin olive oil

1 cup uncooked long-grain white rice

1¾ cups water

½ teaspoon salt

⅓ cup chopped pieces (about ¼ inch) Parmigiano-Reggiano cheese (see Basics, page 267)

Salsa di Pomodoro Crudo

2 cups diced ripe tomatoes

⅓ cup extra-virgin olive oil

⅓ cup chopped fresh basil

½ teaspoon salt

1 small clove garlic, crushed

1. Heat the tablespoon of oil in a medium-sized saucepan. Add the rice and sauté, stirring, over medium-low heat for 2 minutes. Add the water and salt. Heat to boiling, stirring well. Cover and cook until the water is absorbed and the rice is tender, about 15 minutes.

2. Meanwhile, prepare the salsa: Combine the tomatoes, olive oil, basil, salt, and garlic. Stir to blend and set aside until ready to serve.

3. Spoon the rice into a large shallow serving bowl. Sprinkle with the pieces of cheese. Spoon the salsa over the top and fluff with a spoon and a fork just to blend. Serve immediately.

MAKES 4 SERVINGS AS A SEPARATE COURSE OR 6 SERVINGS AS A SIDE DISH

Brown Rice and Wheat Berries
with Crisp-cooked Eggplant

Strips of eggplant fried in olive oil and sprinkled with salt are a favorite snack with drinks. I also like these strips of fried eggplant tossed with rice and chopped fresh tomato. The addition of the wheat berries is what my good friend and fellow food enthusiast Anne Mendelson would call an "accident in the kitchen"—the soaking wheat berries and draining eggplant slices just happened to be side by side on the kitchen counter, and I said, "Why not?"

¹/₂ cup wheat berries

1 firm eggplant (about 1 pound)

2 teaspoons salt

Olive oil

1 tablespoon thinly sliced garlic (about 3 cloves)

Pinch of hot red pepper flakes (optional)

3¹/₂ cups cooked short-grain brown rice

1 cup seeded and diced (¹/₄ inch) fresh tomato (from 1 large
    tomato)

¹/₄ cup coarsely chopped fresh parsley

1 tablespoon chopped fresh basil

1. Soak the wheat berries in 1 quart of water overnight, then drain. Cook the wheat berries, uncovered, in 1 quart of simmering water until tender, about 1 hour, then drain. (These can be prepared up to 2 days ahead. Refrigerate, covered, until ready to use.)

2. Trim the ends from the eggplant. Remove the skin with a vegetable parer. Cut into 1/4-inch-thick slices and arrange in layers in a colander, sprinkling each layer lightly with salt. Place a small plate on the top layer of eggplant and weight it with something heavy (a 28-ounce can of tomatoes works well). Place a soup dish under the colander and let stand at least 3 hours. Blot the eggplant dry with a paper towel. Stack the slices and cut them in 1/4-inch-wide strips.

3. Heat about 1/2 inch of olive oil in a large skillet until hot enough to sizzle a piece of eggplant on contact. Fry the eggplant in two batches until they are dark golden brown, stirring to keep the strips separate. Remove from the oil with a slotted spoon and drain on a double thickness of paper towels.

4. Discard the frying oil and wipe the skillet. Add 1/3 cup of olive oil to the skillet. Stir in the garlic slices and red pepper, if using. Cook and stir the garlic until it begins to turn golden. Immediately add the rice and the cooked wheat berries. Stir to coat and heat through, about 3 minutes. Add the diced tomato, parsley, and basil. Stir to heat through, about 2 minutes. Stir in the eggplant until blended.

5. Serve hot or at room temperature.

MAKES 6 TO 8 SERVINGS

Rice Primavera

Serve Rice Primavera as a separate course before an entree of roasted meat or chicken, or as the main course for a light lunch or dinner. The flavors of the vegetables are delicate, so use a light hand when adding the grated Parmigiano-Reggiano cheese. The ability of converted or parboiled rice to remain in separate and distinct grains makes it a good choice for this dish.

2½ cups unsalted chicken broth, preferably homemade
1 cup uncooked converted or parboiled white rice
Pinch of salt
3 tablespoons unsalted butter
2 tablespoons minced shallots
1 cup diagonally sliced (¼ inch) green beans (about 3 ounces)
1 cup diced (¼ inch) carrot
1 cup tiny green peas (thawed, if frozen)
1 cup diced (¼ inch) zucchini and/or yellow squash
¼ cup freshly grated Parmigiano-Reggiano cheese, plus more
    to serve on the side (see Basics, page 267)
Freshly ground black pepper to taste
1 tablespoon thinly sliced scallion tops
2 tablespoons pignoli (pine nuts), toasted in a small skillet
1 tablespoon finely chopped parsley

1. Heat the broth to boiling and stir in the rice and salt. Cook, covered, over medium-low heat until the rice is tender and the broth is absorbed, about 25 minutes.

2. Meanwhile, heat the butter in a large skillet over low heat. Add the shallots, green beans, and diced carrot, and sauté, stirring, for 2 minutes. Stir in the peas, cover, and cook for 2 minutes. Remove from the heat and stir in the zucchini. Cover and let stand off the heat.

3. Stir the cheese into the cooked rice until creamy. Add the rice to the skillet and

stir until blended with the vegetables. Add a grinding of black pepper. Spoon into a serving dish and sprinkle with the scallion tops, pignoli, and parsley. Serve additional grated cheese on the side.

MAKES 4 SERVINGS

Baked Stuffed Tomatoes, Sicilian Style

This is a perfect summer food when tomatoes are lush and ripe. I like the combination of anchovy and olive, but any mixture of fresh vegetables can be used—try fresh corn kernels, scallions, red bell pepper, shredded mozzarella or grated Parmesan, whatever your pantry or your mood dictates.

4 large or 6 medium-sized tomatoes, moderately ripe
Salt and freshly ground black pepper
Extra-virgin olive oil
2 cups cooked long- or medium-grain white rice or Italian
    arborio rice
1/2 cup diced (1/4 inch) sweet red onion
2 tablespoons pitted and chopped brine-cured black olives
1 tablespoon rinsed, drained, and minced anchovy fillets
1 tablespoon finely chopped Italian (flat leaf) parsley
1 tablespoon finely chopped fresh basil

Garlic Crumbs
1 cup coarse crumbs made from day-old Italian bread
1 tablespoon olive oil
1 clove garlic, crushed

1. Heat the oven to 350°F. Lightly oil a shallow baking dish just large enough to hold the tomatoes side by side.

2. Cut ¹/₂ inch from the tops of the tomatoes. Using a teaspoon scoop out the pulp and seeds, leaving the tomato shell intact. Chop ¹/₂ cup of the pulp and set aside. Discard the remaining pulp or reserve for other use. Sprinkle the inside of each tomato with salt and pepper. Rub the outside lightly with some olive oil. Arrange in the prepared baking dish.

3. In a large bowl combine the rice, red onion, ¹/₂ cup of the chopped tomato pulp, olives, anchovies, parsley, and basil. Add 3 tablespoons of the olive oil and toss to blend. Carefully stuff into the tomatoes, distributing evenly.

4. To make the garlic crumbs: In a small bowl combine the bread crumbs, olive oil, and garlic. Toss to blend, then sprinkle on the tops of the tomatoes, dividing evenly.

5. Bake the tomatoes until the crumbs are golden and the tomatoes are heated through, about 20 to 25 minutes. Serve warm or at room temperature.

SERVES 4 TO 6

Broccoli Rape with Arborio Rice, Hot Red Pepper Oil, and Garlic

I have prepared this dish with both long-grain white rice and Italian arborio rice. Either one works; both are delicious. This dish is special enough to be served as a separate course before the entree or as a vegetable side dish. The flavors are especially good with baked fish.

1½ pounds broccoli rape, rinsed well and with thick stems peeled and trimmed

1½ cups uncooked Italian arborio rice or long- or medium-grain white rice

5 tablespoons extra-virgin olive oil, plus more for molds or cups, if using

½ cup diced red bell pepper

4 garlic cloves, peeled and cut into thin strips

½ teaspoon crushed red pepper flakes, or more to taste

1. Cut the broccoli rape into 1½- to 2-inch lengths. Heat a large saucepan of water to boiling. Stir in the broccoli rape and cook until tender, about 6 to 8 minutes, stirring occasionally. Drain and set aside.

2. Meanwhile, stir the rice into 3 cups of boiling salted water. Cover and cook over medium-low heat until the water is absorbed and the rice is tender, about 15 minutes; let stand, uncovered. Lightly oil the inside of a ring mold or eight 4-ounce custard cups, if using, then set aside.

3. In a small skillet heat 1 tablespoon of the oil. Stir in the red bell pepper and sauté over medium-high heat until the edges begin to brown. Add to the rice along with the broccoli rape and stir just to blend.

4. Add the remaining oil to the skillet with one little sliver of the garlic. When the garlic just begins to sizzle, add the remaining garlic. Fry the garlic in the oil, watching very carefully and stirring just until it begins to turn golden, about 45 seconds. Remove from the oil with a slotted spoon and set aside.

5. Add the red pepper flakes to the oil and sauté, stirring, about 3 minutes.

6. Spoon the rice mixture into a serving bowl or pack into the prepared ring mold or custard cups and unmold on a platter. Drizzle the hot red pepper oil over the top and garnish with the crisp-fried pieces of garlic. Serve at once.

MAKES 6 TO 8 SERVINGS

Brown Rice with Onions, Garlic, and Walnuts

For this delicious side dish use almost any kind of rice, such as brown or white basmati, converted, or long-grain. Cook the onions very slowly so that the natural sugars caramelize and impart a sweetness that goes well with both the rice and the walnuts. This is great with broiled fish fillets.

1 cup uncooked long- or short-grain brown rice or long-grain white rice
3 tablespoons unsalted butter
1 cup coarsely chopped onions
2 cloves garlic, minced
$\frac{1}{2}$ cup broken walnuts
2 tablespoons diagonally slivered green scallion tops

1. Cook the rice according to the package directions.

2. About 15 minutes before the rice is ready, melt the butter in a large heavy skillet over medium-low heat. Add the onion and sauté, stirring often, until the onion is very soft and just begins to color, about 10 minutes.

3. Stir in the garlic and the walnuts. Sauté over medium heat, stirring, until the walnuts and onions are golden and the garlic is tender.

4. Let the rice stand, covered, for 5 minutes. Spoon into a bowl. Spoon the onions and walnuts on top and lightly fluff with a fork or a chopstick. Garnish with the scallions.

MAKES 4 SERVINGS

Brown Rice with Garlic and Cashews

Accompanied by a cooked green vegetable this flavorful rice-and-cashew dish makes a healthful, satisfying menu filled with good-for-you complex carbohydrates.

4 tablespoons peanut or other vegetable oil
2 cups uncooked short-grain brown rice
4½ cups water
Salt
2 cloves garlic, cut lengthwise into thin slivers
1 cup broken unsalted cashews

1. Heat 1½ tablespoons of the oil in a large saucepan over medium-high heat. Add the rice and sauté, stirring, about 2 minutes. Add the water and 2 teaspoons of salt, and heat to boiling, stirring well. Cook, covered, over medium-low heat until the water is absorbed and the rice is tender, about 45 minutes.

2. Just before the rice is cooked heat the remaining 2½ tablespoons of oil in a small heavy skillet over low heat. Add the garlic and sauté gently until golden, about 3 minutes. Stir in the cashews and cook 1 to 2 minutes more. Sprinkle with a pinch of salt.

3. Pour the cashew, garlic, and oil mixture over the cooked rice. Toss with a fork or chopstick and spoon into a serving dish.

MAKES 6 SERVINGS

Brown Rice with Chanterelles, Dried Apricots, and Almonds

This recipe was inspired by Jack Czarnecki, a great chef and respected mycologist. He is the proprietor with his wife, Heidi, of Joe's, a restaurant in Reading, Pennsylvania, specializing in wild mushrooms. The dish can be prepared with fresh shiitake, cremini, or white button mushrooms, although it is at its best when fresh chanterelles are available. The flavors are great with game—pheasant, duck, squab, or quail.

2'/₂ cups unsalted chicken broth, preferably homemade
1 cup uncooked short-grain brown rice
1 teaspoon salt
2 tablespoons sliced natural (unblanched) almonds
3 tablespoons unsalted butter
'/₂ cup chopped onion
1 cup fresh chanterelles, brushed clean and sliced
'/₄ cup cut-up dried apricots

1. In a saucepan combine the broth, rice, and salt. Heat to boiling, stirring well. Cook, covered, over medium-low heat until the rice is tender and the liquid has been absorbed, about 45 minutes.

2. Heat a medium-sized dry skillet over low heat. Add the almonds and sauté, stirring, until lightly toasted, then transfer to a small plate. Add the butter to the skillet and heat until melted. Add the onion and sauté until golden, about 5 minutes. Stir in the chanterelles and apricots, and sauté for 2 minutes.

3. Add the apricot mixture to the rice and fluff with a fork. Spoon into a serving dish and sprinkle with the toasted almonds. Serve at once.

MAKES 4 SERVINGS

Brown Basmati Rice with Crisp Onions and Cumin Seed Butter

1 cup uncooked American basmati-type brown rice
Vegetable oil
2 small onions, cut into thin slices and separated into rings
   (about 1 cup)
1 teaspoon whole cumin seeds
1 tablespoon unsalted butter

1. Cook the rice according to the package directions.

2. Meanwhile, heat about 1 inch of oil in a medium-sized skillet until hot enough to sizzle a small piece of onion on contact. Add the onions and fry until well browned. Using a slotted spoon transfer to a paper towel to drain; discard the oil.

3. Heat the cumin seeds in a small dry skillet set over low heat, stirring, until fragrant. Add the butter and stir until melted.

4. Spoon the hot rice into a serving bowl. Drizzle with the cumin seed butter and toss to blend. Top with the crisp-fried onions.

MAKES 4 SERVINGS

Sonia's Crusty Basmati Rice

Raised in Lebanon, Sonia El-Nawal Malikian is a pastry chef and friend of a friend. This recipe reached me through word of mouth, so I ask Sonia's forgiveness if somewhere along the route from mouth to skillet to printed word it has been changed in any way. The dish is extraordinary. The technique—slowly cooking the rice in a heavy pan until a crust forms on the bottom—is used in many rice-based cuisines; this particular dish is said to be Persian.

12 tablespoons (1½ sticks) cold unsalted butter, cut into ¼-inch pieces
2 cups uncooked imported basmati or American basmati-type white rice
2 teaspoons salt
1 cinnamon stick
3 whole cloves
3 whole black peppercorns
1 cup thinly sliced onions
Generous pinch of saffron threads

1. Place the butter in a small saucepan and melt over low heat; do not brown. Let stand until the solids settle to the bottom of the pan. Skim the foam from the top and spoon the clear liquid (the clarified butter) into a measuring cup; there should be ½ cup. Discard the solids in the bottom of the pan. (Clarified butter is preferred in this recipe because the solids or milk proteins brown when subjected to high temperatures.)

2. Heat 8 cups of water to boiling in a large saucepan. Add the rice, salt, cinnamon stick, cloves, and peppercorns. Cook the rice, uncovered, stirring occasionally, until almost tender, about 10 to 12 minutes. Drain immediately and let stand in a sieve until ready to use. Leave the spices and peppercorns in the rice.

3. Heat the oven to 325°F. Select a 10-inch heavy ovenproof skillet or wide pan. Add 2 tablespoons of the clarified butter to the skillet and the onions, and sauté over

medium-low heat, stirring, until golden. Add the saffron threads and sauté, stirring, for 1 minute. Spread the onions evenly over the bottom of the pan.

4. Spoon the rice on top and drizzle with the remaining clarified butter. Smooth the top and press down with a spatula. Cover and bake in the oven until the bottom is crisp and golden, about 55 to 60 minutes. Let stand, covered, for 10 minutes. Uncover, place a large plate over the skillet, and carefully invert onto the plate.

MAKES 6 TO 8 SERVINGS

Apricot and Brown Rice Stuffing
for Cornish Hens

I use a mixture of short-grain brown rice and Wehani in this stuffing, but you could use all brown rice, preferably short grain, or any combination of rices (3-cup total) of white, brown, long, or short grain—even wild. Dried cherries add a sweet tart flavor and although expensive are well worth it. (See Mail Order Sources, page 271.) If the cherries are not available, dried cranberries or golden raisins can be substituted.

6 tablespoons unsalted butter or olive oil
1 cup chopped onions
1 clove garlic, crushed
1/2 cup diced dried apricots
1/2 cup dried cherries, cranberries, or golden raisins
1/2 cup coarsely chopped natural (unblanched) almonds
1 cup pared, cored, and diced (1/4-inch pieces) tart apple
2 cups cooked short- or long-grain brown rice
1 cup cooked Wehani rice
1/4 cup finely chopped parsley
1 teaspoon salt
1/2 teaspoon ground cinnamon
Freshly ground black pepper to taste

1. Melt the butter in a large (12 inches) skillet. Add the onion and sauté, stirring, until tender, about 5 minutes. Add the garlic and sauté for 1 minute.

2. Add the apricots, cherries, and almonds, and sauté, stirring, until the fruits are plump and the almonds are golden, about 5 minutes. Stir in the apple and sauté until heated through, about 3 minutes. Add the rices, parsley, salt, cinnamon, and pepper.

3. Let the stuffing cool to room temperature before spooning into the birds. Stuffing can be baked separately, covered, in a 350°F. oven for 30 minutes.

MAKES ABOUT 5 CUPS, ENOUGH TO STUFF FOUR CORNISH HENS OR ONE LARGE CHICKEN OR CAPON

Rice, Sausage, and Raisin Stuffing for Turkey

As a young child I remember eating this stuffing when we gathered at Nana and Grandpa's house for Thanksgiving dinner. This recipe makes enough stuffing for a 16- to 20-pound turkey or a roasting chicken, with enough stuffing left to bake in a separate dish. It is also great with Cornish hens. Leftovers are delicious stirred into cooking scrambled eggs.

1/4 cup golden raisins

3 tablespoons pignoli (pine nuts)

6 tablespoons unsalted butter

1 teaspoon salt

1 1/2 cups uncooked long-grain or medium-grain white rice or
  Italian arborio rice

1 cup finely chopped onions

1 pound Italian sweet sausage, removed from the casings

1/4 cup finely chopped fresh Italian (flat leaf) parsley

3 tablespoons freshly grated Parmigiano-Reggiano cheese (see
  Basics, page 267)

1 extra-large egg, well beaten

Freshly ground black pepper to taste

1. Pour boiling water over the raisins to cover in a small heat-proof bowl. Let stand until plump, about 15 minutes, then drain. Meanwhile, toast the pignoli in a small dry skillet set over low heat, stirring constantly, until golden, about 3 minutes. Cool.

2. Combine 3 cups of water, 2 tablespoons of butter, and the salt in a medium-sized saucepan, and heat to boiling. Stir in the rice and turn the heat to low. Cook, covered, until the rice is tender and the liquid is absorbed, about 15 minutes. Remove from the heat and fluff with a fork.

3. Melt the remaining 4 tablespoons of butter in a large heavy skillet over low heat. Add the onion and sauté, stirring, until tender, about 5 minutes. Crumble the sausage into the onions and sauté, stirring frequently, until the sausage is cooked through. Remove from the heat and drain the sausage mixture in a sieve set over a bowl. Reserve the sausage mixture and drippings separately.

4. Combine the cooked rice, raisins, pignoli, sausage mixture, parsley, cheese, egg, and pepper in a large bowl, and stir to blend. Stir in just enough of the reserved drippings to moisten the stuffing (about 3 to 4 tablespoons).

5. Let the stuffing cool to room temperature before spooning into the bird. Stuffing can be baked separately, covered, in a 350°F. oven for 30 minutes.

MAKES ABOUT 8 CUPS

Quick Hits with Rice

Plain cooked rice provides a tempting blank canvas for the creative cook. In addition to the many types of rice available, the cook need have on hand only a few basics—a palette of ingredients—from which to choose. It is exciting to see how easily a handful of raisins, a sautéed onion, or a spoonful of spice can transform plain rice. It all depends on the cook's resources and imagination. Here are a few ideas to get you started.

GLORIA'S PARMESAN RICE

Stir 3 tablespoons of cut-up butter and ¼ cup of freshly grated Parmesan cheese into 3 cups of hot cooked rice.

GARLIC RICE

Sauté uncooked rice and 1 clove of garlic, crushed, in 2 tablespoons of butter or olive oil until fragrant. Add broth or water and cook until tender.

PECAN, ALMOND, OR WALNUT RICE

Sauté 2 tablespoons of coarsely chopped walnuts, almonds, or pecans in 1 tablespoon of butter or olive oil. Sprinkle over hot cooked rice just before serving.

LEMON RICE

Stir 2 tablespoons of fresh lemon juice, 1 tablespoon of unsalted butter, and ½ teaspoon of grated lemon zest into 3 cups of hot cooked rice before serving.

DOUBLE SESAME RICE

Stir 1 tablespoon of sesame seeds in a small dry skillet over low heat until golden, about 2 minutes. Add to hot cooked rice along with 1 teaspoon of Oriental sesame oil. Sprinkle with 1 tablespoon of thinly sliced scallion. (This is also good served at room temperature.)

RICE WITH PEAS AND MINT

Add 1 cup of thawed frozen tiny peas (or fresh peas) to a saucepan of simmering rice 5 minutes before cooking time is completed. Just before serving stir in 1 tablespoon of finely chopped fresh mint, preferably spearmint.

CURRIED RICE

Melt 1 tablespoon of butter in a saucepan. Stir in 1 to 2 teaspoons of good-quality curry powder and 1/2 teaspoon of turmeric. Sauté for 30 seconds, then stir in the uncooked rice to coat. Add broth or water and cook until tender. Garnish with whole cashews, if desired.

RICE WITH TOASTED PIGNOLI

Stir 1 to 2 tablespoons of pignoli in a small dry skillet over low heat until golden, about 2 minutes. Sprinkle over cooked rice. This is also good sprinkled over Garlic Rice (page 111).

ORANGE RICE WITH DRIED CURRANTS

Heat 1 tablespoon of butter or oil in a saucepan. Add the uncooked rice, 2 tablespoons of dried currants, and 1 teaspoon of grated orange zest. Sauté for 2 minutes. Add the water or broth and cook until tender.

ANNA LISA'S BROWN RICE WITH RAISINS AND SUNFLOWER SEEDS

To a steaming pot of cooked brown rice add $\frac{1}{4}$ cup of sunflower seeds and $\frac{1}{4}$ cup of raisins. Toss and serve. Sunflower seeds can first be toasted in a hot skillet, if desired.

MUSHROOM RICE

Sauté 1 cup of sliced or chopped white button, cremini, or shiitake mushrooms in 2 tablespoons of butter or olive oil until browned, about 5 minutes. Add garlic and sauté for 1 minute. Season with salt and pepper. Add to 3 cups of hot cooked rice, sprinkle with parsley, and toss to blend.

INDIAN-STYLE RICE WITH OR WITHOUT COCONUT

Cook rice in broth or water with a piece of cinnamon stick, a whole cardamom pod, and a thick slice of fresh ginger. Serve plain spiced rice or add $\frac{1}{4}$ cup of fresh or packaged grated coconut before serving.

RAISIN AND PEANUT RICE

Stir $\frac{1}{4}$ cup of coarsely chopped dry-roasted peanuts in a dry skillet over low heat until fragrant. Add to hot cooked rice that has been cooked with 1 tablespoon of raisins.

SAFFRON RICE

Heat a pinch of saffron threads (about 4) in $\frac{1}{4}$ cup of water or broth. Cover and soak 10 minutes. Stir in the required remaining liquid and rice. Cook until tender.

SUMMER GARDEN RICE

Stir $\frac{1}{4}$ cup of torn fresh basil leaves into 3 cups of hot cooked rice just before serving. Also good with 1 cup of chopped ripe tomatoes and/or the kernels cut from 1 ear of fresh sweet corn.

MAIN DISHES

Rice, Eggs, and Cheese

Green Rice Frittata with Sautéed Tomatoes and Red Onions
Rice Frittata with Sausage and Red Pepper
Scrambled Eggs with Rice and Tomato-Jalapeño Salsa
Curried Scrambled Eggs and Rice with Cream Cheese and Chutney
Rice-stuffed Poblano Chilies with Tomato Sauce and
Monterey Jack Cheese
Pizza Rustica
Leek and Rice Pie with Roasted Red Peppers

Rice and Beans

Josephine's Rice and Beans, Puerto Rican Style
Aunt Millie's Cannellini Beans and Rice
Cannellini Beans and Rice with Tomatoes and Parmesan Cheese
Yellow Rice with Creamy Black Beans
Indian-style Lentils and Basmati Rice with Green Chili Oil
Cumin-flavored Brown Basmati Rice with Winter Squash,
Chick-peas, and Crispy Garlic
Indian-style Rice and Vegetables

Rice and Meat

Rice, Spinach, and Tomato Meat Loaf
Veal Loaf with Rice, Hard-boiled Egg, and Asparagus
Savoy Cabbage Stuffed with Sausage and Rice, and with
Tomato and Fennel Sauce
Eggplant Stuffed with Ground Lamb and Brown Rice
Red Peppers Stuffed with Rice, Spinach, and Sausage
Rice with Chicken
Afghan-style Rice with Chicken, *Shireen Palow*
Chicken Biryani
One "Mean" Jambalaya

Rice and Seafood

Mussels with Curried Rice
Mussels Stuffed with Curried Rice
Provençal-style Stuffed Red Snapper
Squid Stuffed with Rice, Basil, and Orange
Sautéed Shrimp and Rice with Fresh Corn
Paella

Sauces over Rice

Hot Italian Sausage in Red Sauce over Rice
Orange Pork with Vegetables and Peanuts over Brown Rice
Baby Artichoke Sauce over Parmesan Rice
Anchovy Sauce over Rice and Cauliflower

Rice Stir-fries

Stir-fried Rice and Broccoli with Sesame Seeds and Garlic
Stir-fried Glazed Chicken, Rice, and Cashews
Stir-fried Fiery Shrimp, Orange Rice, and Spinach

Rice, Eggs, and Cheese

Combined with eggs, beans, meat, or seafood; topped with with a zesty sauce; or stir-fried with a myriad of ingredients, rice is essential to the good taste of the following main dishes. For all of these egg and rice main dishes use either long- or medium-grain white rice, Italian arborio rice, or any of the aromatic basmati-type rices.

The Italian frittata, which is simply a flat omelet with a musical name, is just one of many ways to create a main dish using rice with eggs and cheese. Approximately 1 cup of cooked rice to 8 extra-large eggs makes a frittata large enough to serve four. Add meats, seafood, vegetables, or herbs—the variations are endless. Leftover frittata is great served cold or at room temperature.

Simply stirring cooked rice into eggs while they are scrambling might sound dull until you have tried some of the following combinations.

Green Rice Frittata with Sautéed Tomatoes and Red Onions

A frittata is the perfect quick and nourishing meal after a long workday. Serve this plain or with a sauce of chopped raw tomato seasoned with a little olive oil and basil or topped with Sautéed Tomatoes and Red Onions (see Basics, Page 270). Round out the menu with a loaf of crusty bread and a few brine-cured black olives.

1½ cups cooked long-grain white rice
½ cup packed parsley sprigs
1 scallion, trimmed and cut in ½-inch lengths
1 small clove garlic, chopped
8 large eggs
2 tablespoons freshly grated Parmigiano-Reggiano cheese (see
     Basics, page 267)
Freshly ground black pepper to taste
1 tablespoon olive oil
1 cup shredded mozzarella cheese
6 thin slices provolone cheese (about 3 ounces)

1. If using freshly cooked rice spread on a towel until cooled before using. Finely chop the parsley, scallion, and garlic together in the food processor.

2. Whisk the eggs, Parmigiano-Reggiano cheese, and pepper together, then set aside. Heat oil in a heavy 10-inch skillet, preferably nonstick, over medium heat. Add the rice and the parsley mixture. Sauté, stirring, until blended and hot, about 1 minute.

3. Pour the egg mixture over the rice. Sprinkle with the mozzarella cheese and cook over low heat, stirring gently, just until the eggs begin to set, about 1 minute. Cover and cook until the eggs are set and the edge of the frittata begins to brown, about 8 minutes.

4. Uncover and arrange the provolone cheese slices on top. Cover again and cook over low heat just until melted, about 1 minute.

5. Carefully loosen the sides and bottom of the frittata with a rubber spatula and slide onto a serving dish. Cut into wedges and serve with the sautéed tomatoes, if desired.

MAKES 4 SERVINGS

Rice Frittata with Sausage and Red Pepper

This hearty frittata is richly flavored with slowly cooked onion and slivers of red bell pepper. Season with a little grated Parmigiano-Reggiano cheese and either plain or smoked mozzarella cheese.

8 ounces Italian sweet sausage, removed from casings
2 tablespoons olive oil
½ large sweet yellow onion, cut vertically into ¼-inch slices
   (about 1 cup)
½ cup slivered (1 × ⅛ inch) red bell pepper (optional)
½ to 1 cup cooked long- or medium-grain white rice
2 tablespoons chopped fresh Italian (flat leaf) parsley or fresh
   basil
Pinch of salt
Freshly ground black pepper to taste
8 large eggs, beaten
2 tablespoons freshly grated Parmigiano-Reggiano cheese (see
   Basics, page 267)
4 ounces plain or smoked mozzarella cheese, thinly sliced

1. Brown the sausage in a heavy 10-inch skillet, preferably nonstick. Transfer to a sieve to drain off the fat. Wipe out the skillet.

2. Heat the olive oil in the skillet. Stir in the onion and sauté over low heat, stirring occasionally, until golden brown, about 10 minutes. Add the red bell pepper, if using, and sauté for 3 minutes. Stir in the sausage, rice, parsley or basil, salt, and a grinding of pepper.

3. Whisk the eggs with the Parmigiano-Reggiano cheese until blended. Pour over the sausage and rice mixture and cook, stirring, just until the eggs begin to set, about 1 minute. Cover and cook over medium-low heat, shaking the pan occasionally, until the eggs are set around the edges and are almost set in the center, about 12 minutes.

4. Uncover the frittata and arrange the mozzarella cheese on top of the eggs. Cover and cook until the cheese melts. Otherwise, if using the broiler, preheat it. Place the skillet about 3 inches from the heat and broil until the cheese is browned and bubbly, about 3 minutes.

5. Loosen the edges of the frittata with a plastic spatula and slide onto a large round platter. Cut into wedges to serve.

MAKES 4 TO 6 SERVINGS

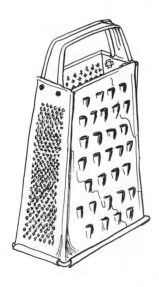

Scrambled Eggs with Rice and Tomato-Jalapeño Salsa

Try these cumin-flavored scrambled eggs and rice for brunch or supper. The accompaniments—salsa, sliced avocado, and cilantro—give the dish a southwestern flavor. To make the entree heartier add 1 or 2 cups of cooked black beans to the tomato salsa. The recipe can be doubled.

Tomato-Jalapeño Salsa
1 cup diced ripe tomatoes
1 scallion, trimmed and thinly sliced
1 tablespoon chopped fresh cilantro leaves
1 fresh jalapeño chili pepper, or more to taste, seeded and
   minced (see Basics, page 263)
2 tablespoons olive oil
2 teaspoons fresh lime juice
1 teaspoon minced fresh mint leaves (optional)
Salt to taste

Scrambled Eggs with Rice
5 extra-large eggs
3 tablespoons cold water
Pinch of salt
Freshly ground black pepper to taste
$1/2$ teaspoon ground cumin
1 tablespoon unsalted butter
1 cup cooked long-grain white rice
1 tablespoon thinly sliced green tops of scallion
Sprigs of cilantro
2 tablespoons sour cream (optional)
$1/2$ ripe avocado, peeled, pitted, and thinly sliced

1. To make the salsa: Combine the tomatoes, scallion, cilantro, jalapeño chili, olive oil, lime juice, and mint in a small bowl and season with salt. Cover and set aside at room temperature until ready to serve.

2. To make the eggs: Whisk the eggs and cold water until thoroughly blended. Add the salt and a grinding of black pepper, and set aside.

3. Sprinkle the cumin in a medium-sized dry skillet. Heat over medium-low heat, stirring gently, until fragrant, about 30 seconds. Transfer to a side dish. Melt the butter in the skillet. When the foam subsides, stir in the rice. Sauté, stirring, until the rice is coated with butter and heated through, about 2 minutes. Stir in the toasted cumin and scallion tops.

4. Add the eggs all at once. Cook, stirring gently with a wooden spoon, just until the eggs begin to set. Immediately spoon onto serving dishes or a platter. Top with cilantro sprigs and a spoonful of sour cream, if using. Garnish the platter with avocado slices. Serve with the tomato salsa on the side.

MAKES 2 SERVINGS

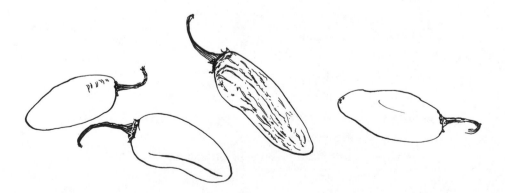

Curried Scrambled Eggs and Rice
with Cream Cheese and Chutney

*I once thought that scrambled eggs were easier to prepare than an omelet,
but the truth is that each dish takes a fair amount of skill acquired only by
lots of practice. Have all the ingredients cut, measured, and ready to go.
Scrambled eggs—like a stir-fry—wait for no one. Once the whisked eggs
hit the hot skillet, they will be cooked in a matter of minutes. Serve with
thickly sliced peasant bread toasted and spread with butter. This recipe can
be doubled; use a larger skillet.*

5 extra-large eggs
3 tablespoons cold water
1/4 teaspoon salt
Freshly ground black pepper to taste
1 tablespoon slivered natural (unblanched) almonds (optional)
2 tablespoons unsalted butter
1 teaspoon curry powder
1 cup cooked long-grain white or brown rice
1 scallion, trimmed and cut diagonally into thin slices (set aside
    1 tablespoon of the sliced green tops for garnish)
1 1/2 ounces cream cheese, cut into small squares, or use a
    young creamy goat cheese, if available
1/4 cup chutney, plus additional on the side, if desired
Thick diagonal slices French bread, toasted

1. In a bowl whisk the eggs, cold water, salt, and a grinding of pepper until frothy.
Toast the almonds, if using, by stirring in a hot, dry skillet over medium-low heat for 1 to
2 minutes, then set aside.

2. Melt the butter in a heavy 10-inch, preferably nonstick, skillet over low heat. Stir
in the curry and sauté for 1 minute. Add the rice and scallion slices. Sauté, stirring, until
the ingredients are blended and the rice is heated through.

3. Turn the heat to medium-high and add the eggs all at once. Using a rubber spatula carefully stir the eggs from the edges of the pan to the center. After about 2 minutes the eggs should be half cooked; add the cubes of cream cheese. Carefully turn the eggs in large chunks so that the cream cheese heats through and begins to melt and the eggs finish cooking.

4. Immediately spoon onto a platter. Place spoonfuls of the chutney down the center of the eggs and sprinkle with the reserved tablespoon of scallion tops. Sprinkle with the almonds, if using.

5. Serve with hot buttered toasted French bread and extra chutney on the side.

MAKES 2 GENEROUS SERVINGS

Rice-stuffed Poblano Chilies with Tomato Sauce and Monterey Jack Cheese

At Cafe Annie in Houston, Texas, Robert Del Grande serves enchiladas stuffed with rice and cheese with a wonderful black bean sauce; in Miami one of Norman Van Aken's signature dishes is poblano chilies stuffed with seafood seviche. Here I take the creamy rice and cheese from the enchiladas and stuff it into roasted and peeled poblano chili peppers, smother them in a chunky tomato sauce and lots of Monterey Jack cheese, and bake until bubbly to make a wildly spicy Southwest-style dish. Poblano chilies are mildly hot but complex in flavor. If you suffer from a fear of fiery food, substitute sweet Italian roasting peppers. Read about chilies and how to handle chilies in Basics, page 263, before beginning this recipe.

12 unblemished, evenly sized fresh poblano chili peppers

Tomato Sauce (see Basics, page 269)

4 ounces cream cheese, at room temperature

4 ounces mildly flavored fresh goat cheese, crumbled

7 ounces Monterey Jack cheese, coarsely shredded (about 2
    cups)

½ cup sour cream

2½ cups warm cooked long-grain white rice

2 tablespoons pignoli (pine nuts), toasted

¼ cup finely chopped sweet red onion

1 jalapeño chili pepper, seeded and minced

¼ cup grated Pecorino-Romano cheese

Sprigs of cilantro (optional)

1. Roast and peel the poblano chilies (see Basics, page 263). Place the chilies on a work surface and carefully cut through one layer of each chili from stem to pointed end. Using the tip of a teaspoon carefully lift out the clump of seeds and any other stray seeds. Don't be discouraged if the chilies tear or the stem end comes out of a few of the chilies. When they are stuffed and covered with the sauce, no one will even know. (This can be done up to 1 day ahead.)

2. Make the tomato sauce.

3. To make the stuffing: Combine the cream cheese, goat cheese, 4 ounces of the Monterey Jack, and sour cream in a bowl. Stir with a wooden spoon until blended. Add the warm cooked rice, pignoli, red onion, and minced jalapeño chili, and stir to blend.

4. Heat the oven to 350°F. Lightly oil a 13 × 9-inch baking dish. Form an oval of the rice mixture about 3 inches long and 1 inch wide. Place in the cavity of each chili. Wrap the chili around the rice filling and place, seam side down, in the baking dish. Repeat with the remaining chilies and stuffing. Spoon the tomato sauce over the top. Sprinkle with the remaining 3 ounces of Monterey Jack and the Pecorino-Romano cheeses. (These can be assembled several hours before baking.)

5. Bake for 30 minutes or until the cheese is melted. Garnish with cilantro sprigs before serving, if using.

MAKES 6 SERVINGS

Pizza Rustica

This pie is inspired by the Easter pie my grandmother used to make. This one is enormous, but so was Nana's. I do as she always did: Offer a sliver (it is very rich) to every guest and then send everyone home with a nice healthy portion. It tastes wonderful cold for breakfast or with espresso in the afternoon.

Pie Crust

3 cups all-purpose flour

1 tablespoon sugar

1 teaspoon salt

1 ⅓ cups lard or vegetable shortening, or half of each

1 large egg, beaten

½ cup ice water, or more as needed

Filling

1 tablespoon olive oil

½ cup chopped onion

⅔ cup finely diced salami or prosciutto

6 extra-large eggs, beaten

2 containers (15 ounces each) ricotta cheese

1 cup cooked medium- or long-grain white rice or Italian arborio rice

1 cup shredded mozzarella cheese

½ cup shredded Provolone cheese

½ cup freshly grated Parmigiano-Reggiano cheese (see Basics, page 267)

¼ cup grated Pecorino-Romano cheese

½ cup milk

½ teaspoon salt

Freshly ground black pepper to taste

Generous pinch of ground cloves

1 large egg yolk beaten with 1 tablespoon milk

1. To make the pie crust: Stir the flour, sugar, and salt together in a large bowl. Add the shortening of choice and cut in with a pastry blender until the mixture resembles coarse meal.

2. In a cup mix the egg and ice water with a fork until blended. Gradually stir into the dry ingredients while tossing lightly with a fork. Add additional ice water, a tablespoon at a time, until the mixture is moist enough to press into a ball. Flatten into a disk shape, wrap in foil, and refrigerate at least 1 hour.

3. To make the filling: Heat the olive oil in a medium-sized skillet. Add the onion and sauté until golden, about 5 minutes. Stir in the salami or prosciutto, and sauté for 2 minutes. Remove from the heat.

4. In a large bowl whisk the eggs until frothy. Stir in the sautéed onion mixture, ricotta, rice, mozzarella, Provolone, Parmigiano-Reggiano and Pecorino-Romano cheeses, milk, salt, pepper, and cloves until blended.

5. Heat the oven to 400°F. Divide the pastry into two unequal portions, the larger one for the bottom crust and the smaller one for the top crust. Roll the larger portion into a large circle (about 16 inches in diameter) on a lightly floured board. Drape over the rolling pin and fit into a 10 × 3-inch springform cake pan. Press the edges of the pastry to the rim of the pan to prevent its falling in.

6. Carefully pour the filling into the prepared pan. Roll out the remaining smaller portion of dough to a diameter of about 11 inches and carefully place on top of the filling. Fold the edges of the bottom crust over the edges of the top crust, and then pinch them together to form a thick band just inside the cake pan. Make 5 large slashes on the top crust in a sunburst pattern. Whisk to blend the egg yolk and milk and brush over the top crust.

7. Bake for 20 minutes. Lower the heat to 350° and bake 1 hour more or until the crust is golden and the pie begins to pull away from the sides of the pan. Cool thoroughly on a wire rack before running a spatula around the edges of the pie and removing the outer rim.

MAKES ONE 10-INCH PIE THAT SERVES 10 TO 12

Leek and Rice Pie with Roasted Red Peppers

Serve this delicious pie for breakfast, lunch, or supper. The filling is also good with a small amount of minced smoked ham added.

1/2 recipe for Pie Crust (see page 126; use only 1 tablespoon of
    beaten egg and substitute unsweetened butter *or* half butter
    and half vegetable shortening for the lard)
2 tablespoons olive oil
3 or 4 medium-sized leeks, bottoms and dark green tops
    trimmed, washed well, and chopped (about 3 cups)
1 cup cooked medium- or long-grain white rice or Italian
    arborio rice
1/2 cup peeled and diced roasted red peppers, homemade (see
    Basics, pages 267–268) or jarred (if using jarred peppers,
    rinse and drain first)
1 teaspoon grated lemon zest
1/2 teaspoon fresh thyme leaves, stripped from stems
1/2 teaspoon salt, or to taste
Freshly ground black pepper to taste
4 extra-large eggs
2 1/2 cups milk or half-and-half
1/2 cup freshly grated Parmigiano-Reggiano cheese (see Basics,
    page 267)
1 cup coarsely shredded Italian Fontina, Gruyère, or other
    flavorful cheese with good melting properties

1. Make the pie crust dough.
2. Roll out the pastry on a lightly floured board or pastry cloth into a large circle. Drape over a rolling pin and transfer to a deep 9-inch or 10-inch pie plate. Trim the edges, leaving about a 1 1/2-inch overhang. Fold under and form a rim around the edges. Crimp the edges with thumb and forefinger. Refrigerate until ready to bake.

3. Heat the oil in a large skillet. Add the leeks and sauté over medium-low heat, stirring, until very tender, about 10 minutes. Do not brown. Stir in the rice, roasted peppers, lemon zest, thyme, salt, and a generous grinding of black pepper.

4. Heat the oven to 400°F. Whisk the eggs in a large bowl. Stir in the milk or half-and-half and the grated Parmigiano-Reggiano cheese. Spoon the leek and rice mixture into the prepared pan. Place the shredded cheese on top. Carefully add the egg mixture.

5. Bake for 20 minutes, then lower the heat to 350°F and continue to bake until the crust is golden and the custard is set, about 25 to 30 minutes. Cool on a rack before cutting into wedges. This is best served warm or at room temperature.

MAKES 6 GENEROUS SERVINGS

Rice and Beans

In today's world the informed person has at least a modicum of knowledge of the advantages of eating a plate of high-complex carbohydrate, protein-complementary, low-fat rice and beans. In a topsy-turvy world these dishes, once considered merely sustainable, are now considered healthy (therefore chic) and are reverently called "peasant food."

Worldwide, the popularity of rice and beans is impressive. From *Fejoida,* the national dish of Brazil—a complex and sophisticated meal of black beans, rice, greens, and meats—to street vendors in Cairo, Egypt, who serve bowls of *Kosheri,* a combination of lentils, rice, and elbow macaroni topped with a fiery sauce, and dozens of countries and cuisines in between, the combination is truly international in scope. The recipes that follow are only a few of my favorites.

Josephine's Rice and Beans, Puerto Rican Style

Josephine was our daughter's baby-sitter and my savior when I was a working mother with a young child. There were many evenings when I would stop by to collect our daughter and be greeted not only by a bright-eyed happy child but by the inviting aroma of Josephine's rice and beans as well. As the beans cook, they create a rich sauce that Josephine ladled over a dish of plain hot rice. Here is my interpretation of this memorable dish.

Beans

1/4 cup flavorful extra-virgin olive oil

2 cups chopped onions

1 tablespoon minced garlic

1 pound dried red kidney beans, rinsed and soaked (see Basics, page 264)

4 to 5 cups unsalted chicken broth, preferably homemade

2 bay leaves

1 piece (about 1 1/2 inches) cinnamon stick

Salt to taste

Hot pepper sauce to taste

Rice

3 tablespoons flavorful extra-virgin olive oil

1/2 cup chopped onion

2 cloves garlic, minced

2 cups uncooked long-grain white rice

3 1/2 cups water or half unsalted chicken broth and half water

2 teaspoons salt

1/2 cup pared and finely chopped carrot

1/2 cup finely chopped celery

1/2 cup diced (1/4 inch) sweet red onion

1/2 cup diced (1/4 inch) green bell pepper

1. To make the beans: Heat the oil in a large heavy saucepan. Add the onions and sauté, stirring, until coated with oil. Cover and cook over very low heat, stirring occasionally, until golden brown, about 15 minutes. Stir in the garlic and sauté, uncovered, for 3 minutes.

2. Drain the beans, then add them and the broth to the onion. Heat to boiling and cook, covered, over low heat for 2 hours. Add the bay leaves and cinnamon. Cover and continue to cook until the beans are very tender, about 1 hour. Season with salt and hot red pepper sauce. (The beans can be prepared up to 24 hours before serving. Reheat, adding additional broth if necessary.)

3. To prepare the rice: Heat 1 tablespoon of oil in a heavy saucepan. Stir in the onion and garlic, and sauté, stirring, just until tender, about 5 minutes. Stir in the rice until coated with oil. Add the water (or broth and water) and salt, then heat to boiling. Cover and cook the rice over medium-low heat until the liquid is absorbed and the rice is tender, about 15 minutes.

4. Meanwhile, heat the remaining 2 tablespoons of oil in a large skillet. Add the carrot, celery, and red onion, and sauté, stirring, until tender but not browned, about 5 minutes. Add the green bell pepper and sauté until crisp-tender, about 2 minutes. Set aside.

5. Toss half of the sautéed vegetables with the cooked rice just before serving. Spread a mound of the rice in shallow soup plates and top with the beans. Garnish each with a spoonful of the remaining sautéed vegetables.

MAKES 6 SERVINGS

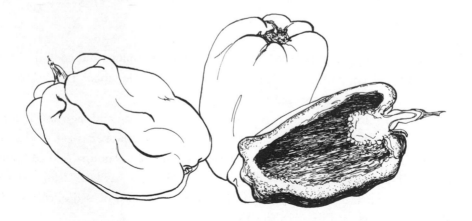

Aunt Millie's Cannellini Beans and Rice

*When members of my family told me about Aunt Millie's cannellini beans
and rice, I thought it sounded too pale, an all-white uninteresting food.
When I suggested the addition of a few pieces of diced tomato or maybe
bits of carrot, family members were insistent: "No, it was all white. It
was delicious. We ate it by the bowlful." Amen! The following recipe is
dedicated to the late Mildred Castano Cosentino. I have tried to stay true to
her undocumented recipe.*

1/4 cup olive oil, preferably extra-virgin
2 cups chopped onions
1 clove garlic, finely chopped
4 to 5 cups unsalted chicken broth, preferably homemade
1 1/2 cups dried cannellini beans, rinsed and soaked (see Basics,
   page 264)
1 bay leaf
1 fresh or dried sage leaf (optional)
Salt and freshly ground black pepper to taste
3 cups freshly cooked long-grain white rice
Freshly grated Parmigiano-Reggiano cheese (see Basics, page
   267)

1. Heat the olive oil in a large wide saucepan. Add the onions and cook over very
low heat, stirring often, until the onions are tender and golden, about 15 minutes. Do
not brown. Stir in the garlic and sauté for 1 minute.

2. Add 4 cups of the chicken broth, drained beans, bay leaf, and sage leaf, if using.
Heat to boiling. Cook, uncovered, stirring occasionally, until the beans are tender and
the liquid is reduced to an almost creamy consistency, about 1 1/2 hours. Add additional
broth if needed (the mixture should be saucelike). Remove the bay leaf. Using a slotted
spoon transfer about 1 cup of the beans to the bowl of a food processor. Process until
pureed, then stir back into the remaining beans.

3. Season with salt and pepper. Ladle the sauce over mounds of hot steaming rice and sprinkle generously with grated cheese.

MAKES 4 SERVINGS

Cannellini Beans and Rice with Tomatoes and Parmesan Cheese

This is peasant food at its best. Healthy and robust rice and beans flavored with chewy Parmigiano-Reggiano cheese rinds. The perfect meal for a winter day.

1³/₄ cups dried cannellini beans, rinsed and soaked (see Basics, page 264)

1 small onion, halved, plus 1 cup diced (¹/₄ inch) onions

1 leafy celery top, plus ¹/₂ cup diced (¹/₄ inch) celery

2 bay leaves

3 cloves garlic

¹/₄ cup extra-virgin olive oil

¹/₂ cup diced carrot

Pinch of crushed red pepper flakes (optional)

1¹/₂ cups uncooked medium- or long-grain white rice or Italian arborio rice

8 pieces (approximately ¹/₄ × 1 inch) Parmigiano-Reggiano cheese rinds (see Basics, page 267) *or* ¹/₂ cup coarsely chopped cheese pieces, plus additional freshly grated cheese to taste

1 can (14¹/₂ ounces) Italian-style plum tomatoes with juice

1¹/₂ to 2 cups (approximately) unsalted chicken broth, preferably homemade

1 teaspoon salt, or to taste

1. Drain the soaked beans and cover with 8 cups of water. Add the halved onion, celery top, 1 bay leaf, and 1 garlic clove bruised with the side of a knife, and heat to boiling. Cook, uncovered, over medium-low heat until the beans are tender but not mushy, about 1½ hours. Drain and discard the vegetables and bay leaf.

2. Heat the oil in a large wide saucepan. Stir in the cup of diced onions and sauté over low heat, stirring, until the onions are golden, about 15 minutes. Finely chop the remaining 2 garlic cloves and stir it in along with the carrot, diced celery, and hot pepper flakes, if using. Sauté for 1 minute. Add the rice and sauté, stirring, about 2 minutes more. Stir in the beans, remaining bay leaf, and cheese rinds, if using.

3. Pour the tomatoes and their juice into a 4-cup measure. Cut up the tomatoes with kitchen shears and add enough chicken broth to measure 3½ cups. Add to the rice and heat to boiling. Add the salt.

4. Cover and cook over medium-low heat until the broth is absorbed and the rice is tender, about 25 minutes. Let stand, covered, for 5 minutes before serving. If you didn't add the cheese rinds in step 2, add the ½ cup of chopped cheese pieces now.

5. Spoon into a large serving bowl and sprinkle grated cheese generously over the top.

MAKES 6 TO 8 SERVINGS

Yellow Rice with Creamy Black Beans

This recipe can be converted to a wonderful black bean soup simply by thinning the consistency of the beans with broth. If you prefer a soup with a smoother texture, puree half of the black beans (remove the bay leaf) in a food processor after step 2 is completed. The recipe below makes a richly flavored bean sauce with many different levels of heat attributed to the various chilies and seasonings used. It makes a striking presentation against the bold yellow background of rice crowned with green cilantro leaves.

Beans

1 pound dried black beans, rinsed and soaked (see Basics, page 264)

1 large green bell pepper, halved, seeded, and cut in wedges, plus ¹/₂ cup chopped green bell pepper

1 bay leaf

4 cloves garlic

2 tablespoons olive oil

2 cups chopped onions

¹/₂ cup chopped red bell pepper

1 jalapeño chili pepper, seeded and finely chopped (see Basics, page 263)

1 serrano chili pepper, seeded and finely chopped (see Basics, page 263)

1¹/₂ teaspoons ground cumin, or more to taste

Salt and freshly ground black pepper to taste

2 to 3 cups unsalted chicken broth, preferably homemade, or half water and half broth

¹/₂ cup heavy cream, at room temperature

Yellow Rice

1¾ cups unsalted chicken broth, preferably homemade

Generous pinch of saffron threads (optional)

1 tablespoon olive oil

1 cup uncooked long-grain white rice

1 clove garlic, minced

½ teaspoon turmeric

1 teaspoon salt, or to taste

¼ cup peeled and diced roasted red pepper (optional)

Whole cilantro leaves

1. To make the beans: Drain the beans and combine them in a large saucepan with 10 cups of water, green pepper wedges, bay leaf, and 1 garlic clove bruised with the side of a knife. Cook over medium-low heat, stirring occasionally, until the beans are tender enough to crush with a spoon on the side of the pan and most of the liquid is absorbed, about 2½ hours. Remove and discard the bay leaf and any visible green pepper skins.

2. Meanwhile, heat the oil in a medium-sized skillet over low heat. Add the chopped onions, chopped green and red peppers, and remaining 3 garlic cloves. Sauté over medium-low heat, stirring, until the onions and peppers are golden, about 15 minutes. Add the chilies and cumin, and sauté for 1 minute. Season with salt and pepper.

3. Stir the sautéed vegetables into the beans. Cook for 1 to 1½ hours, stirring often and adding as much of the chicken broth (or half water and half broth) as needed to keep the beans a thick consistency without sticking. Stir in the heavy cream. Taste and correct the seasoning.

4. To cook the yellow rice: Heat ¼ cup of the chicken broth to boiling in a small saucepan. Add the saffron threads, if using. Cover and let stand for 5 minutes. Meanwhile, in a heavy saucepan heat the olive oil over low heat. Add the rice and garlic, and sauté, stirring, just until the rice is coated and the garlic is fragrant, about 2 minutes. Do not brown. Stir in the turmeric, the remaining chicken broth, the saffron and broth mixture, and salt if the broth is unsalted. Heat to boiling, stirring once. Cook, covered, over low heat until the broth is absorbed and the rice is tender, about 12 minutes.

5. Spoon the rice into a large shallow serving bowl. Ladle the black beans on top. Garnish with the diced roasted pepper, if using, and a halo of cilantro leaves.

MAKES 6 TO 8 SERVINGS

Indian-style Lentils and Basmati Rice
with Green Chili Oil

I am partial to the flavors of India. Like the country, the flavors may assault the senses at first, but gradually they grab—and then you are either hooked for life or never go back. I'm hooked for life. I am reasonably successful at duplicating in my own kitchen some of the flavors, and this particular dish is one of my favorites. It is hearty and filling, good cold weather food, and it makes enough to feed a small crowd. Serve with glasses of cold beer, preferably Indian.

1 1/2 cups brown lentils, rinsed and sorted

2 tablespoons unsalted butter or vegetable oil

2 cups finely chopped onions

1 clove garlic, finely chopped

2 teaspoons ground cumin

1/2 teaspoon ground coriander

1/4 teaspoon crushed hot red pepper, or more to taste

1 1/2 cups uncooked imported basmati or American basmati-type white rice

1 slice (about 1/4 inch thick) fresh ginger

1 piece (about 2 inches) cinnamon stick

2 whole cardamom

1 can (14 1/2 ounces) whole tomatoes, cut into chunks, plus juice

1 1/2 cups (approximately) unsalted chicken broth, preferably homemade

1 teaspoon salt

Green Chili Oil

$^1/_3$ cup vegetable oil

$^1/_3$ cup seeded and thinly sliced rounds of moderately hot fresh
  green chili peppers (see Basics, page 263)

2 cloves garlic, minced

2 tablespoons torn fresh cilantro leaves (optional)

1. Combine the lentils and 8 cups of water in a large saucepan and heat to boiling. Lower the heat and simmer, uncovered, for 15 minutes, or until the lentils are almost tender (they will continue cooking with the rice). Drain and set aside.

2. Meanwhile, heat the butter or oil in a large wide saucepan. Add the onion and sauté over low heat, stirring, until golden, about 10 minutes. Stir in the garlic, cumin, coriander, and red pepper. Sauté, stirring, for 2 minutes. Add the rice and ginger, cinnamon, and cardamom. Sauté, stirring, about 2 minutes. Stir in the drained lentils.

3. Pour the tomatoes and their juice into a 4-cup measure. Add enough of the chicken broth to measure 3$^1/_2$ cups. Stir into the rice and add the salt. Heat to a full boil, stirring once. Cover and cook over medium-low heat for 25 minutes, or until the liquid is absorbed and the rice is tender.

4. To make the green chili oil: Heat the oil in a small skillet until hot enough to sizzle a slice of the chilies. Add the chilies and sauté, stirring, just until wilted, about 2 minutes. Add the garlic and sauté for 30 seconds. Remove from the heat.

5. Spoon the rice and lentils into a large shallow bowl. Pour the chili oil mixture over the top and garnish with the coriander leaves, if using. Serve at once.

MAKES 6 SERVINGS AS A MAIN DISH AND MORE AS A SIDE DISH

Cumin-flavored Brown Basmati Rice with Winter Squash, Chick-peas, and Crispy Garlic

3 tablespoons olive oil

1/2 cup chopped onion

1 fresh jalapeño chili pepper, seeded and finely chopped (see
    Basics, page 263)

1 clove garlic, minced

2 teaspoons ground coriander

1 teaspoon ground cumin

1 cup uncooked American basmati-type brown rice

2 cups pared and diced (1/2-inch cubes) uncooked butternut or
    acorn squash

1 can (16 ounces) chick-peas, rinsed and drained

2 1/4 cups unsalted chicken broth, preferably homemade

1 teaspoon salt, or to taste

Garlic Threads

2 tablespoons olive oil

2 cloves garlic, cut lengthwise into thin strips

1. Heat the olive oil in a large wide saucepan. Add the onion and sauté, stirring, until golden, about 5 minutes. Stir in the jalapeño chili and garlic, and sauté for 1 minute. Stir in the coriander and cumin, and sauté 1 minute more. Add the rice, squash, and chick-peas. Stir to coat with the onion and seasonings.

2. Stir in the broth and salt. Heat to boiling, stirring well. Cover and cook over medium-low heat until the broth is absorbed and the rice is tender, about 45 minutes. Let stand, uncovered and off the heat, for 5 minutes before serving.

3. To prepare the crispy garlic threads: Heat the oil in a small skillet. Add the garlic and sauté, stirring, just until golden, about 1 minute. Immediately lift the garlic from the oil with a slotted spoon. Drain on paper towels and sprinkle over the rice.

MAKES 4 GENEROUS SERVINGS

Indian-style Rice and Vegetables

2 tablespoons unsalted butter

2 tablespoons vegetable oil

1 large yellow onion, cut into 1-inch cubes

1 tablespoon finely chopped fresh ginger

2 cloves garlic, minced

1 tablespoon curry powder

1 teaspoon ground cumin

1 piece (about 2 inches) cinnamon stick

$1/2$ teaspoon ground coriander

$1/2$ teaspoon ground cardamom

$1/4$ teaspoon crushed red pepper flakes, or to taste

1 cup uncooked imported basmati or American basmati-type
    white rice

2 cups cauliflower florets, broken into 1-inch pieces

2 cups peeled and cubed ($1/2$ inch) sweet potato

1 cup cut (1-inch lengths) fresh green beans

1 cup frozen lima beans, thawed

1 cup pared and cubed ($1/2$ inch) carrot

2 cups unsalted chicken broth, preferably homemade

1 teaspoon salt

Freshly ground black pepper to taste

$1/4$ cup flaked coconut

$1/2$ cup heavy cream

$1/2$ cup coarsely chopped unsalted roasted cashews

Chopped fresh cilantro leaves (optional)

1. Heat the butter and oil in a large wide saucepan. Add the onion, ginger, and garlic, and sauté over medium heat, stirring, until the onion is golden, about 10 minutes. Stir in the curry powder, cumin, cinnamon stick, coriander, cardamom, and red pepper flakes. Sauté over low heat, stirring constantly, for 2 minutes. Add the rice and stir to coat with butter and spices for 1 minute.

2. Add the cauliflower, sweet potato, green beans, lima beans, and carrot. Stir to blend with the rice. Add the chicken broth, salt, and a grinding of black pepper. Heat to boiling over high heat, stirring thoroughly. Cover and cook over low heat until the broth is absorbed, about 15 minutes. Let stand, covered and off the heat, for 15 minutes before serving.

3. Just before serving finely chop the coconut in a food processor. Add the heavy cream and process for 1 minute. Drizzle over the vegetables and rice, and gently fold to blend.

4. Spoon into a large shallow bowl. Sprinkle with the chopped cashews and chopped fresh cilantro leaves, if using. Serve at once.

MAKES 4 SERVINGS AS A MAIN DISH OR 6 TO 8 SERVINGS AS A SIDE DISH

Rice and Meat

"What was left from dinner," writes M. F. K. Fisher, on the subject of rice, "went into a baked custard full of raisins, with nutmeg on top. Or into a meat loaf or a stuffing."

Rice, Spinach, and Tomato Meat Loaf

Combining sweet and sour or sweet and salty in the same dish is a popular theme in many southern Italian dishes. Here the sweetness of dried currants sets off the saltiness of anchovies in a meat loaf with rice, spinach, and tomato. Serve this with thin slices of crisp-roasted potatoes. Leftover meat loaf is delicious served cold.

3 tablespoons olive oil

½ cup chopped onion

1 teaspoon minced garlic

1 tablespoon rinsed, drained, and minced anchovy fillets

2 cups cooked long- or medium-grain white rice or Italian arborio rice

1½ pounds meat loaf mixture (1 pound ground beef, ¼ pound each ground veal and pork)

1½ cups water

1 extra-large egg

1 package (10 ounces) frozen chopped spinach, cooked, drained, and squeezed dry

2 sun-dried tomatoes, halved, soaked, drained, and minced *or* 2 tablespoons tomato paste

2 tablespoons dried currants or chopped raisins

½ teaspoon ground cinnamon

¼ teaspoon freshly ground pepper

1. Heat the oil in a large skillet. Add the onion and sauté, stirring, until soft and golden, about 5 minutes. Add the garlic and sauté for 1 minute. Add the anchovies and sauté, stirring and crushing with the back of a spoon until the anchovies are "melted" or dissolved. Stir in the rice until blended. Set aside.

2. Heat the oven to 350°F. In a large bowl combine the meat loaf mixture with the water and egg until the meat is lightened. Add the anchovy mixture, spinach, tomatoes or tomato paste, currants or raisins, cinnamon, and pepper. Stir to blend.

3. Spoon into a 9 × 5-inch loaf pan and smooth the top with a spatula. Bake for 1 hour and 30 minutes, or until the juice runs clear when the center is pierced with a skewer. Let stand for 15 minutes before lifting from the loaf pan and setting on a serving platter. To serve, cut into thick slices.

MAKES 8 SERVINGS

Veal Loaf with Rice, Hard-boiled Egg, and Asparagus

This delicately flavored meat loaf makes an attractive presentation and is perfect for a spring dinner or served cold in neat slices on a buffet table. It takes 1½ hours to bake and needs at least 20 minutes and preferably longer to stand before slicing and serving. To serve cold, it should be prepared one day ahead.

3 large hard-boiled eggs
8 to 10 thin asparagus spears, trimmed
2 tablespoons butter
1 medium-sized leek, trimmed, soaked, rinsed, and finely
    chopped (about 1 cup)
¼ cup minced carrot
1½ pounds ground veal
1½ cups cooked long- or medium-grain white rice or Italian
    arborio rice
¾ cup milk
1 extra-large egg, beaten
Whole-grain mustard
1 teaspoon salt
⅛ teaspoon freshly ground black pepper
½ cup dry white wine

1. Peel the hard-boiled eggs and set aside. Steam the asparagus in a steamer set over gently boiling water for 4 minutes or until crisp-tender. Rinse and drain, then set aside.

2. Heat the butter in a skillet. Add the leek and sauté over low heat, stirring, until tender, about 10 minutes. Add the carrot and sauté for 2 minutes.

3. Combine the veal, sautéed vegetables, rice, milk, beaten egg, 1 teaspoon of mustard, salt, and pepper. Meanwhile, heat the wine in the skillet over medium-high heat until boiling. When reduced by half, add to the meat loaf mixture. Stir or work together with your hands until the mixture is thoroughly blended.

4. Heat the oven to 350°F. Select a 9 × 5-inch loaf pan. Spread about $1/3$ of the meat loaf mixture in the bottom of the pan. Arrange 4 or 5 asparagus spears lengthwise, alternating the stem and blossom ends and spacing them evenly on top of the meat loaf. Line up the eggs end to end down the center of the pan. Spoon about half of the remaining meat loaf mixture around the sides and over the top of the eggs, then smooth the surface. Arrange the remaining 4 or 5 asparagus spears on this layer of meat loaf. Top with the remaining meat loaf mixture and make the top smooth.

5. Using a small metal or rubber spatula, spread about 1 tablespoon of mustard on the surface of the meat loaf.

6. Bake until the top is browned and the juice runs clear when the meat loaf is pierced with a skewer, about 1 hour and 30 minutes. Cool at least 20 minutes before turning out of the pan. Serve with the mustard-glazed side up. To slice use a very sharp knife and a careful sawing technique so that the asparagus spears and the eggs cut cleanly.

MAKES 8 SERVINGS

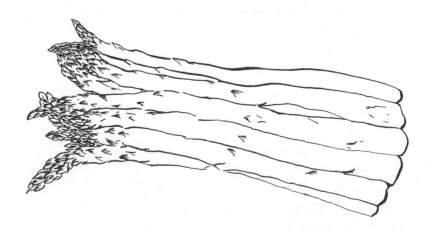

Savoy Cabbage Stuffed with Sausage and Rice, and with Tomato and Fennel Sauce

This interesting recipe was developed by Susan Sarao Westmoreland, a good friend and wonderful cook. It is perfect when the menu commands a hearty but extra-special dish.

1 large head (about 2¹/₂ pounds) Savoy cabbage, trimmed
1 tablespoon olive oil
1¹/₂ pounds sweet Italian sausage with fennel seeds, casings removed
1 cup chopped onions
2 cloves garlic, finely chopped
¹/₂ teaspoon grated orange zest
2¹/₂ cups cooked long-grain white rice
2 extra-large eggs, lightly beaten
¹/₄ teaspoon salt
¹/₄ teaspoon freshly ground black pepper
¹/₃ cup water

Tomato and Fennel Sauce
2 tablespoons olive oil
¹/₂ cup chopped onion
1 strip (2 × ¹/₂ inches) orange zest
¹/₈ teaspoon dried fennel seeds
1 clove garlic, crushed
1 can (35 ounces) imported Italian plum tomatoes, drained and with juice reserved separately and tomatoes coarsely chopped
Sprig of fresh basil
Salt and freshly ground black pepper to taste

1. Heat a large stockpot half-filled with water to boiling. Slip the whole cabbage into the water. Boil, uncovered, until the outer leaves are pliable, about 5 minutes. Carefully remove the cabbage to a colander set over a bowl to drain. Cool slightly.

2. Cutting at the base of the cabbage, carefully remove 5 or 6 of the large outer leaves of cabbage and set aside. Using a sharp knife, cut most of the core from the cabbage and discard. Coarsely chop the remaining cabbage.

3. Heat the oil in a large skillet. Add the sausage and sauté until lightly browned, stirring and breaking up with the side of a spoon. Using a slotted spoon, transfer the sausage to a side dish, leaving the fat in the skillet. Add the reserved chopped cabbage, onions, garlic, and orange zest to the skillet. Stir to blend the mixture. Cover and cook over low heat, stirring occasionally, until the cabbage is wilted, about 15 to 20 minutes.

4. Meanwhile, trim the thick rib from each of the reserved cabbage leaves so that it is almost flush with the rest of the leaf. Line an 8 or 9 × 4½-inch ovenproof bowl or casserole that has rounded sides with 4 or 5 of the leaves, setting aside at least one very large leaf for the top. Arrange the leaves so that the top ends are on the bottom of the casserole and overlap, covering the entire inside of the bowl, and about 2 inches of the leaves extend above the outside rim of the bowl.

5. Heat the oven to 350°F. Add the sausage meat, rice, eggs, salt, and pepper to the cabbage mixture. Stir until well blended. Fill the cabbage-lined bowl with the mixture, mounding it slightly. Cover the filling with the remaining cabbage leaf and fold the overhanging leaves toward the center. Pour the water around the cabbage. Lightly butter a piece of aluminum foil large enough to cover the bowl. Place the foil on the bowl, buttered side down, and secure the ends tightly.

6. Bake for 1 hour and 15 minutes.

7. Meanwhile, make the fennel and tomato sauce: Heat the oil in a large skillet. Add the onion, orange zest, fennel, and garlic. Sauté, stirring, until the onion is tender but not browned, about 5 minutes. Stir in the tomatoes and their juice and fresh basil. Heat to boiling, then turn the heat to low and simmer, uncovered, stirring occasionally, until the sauce is thickened, about 25 minutes. Remove the orange zest and basil before serving. Season with salt and pepper.

8. Let the cabbage stand 5 minutes before serving. Remove the foil and pour off any juice in the bowl. Place a serving platter over the bowl and carefully invert. Serve cut in wedges and topped with the tomato and fennel sauce.

MAKES 6 TO 8 SERVINGS

Eggplant Stuffed with Ground Lamb and Brown Rice

The lamb, feta cheese, mint, and eggplant make this dish Greek in spirit. The nutty taste of short-grain brown rice blends successfully with the other ingredients, but feel free to use long-grain brown or white rice. This makes a hearty supper served with a simple green salad and a robust glass of wine. You can vary the presentation slightly by using an equal weight of smaller eggplants and serving them as a first course or side dish. Also feel free to use all beef or a combination of beef and lamb.

2 eggplants (about 1 pound each)

1 teaspoon coarse salt

3 tablespoons extra-virgin olive oil

8 ounces ground lean lamb or beef and lamb or all beef

1 cup coarsely chopped onions

$\frac{1}{2}$ cup diced (about $\frac{1}{4}$ inch) green bell pepper

2 cloves garlic, crushed

1 cup seeded and diced fresh or canned tomatoes

2 tablespoons finely chopped parsley

2 tablespoons finely chopped fresh dill

2 tablespoons finely chopped fresh mint

$\frac{1}{2}$ teaspoon ground cinnamon

Salt and freshly ground black pepper to taste

2 cups cooked short-grain brown rice or long-grain brown or white rice

1 cup crumbled feta cheese (about 4 ounces)

1 cup shredded mozzarella cheese (about 4 ounces)

1. Wash the eggplants and halve them lengthwise. Score the cut sides at 1-inch intervals with a small paring knife. Sprinkle the surface with salt and place the eggplants,

cut side down, on a wire rack set on a tray. Let them drain at least 2 hours. Carefully squeeze the excess water from the eggplants and blot them dry with paper towels.

2. Heat the oven to 400°F. Rub the cut sides of the eggplant with 1 tablespoon of the olive oil and place, oiled side down, in a 13 × 9-inch baking pan. Bake for 15 minutes or until partially softened. Remove from the oven, turn cut side up, and let stand until cool enough to handle. Turn the oven down to 350°F.

3. Meanwhile, crumble the lamb (or beef and lamb or all beef) in a large skillet and sauté, stirring, until well browned. Transfer the lamb to a large bowl. Heat the remaining 2 tablespoons of olive oil in the skillet. Add the onions and green pepper, and sauté over medium-low heat, stirring, until golden, about 10 minutes. Add the garlic and sauté 1 minute more.

4. Using a tablespoon carefully scoop out the cooked eggplant, leaving the flesh about ¼ inch thick around the edges so that the shells stay intact and can be stuffed. Coarsely chop the partially cooked eggplant and add to the skillet with the onions. Leave the eggplant shells, scooped side up, in the baking pan.

5. Cook the eggplant with the onion mixture, stirring occasionally, about 10 minutes or until the eggplant is evenly cooked. Stir in the tomatoes, parsley, dill, mint, cinnamon, salt, and pepper. Transfer to the large bowl with the cooked lamb.

6. Add the rice and feta cheese to the bowl, and stir to blend. Taste and add more seasonings, if desired. Carefully spoon into the eggplant shells, dividing the mixture evenly. Sprinkle the tops with the mozzarella cheese, dividing evenly.

7. Bake the eggplants for 45 minutes or until the cheese is well browned and bubbly. Serve warm or at room temperature.

MAKES 4 SERVINGS AS A MAIN DISH

Red Peppers Stuffed with Rice, Spinach, and Sausage

Roasting the peppers before stuffing them adds a lot of flavor to the pepper. What is lost in height (the peppers won't stand as rigidly) will be gained in flavor. These are great on a buffet or for a picnic supper.

2 large (about 12 ounces each) red bell peppers *or* 4 medium-sized peppers
1 clove garlic, bruised with the side of a knife
4 tablespoons olive oil
Sprig of fresh thyme
1 pound well-seasoned breakfast or Italian-style pork sausage, removed from casings and crumbled
¹/₂ cup chopped onion
1 cup chopped red or yellow bell pepper
1 tablespoon fresh thyme leaves, stripped from stems
1 clove garlic, crushed
3 cups packed trimmed and shredded fresh spinach leaves
2 cups cooked long-grain white rice or imported basmati or American basmati-type white rice (use half brown and half white rice, if preferred)
2 tablespoons finely chopped parsley
2 tablespoons pignoli (pine nuts), toasted
Salt and freshly ground black pepper to taste
¹/₂ cup freshly grated Parmigiano-Reggiano (see Basics, page 267) or shredded mozzarella, Monterey Jack, or other flavorful cheese

1. Heat the oven to 400°F. Cut the peppers in half lengthwise, cutting through the stem end. Leaving the stems intact, if possible, cut out the seeds and ribs with a small sharp knife. Rub the baking dish with the garlic. Add the peppers, cut side up. Drizzle

with 2 tablespoons of the oil and turn the peppers to coat evenly. Add the sprig of thyme to the baking dish. Bake for 25 to 30 minutes, turning once, or until the peppers begin to char. Remove from the oven and let cool while preparing the stuffing. Lower the oven to 350°F.

2. Sauté the sausage in a large skillet over medium heat until well browned, stirring to break it into small pieces. Drain the sausage in a sieve, discard the fat, and set the sausage aside. Wipe out the skillet with a damp paper towel.

3. Heat the remaining 2 tablespoons of oil in the cleaned skillet. Add the onion and sauté, stirring until tender, about 5 minutes. Add the chopped bell pepper and sauté, stirring, until the pepper and onion begin to brown. Add the thyme and garlic, and sauté for 1 minute. Stir in the spinach until well blended. Cover and cook over low heat for 5 minutes, or until the spinach is wilted.

4. Stir in the reserved sausage, rice, parsley, and pignoli. Taste and add salt (remember that the sausage may be salty) and pepper. Stir until blended. Carefully spoon into the roasted red pepper halves, packing the rice mixture and lifting the sides of the peppers as they are stuffed. Sprinkle the tops with the grated or shredded cheese.

5. Bake in the oven until browned, about 25 minutes. Serve warm or at room temperature.

MAKES 4 SERVINGS

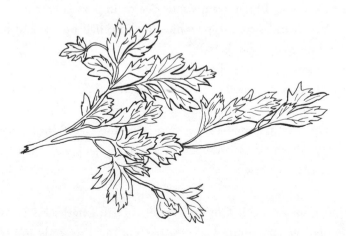

Rice with Chicken

Arroz con pollo, *or rice with chicken, is a favorite Spanish dish similar to, but much simpler than, paella. In this version the saturated fat calories can be cut by removing the skin from the chicken before browning and by draining all the fat from the sautéed chorizos. If chorizos are unavailable, use hot Italian sausage and perhaps a pinch of crushed hot red pepper flakes to add a little more fire. The saffron flavor is rich and pungent, but if preferred one can substitute $^1/_2$ teaspoon of turmeric and 1 teaspoon of ground cumin.*

This version makes four generous portions; add another 4 pieces of chicken to make six servings.

1 tablespoon olive oil

5 ounces (about 2 links) chorizos, with casings removed and
   finely diced ($^1/_8$ inch)

1 whole chicken breast, split, fat trimmed, and each piece
   halved crosswise

4 chicken thighs, fat trimmed

Salt and freshly ground black pepper

1 can (14$^1/_2$ ounces) whole tomatoes, drained and with juice
   reserved separately and tomatoes cut into large chunks

2$^1/_2$ cups unsalted chicken broth, preferably homemade

Generous pinch of saffron threads

$^1/_2$ cup chopped onion

$^1/_2$ cup diced ($^1/_4$ inch) green bell pepper

1 clove garlic, crushed

1$^1/_2$ cups uncooked medium-grain white rice, Italian arborio,
   or Spanish Valencia rice

$^1/_2$ cup tiny green peas (thawed, if frozen)

1 to 2 tablespoons chopped pimento-stuffed green olives

1. Select a 10-inch nonstick skillet with a tight-fitting lid. Heat the olive oil in the skillet, add the chorizos, and sauté over medium heat, stirring, until browned and the fat is rendered, about 3 minutes. With a slotted spoon transfer the sausage to a side dish, discarding all but 1 tablespoon of the fat in the skillet.

2. Sprinkle the chicken on both sides with salt and pepper. Add the chicken to the hot skillet and sauté until browned on both sides, about 5 minutes; the chicken will be partially cooked. Transfer to a side dish and drain off and discard all but about 1 tablespoon of the fat in the skillet.

3. Combine the liquid from the tomatoes and the chicken broth in a 1-quart glass measuring cup. Add enough water so that the liquid measures 3$\frac{1}{4}$ cups; set aside. In a separate bowl or cup combine the saffron threads with $\frac{1}{4}$ cup of boiling water. Cover and set aside until ready to use.

4. Sauté the onion and green pepper in the skillet over medium heat, stirring, until the edges are browned, about 3 minutes. Add the garlic and sauté for 1 minute. Stir in the rice and sauté over low heat, stirring, until the rice is thoroughly coated with oil. Do not brown. Stir in the reserved tomato and broth liquid. Add the saffron, $\frac{1}{2}$ teaspoon of salt, and $\frac{1}{8}$ teaspoon of pepper, or to taste, and heat to boiling. Stir in the reserved chorizos and tuck the pieces of chicken into the boiling rice mixture. Place the tomatoes on top.

5. Cover and cook over medium heat for 15 minutes, or until most of the liquid has been absorbed. Uncover, add the peas, cover again, and cook for 5 minutes.

6. Uncover and cook over medium-high heat about 2 to 5 minutes to cook off any excess moisture. Sprinkle with chopped olives before serving.

MAKES 4 SERVINGS

Afghan-style Rice with Chicken, Shireen Palow

The surprise ingredient in this wonderful rice dish is sugar. This recipe was inspired by a similar dish served at a modest little restaurant called Caravan located in the theater district of New York City. I keep trying to duplicate the taste at home, and the version that follows is very, very close—albeit not exactly the same. At Caravan this dish, called Shireen Palow, *is served spooned over a small mound of tender pieces of cooked chicken.*

1 whole chicken (about 2¹/₂ pounds), cooked, skinned, and
    boned (see Basics, page 262)
Generous pinch of saffron threads
1³/₄ cups chicken broth
2 tablespoons unsalted butter
1 tablespoon thinly slivered orange zest (about 1 inch long)
2 tablespoons granulated sugar
1 cup uncooked imported basmati or American basmati-type
    white rice
1 tablespoon dried currants
¹/₂ teaspoon salt
2 tablespoons unsalted shelled pistachios

1. Cut the chicken meat into large pieces, wrap in foil, and keep warm in the oven set at the lowest temperature. Set aside 1³/₄ cups of the chicken broth and freeze the remainder for later use.

2. Combine the saffron threads with ¹/₄ cup of boiling broth. Cover and let stand for 15 minutes.

3. Meanwhile, heat the butter over low heat in a large shallow saucepan until the foam subsides. Add the orange zest and sprinkle with sugar. Sauté, stirring, for 1 minute.

4. Add the rice and sauté, stirring, until the rice is coated with butter and sugar,

and begins to turn milky white. Add the remaining broth and the broth and saffron mixture, and heat to boiling. Stir in the currants and salt.

5. Cook, covered, over medium-low heat for 15 minutes, or until the liquid is absorbed. Turn off the heat and let the pan sit, covered, for 10 minutes.

6. Add the chicken and fluff with a fork. Quickly warm the pistachios in a small dry skillet set over low heat. Sprinkle on the rice before serving.

MAKES 4 SERVINGS

Chicken Biryani

Biryani is an elaborate Moghul dish from the north of India. It is traditionally prepared with lamb, the preferred meat of the Muslims, who don't eat pork, and the Hindus, who consider the cow a sacred beast. Here it is prepared with chicken. A hearty dish, it is perfect for a buffet dinner party. The preparation is lengthy, but it is well suited to doing ahead of time. There are hundreds of versions of biryani—here is one using both brown and white rice.

Brown Rice with Garlic and Chili Peppers

1 tablespoon unsalted butter

1 clove garlic, minced

1 cup uncooked long- or short-grain brown rice or American basmati-type brown rice

2¹/₂ cups water or half water and half chicken broth

1 tablespoon seeded and finely chopped jalapeño or other hot green chili pepper (see Basics, page 263)

Saffron Rice

Generous pinch of saffron threads

1 cup uncooked imported basmati or American basmati-type white rice

1 tablespoon unsalted butter

1 teaspoon salt

¹/₂ teaspoon ground turmeric

1 bay leaf

1 piece cinnamon stick (about 2 inches)

1 slice (about ¹/₄ inch thick) ginger

Chicken and Yogurt

2 tablespoons unsalted butter

2 medium onions, cut into $1/2$-inch chunks (about 2 cups)

2 to 3 carrots, pared and cut into $1/2$-inch chunks (about 1
  cup)

3 cloves garlic, coarsely chopped

$1\,1/2$ pounds boneless and skinless chicken breasts and thighs,
  with fat trimmed and cut into 1- to 2-inch pieces

2 to 3 teaspoons curry powder

$1/2$ teaspoon ground cumin

$1/2$ teaspoon ground ginger

$1/2$ teaspoon salt, or more to taste

$1/4$ teaspoon ground red pepper (cayenne), or more to taste

$1/8$ teaspoon freshly ground black pepper

2 cups plain yogurt

$1/4$ cup raisins

$1/2$ cup chicken broth

Toppings

1 cup thinly sliced onion rings fried until browned in 2
  tablespoons of vegetable oil (optional)

$1/2$ cup chopped salted dry-roasted cashews or peanuts

$1/4$ cup coarsely chopped fresh cilantro

Mango chutney (store-bought)

1. To make the brown rice with garlic and chili peppers: Heat the butter in a heavy saucepan. Stir in the garlic and sauté over low heat just until fragrant. Stir in the rice just to coat, add the water (or water and broth), and heat to boiling. Cook, covered, over medium-low heat about 40 minutes (the rice will be slightly undercooked), then let stand off the heat, uncovered. Just before using add the jalapeño or other chili pepper and toss with a fork to blend.

2. Meanwhile, cook the saffron rice: Combine the saffron threads and $1/4$ cup of boiling water in a small bowl. Cover and let stand for 15 minutes. In a heavy saucepan heat $1\,1/2$ cups of water to boiling; add the rice, butter, salt, turmeric, bay leaf, and cinnamon stick and ginger. Stir in the soaked saffron threads and water. Cover and cook

over medium-low heat for 12 minutes (the rice will be slightly undercooked). Uncover and let stand off the heat. Remove and discard the bay leaf and cinnamon stick.

3. To make the chicken and yogurt: Melt the butter in a large heavy skillet until the foam subsides. Add the onions, carrots, and garlic, and sauté over medium heat, stirring, until the edges are browned and the vegetables are tender, about 10 minutes.

4. Add the chicken and sauté over high heat, stirring, until the chicken is just browned on the outside (do not cook through), about 5 minutes. Season with the curry, cumin, ginger, salt, cayenne, and black pepper. Sauté, stirring, for 2 minutes, just to release the flavors of the spices and coat the chicken and vegetables evenly. Stir in the yogurt and raisins until blended.

5. Heat the oven to 350°F. Select a shallow baking or serving dish about 13 × 9 inches. Spread half of the brown rice mixture in a shallow layer along one side of the bottom of the baking dish. Spread half of the saffron rice on the other side of the brown rice mixture.

6. Spoon the chicken and yogurt mixture in an even layer on top of the rice and top with the remaining rices (half of the brown and half of the saffron) in two even strips.

7. Drizzle with the broth, cover tightly with foil, and heat in the oven for 45 minutes, or until it is steaming hot.

8. Sprinkle the top of the dish with the fried onion rings, cashews or peanuts, and cilantro. Serve with chutney on the side.

MAKES 8 SERVINGS

One "Mean" Jambalaya

I have eaten jambalaya from Savannah to Houston and points in between, and have yet to experience the same recipe twice. Jambalaya often contains tomatoes, pork, ham (tasso, a highly seasoned Cajun smoked ham is popular), or seafood. This version, from Kristen O'Brien of the Rice Council in Houston, Texas, uses boneless and skinless chicken. Kris says, "This is a great do-ahead dish; in fact, the flavors are better if the dish is made a day ahead." It is also an enormous dish that is perfect for entertaining. The recipe can be halved.

1 1/2 pounds smoked spiced beef sausage, cut into 1/4-inch-thick
  slices
3 skinless and boneless chicken breasts, halved
8 skinless and boneless chicken thighs
Salt and freshly ground black pepper to taste
1 tablespoon vegetable oil (optional)
4 cups chopped onions
2 cups chopped celery
2 cups chopped green bell peppers
3 cloves garlic, minced
4 cups uncooked converted or parboiled long-grain white rice
5 cups unsalted chicken broth, preferably homemade
1/2 teaspoon ground red pepper (cayenne)

1. In a large Dutch oven over medium heat cook the sausage until browned. Remove from the pan to a side dish. Add the chicken pieces to the drippings in the pan and sauté, in batches if necessary, for 3 minutes on each side or until lightly browned. Transfer the chicken to a side dish and generously salt and pepper.

2. Add vegetable oil to the pan if needed. Add the onions, celery, green peppers, and garlic. Sauté over low heat, stirring, until tender and just beginning to brown, about 15 minutes.

3. Heat the oven to 325°F. Stir in the rice, broth, red pepper, and additional salt if needed. Heat to boiling. Add the chicken and sausage to the pot. Cover and bake for 30 minutes, or until the liquid is absorbed and the rice is tender, stirring once or twice.

MAKES 8 TO 10 SERVINGS

Rice and Seafood

Rice has a natural affinity for seafood, perhaps because they both grow in water. Consider just a handful of famous rice dishes: Spanish paella, Japanese sushi, jambalaya from the American South, and Italian seafood risotti. In Asia, it is not unusual for rice paddies to double as fish ponds between rice-growing seasons. In many rice-growing cultures the frogs living in the paddies control the insect population, while the people eat the frogs—an important source of protein in many rice-based cuisines.

Mussels with Curried Rice

Serve this wonderful mussel and rice dish in a large bowl garnished with whole cooked mussels or divide the rice among halved mussel shells and tuck a cooked mussel into each shell. Good served warm or at room temperature.

Mussels

1 bag (2 pounds) mussels
1 tablespoon olive oil
1 small onion, sliced
1 clove garlic, bruised with the side of a knife
1 strip (2 × ¹/₂ inch) orange zest
1 cup dry white wine
Sprig each of fresh basil, cilantro, and parsley (or select
    just one)

Curried Rice

1 tablespoon olive oil
¹/₄ cup chopped onion
1 clove garlic, crushed
1 to 2 teaspoons curry powder, or to taste
¹/₂ teaspoon ground cumin
¹/₂ teaspoon ground turmeric
Salt to taste (optional)
1 cup uncooked long-grain white rice or imported basmati or
    American basmati-type white rice
2 tablespoons chopped basil, cilantro, or parsley
Sprigs of basil, cilantro, or parsley

1. Prepare the mussels (see Basics, page 265).

2. Meanwhile, heat the oil in a large wide saucepan. Add the onion and sauté for 5 minutes. Add the garlic and orange zest, and sauté for 1 minute. Add the wine and

herbs, and heat to boiling. Drain the mussels and add to the boiling wine. Cover and cook over high heat for 4 to 5 minutes, or until all the mussels are open. Remove the mussels to a platter with a slotted spoon and cover with foil to keep warm. Carefully strain the broth through a sieve set over a 2-cup glass measure. Discard the solids. Add enough water to the broth to equal 2 cups, then set aside.

3. To prepare the curried rice: Heat the oil in a medium-sized saucepan. Add the onion and sauté for 5 minutes. Add the garlic and sauté 1 minute more. Stir in the curry powder, cumin, and turmeric. Heat over low heat, stirring, for 1 minute. Add the reserved 2 cups of mussel broth, salt, if using, and the rice. Heat to boiling, stirring. Cover and cook over low heat until the water is absorbed and the rice is tender, about 15 minutes.

4. Reserve 12 mussels in their shells to use as garnish. Remove the remaining mussels from their shells. When the rice is cooked, spoon onto a large platter. Distribute the mussels on top of the rice and sprinkle with the chopped basil, cilantro, or parsley. Fluff with a fork. Garnish with the reserved mussels left in their shells and sprigs of basil, cilantro, or parsley.

MAKES ABOUT 4 SERVINGS

MUSSELS STUFFED WITH CURRIED RICE

Use 20 evenly sized mussels and prepare and cook as described in the recipe above. Strain the broth and add enough liquid to equal 1⅓ cups. Cook ⅔ cup of rice as directed in step 2 of the recipe above, using 1 teaspoon of curry powder and ¼ teaspoon each of cumin and turmeric. Meanwhile, remove the mussels from their shells. Separate the shells into 2 halves and reserve 20 of the largest halves; discard the remainder. Cool the rice slightly. Add ½ cup of peeled and diced ripe tomato, 1 thinly sliced scallion, 2 tablespoons of finely chopped cilantro or basil, and 1 tablespoon of fresh lime juice. Stuff the rice mixture into the mussel shells, tucking 1 mussel in each mounding and pressing the rice around it. Arrange on a platter and serve at room temperature as an appetizer or as a first course. (This can be made up to 1 day ahead.) Garnish each with a fresh cilantro leaf or a small basil leaf.

Provençal-style Stuffed Red Snapper

This recipe contains many of the flavors and fragrances—fennel, orange, capers, and black olives—I associate with the foods of Provence.

1 large red snapper (about 2 to 2½ pounds) *or* 2 smaller red
    snappers (about 1½ pounds each)
4 tablespoons olive oil
1 cup finely chopped fresh fennel, plus fernlike tops reserved
    separately
½ cup diced sweet red onion
¾ teaspoon dried fennel seeds
2 cloves garlic
2 cups cooked long-grain white or brown rice
2 tablespoons chopped sun-dried tomatoes *or* ½ cup diced
    fresh tomato
¼ cup orange juice
6 brine-cured black olives, pitted and cut up
2 teaspoons rinsed and drained capers
1 teaspoon grated orange zest, plus 2 strips (2 × ½ inch)
Salt and freshly ground black pepper
4 orange slices

1. Heat the oven to 350°F. Rinse the fish thoroughly with cold running water. Pat dry inside and out with a paper towel.

2. Heat 2 tablespoons of the oil in a large skillet. Add the cup of chopped fennel and sauté over medium-low heat, stirring, until the fennel is tender, about 5 minutes. Stir in the onion and ¼ teaspoon of the fennel seeds, and sauté for 5 minutes. Crush 1 clove of the garlic and add to the skillet. Sauté 1 minute more.

3. Stir in the rice, sun-dried tomatoes, orange juice, and 2 tablespoons of finely chopped fernlike fennel tops. Cook over medium heat, stirring, just until blended, about

5 minutes. Remove from the heat. Add the olives, capers, and grated orange zest, and set the stuffing aside.

4. In a large baking pan combine the remaining 2 tablespoons of oil, strips of orange zest, remaining ½ teaspoon of fennel seeds and remaining garlic clove bruised with the side of a knife. Place in the oven and bake for 10 minutes, or until the garlic is sizzling. Remove the oil from the oven.

5. Carefully place the snapper in the baking pan and turn the fish to coat with the aromatic oil. Open the cavity and sprinkle with salt and pepper. Carefully stuff the entire fish cavity (or cavities, if using 2 fish), including the head portion. Mound any excess stuffing around the opening.

6. Arrange any remaining large pieces of the fernlike fennel tops over the fish and top with the orange slices. Bake the smaller fish for 30 to 40 minutes; bake the larger fish for 50 to 60 minutes. To test for doneness use a kitchen knife and cut along the backbone to separate the flesh. If the flesh is opaque to the bone, the fish is cooked. Remember that fish continues to cook after it is removed from the oven.

7. To serve, cut along the backbone and lift off the top fillet, then lift out the entire bone and discard. Serve the fillets (don't forget to retrieve the clumps of meat around the head of the fish) with a spoonful of stuffing and garnish with the roasted orange slices.

MAKES 4 SERVINGS

Squid Stuffed with Rice, Basil, and Orange

Although they require a little more patience to clean and stuff, I prefer small squid for this dish. It is most important to select squid that are uniform in size so they will cook evenly.

1 1/2 pounds small (about 3 to 4 inches in length) squid with
    tentacles, cleaned
2 tablespoons oil
2 tablespoons minced shallots
2 tablespoons minced prosciutto
2 tablespoons raisins
2 tablespoons pignoli (pine nuts)
1 cup cooked Italian arborio rice or medium-grain white rice
2 tablespoons chopped fresh basil
2 tablespoons chopped fresh parsley
1 teaspoon grated orange zest
Salt and freshly ground black pepper to taste

Sauce
2 tablespoons olive oil
1/2 cup thin vertical slices of onion
1 clove garlic, bruised with the side of a knife
1 strip (2 × 1/2 inch) orange zest
2 cups coarsely chopped fresh ripe plum tomatoes, peeled and
    with juice, *or* Italian-style canned tomatoes
1 tablespoon packed 1/8-inch strips fresh basil
Salt and freshly ground black pepper to taste
Sprigs of fresh basil

1. Rinse the insides of the squid thoroughly under cold tap water and lay out on paper towels to drain. Separate the tentacles, cut them into 1-inch lengths, rinse, drain, and set aside.

2. Heat the oil in a large skillet. Add the shallots and sauté, stirring, until tender, about 5 minutes. Add the prosciutto, raisins, and pignoli. Sauté, stirring, until the raisins are plumped and the pignoli are golden, about 5 minutes. Stir in the rice, basil, parsley, and orange zest until blended. Add salt and pepper.

3. Using a teaspoon carefully fill the squid with the rice mixture, dividing evenly. Do not force the stuffing or the squid will break open during cooking. Seal the open end of each squid with a toothpick.

4. To make the sauce: Heat the oil in a large skillet with a tight-fitting lid. Add the onion, garlic, and orange zest, and stir to blend. Add the stuffed squid and the tentacles to the skillet. Sauté the squid, turning gently as they brown.

5. Add the tomatoes and strips of basil, and heat to boiling. Spoon the sauce over the squid. Turn the heat to very low and cook the squid for 45 minutes, turning once halfway through cooking. Taste the sauce and add salt and pepper if needed.

6. Serve with sauce spooned around each serving. Garnish with sprigs of fresh basil.

MAKES 4 SERVINGS AS A MAIN COURSE OR 6 AS AN APPETIZER

Sautéed Shrimp and Rice with Fresh Corn

Save this quick and easy recipe for fresh corn season. Canned or frozen corn can be used, but it will not have the same sweet, crunchy flavor. Use the medium- or smaller-sized shrimp instead of the more popular jumbo type. With a fresh tomato and basil salad, this is a tasty and fast menu when you want to serve an especially nice meal but there is no time to fuss.

3 scallions, trimmed
2 tablespoons unsalted butter
1 cup uncooked long-grain white rice
1¼ cups water
½ cup dry white wine
1 teaspoon salt
1 cup fresh corn kernels (from 2 ears of corn)
8 ounces medium-sized shrimp, shelled and deveined
1 tablespoon torn fresh basil leaves
½ teaspoon fresh thyme leaves, stripped from stems
Lemon wedges

1. Cut the green tops from the scallions. Thinly slice them and set aside. Chop the white and pale-green part of the scallions. Heat 1 tablespoon of the butter in a medium-sized saucepan, add the chopped scallion, and sauté until tender, about 2 minutes.

2. Stir in the rice and sauté 2 minutes more. Add the water, wine, and salt. Heat to boiling, stirring well. Cover and cook over low heat for 12 minutes.

3. Uncover and stir in the corn, shrimp, remaining tablespoon of butter, basil, and thyme. Cover and cook for 3 minutes, or until the liquid is absorbed and the shrimp are cooked.

4. Serve sprinkled with the green scallion tops and garnished with the lemon wedges. Leftovers are good served cold.

MAKES 2 TO 3 SERVINGS

Paella

The expression "There are probably as many recipes as there are cooks" is quite true when it comes to paella, considered by some to be the signature dish of Spain. Paella means pan from the Latin patella or the Greek pateras. A paella eaten in Valenciana could be a simple mixture of rice, beans, snails, and rabbit, or an extravagant one with shellfish, saffron, sausage, and artichokes. This version has rabbit or chicken, clams, shrimp, lima beans, and green beans—and imported medium-grain rice from Spain or Italy or home-grown American medium-grain rice.

¼ cup olive oil

1 rabbit, cut up, *or* 4 chicken thighs and 2 chicken breasts, split

1 teaspoon fresh rosemary, stripped from stems, or ½ teaspoon dried rosemary

Salt and freshly ground black pepper

4 cups unsalted chicken broth, preferably homemade

Generous pinch of saffron threads

2 cups imported Spanish Valencia rice or Italian or American medium-grain white rice

1 can (28 ounces) Italian-style plum tomatoes, drained

12 large shrimp, shelled and deveined

12 Manila (see Basics, page 265) or littleneck clams, scrubbed

1 cup cooked dried small lima beans *or* 1 cup frozen lima beans, thawed

1 cup cut-up (1-inch lengths) trimmed fresh green beans or Italian green beans

Sprigs of rosemary

1. Heat the olive oil in a very large round shallow ovenproof dish or paella pan. Sauté the pieces of rabbit or chicken until golden on both sides and almost cooked

through, about 15 minutes; remove to a side dish. Sprinkle with rosemary, salt, and pepper.

2. Heat the oven to 350°F. Combine ¼ cup of the chicken broth and the saffron threads in a small saucepan. Heat to boiling, then remove from the heat, cover, and let stand for 10 minutes. Add the rice to the fat in the ovenproof dish and sauté, stirring, until coated with the oil, about 2 minutes. Add the remaining chicken broth and the tomatoes to the pan. Cook, stirring, to loosen any browned pieces from the bottom of the pan and break the tomatoes with the side of a spoon until the mixture boils. Stir in the saffron mixture.

3. Add the rabbit or chicken, any meat juice, shrimp, clams, lima beans, and green beans, and season with 2 teaspoons of salt, or to taste, and pepper. Heat to boiling and stir to mix ingredients. Remove from the heat and cover with foil.

4. Place in the oven and bake for 20 minutes. Remove from the oven and let stand 20 minutes before uncovering the pan.

5. Lift the meats and shellfish to the surface of the dish to show them off and garnish with rosemary sprigs.

MAKES 6 SERVINGS

Sauces over Rice

This section was created when my aunt Tess described a favorite childhood supper of rice topped with a spicy red sauce. Three of these recipes are Italian in feeling and one leans toward the Orient.

Hot Italian Sausage in Red Sauce over Rice

My aunt Tess recalled this recipe from her childhood with such detail that I could imagine the taste and aroma long before I began cooking. My grandmother, Antoinette Abbruzzese, cooked for ten every day: her own five children, a niece, her mother, and her mother-in-law (affectionately referred to as "the grannies"), Grandpa, and herself. This recipe was a favorite. Pure and simple, brimming with good flavor and comfort, it is now one of mine.

Select a good-quality well-seasoned sausage. The flavor of the sauce is entirely dependent on the sausage. As Nana would say, "Don't be skimpy."

1½ pounds hot Italian sausage, with casings removed
1 tablespoon olive oil
½ cup finely chopped onion
1 clove garlic
3 cans (14½ ounces each) Italian-style plum tomatoes with
   juice
2 tablespoons tomato paste
1 bay leaf
Pinch of dried oregano
Salt and freshly ground black pepper
2 cups uncooked long-grain white rice
Grated Pecorino-Romano cheese

1. Crumble the sausage into a large skillet and sauté over medium heat, stirring often, until well browned.

2. Meanwhile, heat the olive oil in a wide saucepan. Add the onion and sauté over medium-low heat, stirring, until the onion is tender, about 5 minutes. Add the garlic and sauté 1 minute more.

3. Set a food mill over the saucepan. Add the tomatoes, puree them through the food mill, and discard the seeds. Stir in the tomato paste, bay leaf, and oregano, and heat

to boiling. Add the browned sausage meat and any drippings. Add ¼ cup of water to the skillet and heat, stirring constantly to scrape up any of the browned bits of sausage drippings. Add to the tomato sauce along with salt and pepper to taste.

4. Cook over medium-low heat, stirring occasionally, for 1½ hours, or until the sauce is thick and fragrant. Remove and discard the bay leaf. (This can be made ahead up to this point and reheated later.)

5. Just before serving cook the rice in 3½ cups of boiling salted water over low heat in a medium-sized saucepan, covered, until the water is absorbed and the rice is tender, about 15 minutes.

6. To serve spoon the rice onto serving plates. Top liberally with the sausage in red sauce and sprinkle generously with grated cheese.

MAKES 4 TO 6 SERVINGS

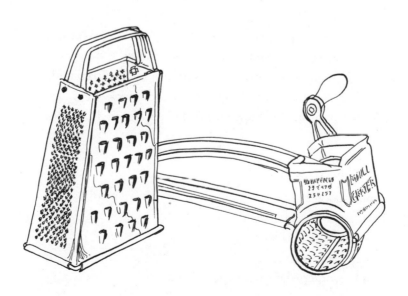

Orange Pork with Vegetables and Peanuts over Brown Rice

6 ounces lean boneless pork, cut into thin strips (1 or 1½ × ¼ inch)

1 teaspoon soy sauce

½ teaspoon grated orange zest, plus 6 strips (2 × ½ inch), cut lengthwise into ⅛-inch pieces

1 clove garlic, crushed, plus 1 teaspoon minced fresh garlic

1 cup uncooked short-grain brown rice

8 ounces green beans, trimmed and diagonally sliced (1-inch lengths)

2 medium carrots, pared and cut into 1 × ¼-inch sticks

1 tablespoon peanut oil

1 tablespoon minced fresh ginger

1 cup trimmed and diagonally sliced (about ½-inch lengths) scallions

1 small red bell pepper, quartered, stem and seeds discarded, and cut crosswise into ¼-inch-wide pieces

1 small (about 3 ounces) yellow summer squash, trimmed, halved lengthwise, and cut into ⅛-inch-thick slices

2 tablespoons finely chopped unsalted dry-roasted peanuts

Orange Sauce

¼ cup fresh orange juice

1 tablespoon honey

1 tablespoon rice vinegar

2 teaspoons soy sauce

1 teaspoon cornstarch

¼ teaspoon crushed red pepper flakes

1. Stir together the pork, soy sauce, grated orange zest, and crushed garlic clove in a small bowl. Marinate, covered and refrigerated, for about 30 minutes before using.

2. Meanwhile, cook the rice according to package directions. Steam the green beans and carrots together in a vegetable steamer set over simmering water, covered, until crisp-tender, about 3 minutes. Rinse and let stand at room temperature.

3. To make the orange sauce: In a small bowl stir together the orange juice, honey, rice vinegar, soy sauce, and cornstarch. Add the red pepper and set aside.

4. Just before serving heat a large heavy skillet, preferably nonstick, or a seasoned wok over high heat until hot enough to evaporate a drop of water on contact. Add the peanut oil and tilt the pan to coat the bottom. Add the strips of orange zest and stir-fry until fragrant and the edges begin to brown, about 30 seconds. Using a slotted spoon remove half of the zest to a side dish and set aside. Immediately add the minced ginger and teaspoon of minced garlic to the hot skillet, and stir-fry for 30 seconds. Add the scallions and cooked green beans and carrots, and stir-fry for 2 minutes. Add the red bell pepper and yellow squash, and stir-fry 30 seconds more. Scrape all the vegetables and seasonings from the skillet or wok into a warmed serving dish and set aside (do not cover).

5. Reheat the skillet or wok over high heat until hot enough to sizzle and instantly brown a piece of the marinated pork. Add the pork a little at a time to the hot skillet and stir-fry, using a chopstick to keep the pieces of pork separated, until the pork is browned on all sides, about 2 minutes.

6. Add the reserved vegetables to the sizzling pork all at once and stir to blend. Stir the orange sauce to mix and pour over the contents of the skillet. Stir-fry over high heat just until the mixture begins to thicken and coat the vegetables.

7. Mound the cooked rice in the center of a platter and top with the stir-fried pork and vegetables. Sprinkle with the reserved crisp pieces of orange zest and the chopped peanuts.

MAKES 4 SERVINGS

Baby Artichoke Sauce over Parmesan Rice

Artichokes come from a perennial plant that produces nearly all year long. Every plant bears its share of large picture-perfect artichokes, but way down among the shaded plant fronds the smallest and most tender artichokes, called "babies," are harvested. These baby artichokes, measuring under 2¹/₂ inches long, are essential for this sauce. For the best flavor use homemade chicken broth in both the sauce and the rice recipes.

Baby Artichoke Sauce
1 lemon, halved
1¹/₂ pounds (about 24) baby artichokes
¹/₂ cup extra-virgin olive oil
1 medium-sized sweet yellow onion, halved lengthwise and cut
    vertically into ¹/₄-inch-thick slices
1 rib celery, trimmed, halved lengthwise, and cut into ¹/₈-inch
    slices
1 medium carrot, pared, trimmed, and cut into ¹/₈-inch slices
4 cloves garlic, bruised with the side of a knife
1 cup chicken broth, preferably homemade
1 teaspoon fresh thyme leaves, stripped from the stems, and
    four sprigs of fresh thyme
Salt and freshly ground black pepper to taste

Parmesan Rice
1 tablespoon extra-virgin olive oil
1 cup uncooked long-grain white rice or Italian arborio rice
1³/₄ cups chicken broth, preferably homemade
Salt
¹/₃ cup freshly grated Parmigiano-Reggiano cheese (see Basics,
    page 267)

1. To make the baby artichoke sauce: Half-fill a large bowl with cold water and squeeze the lemon halves into the water. Pull the thick outside leaves off the artichokes. Trim the dark edge from the stem and cut off the pointed tops about ¼ inch down. Halve the artichokes and with the point of a small paring knife pull out the sharply pointed center leaves and the fuzzy portion. Immediately add to the bowl of lemon water to prevent darkening.

2. Heat the olive oil in a large skillet with a tight-fitting lid. Stir in the onion, celery, carrot, and garlic. Cover and cook over low heat for 10 minutes, or until the vegetables are tender.

3. Drain the lemon water from the artichokes and add them to the skillet. Stir to coat with the oil mixture. Add the chicken broth and thyme leaves. Season with salt and pepper.

4. Cover and cook over low heat for 25 minutes, or until the artichokes are very tender. Uncover and taste the broth. Add additional salt and pepper if necessary. Don't overdo it; remember that the cheese in the rice will add a salty flavor to the dish. (This can be prepared up to 1 day ahead and reheated just before serving.)

5. To make the Parmesan rice: Heat the oil in a medium-sized saucepan over low heat. Stir in the rice to coat; sauté, stirring, until the rice becomes opaque, about 2 minutes. Add the chicken broth and salt to taste, and heat to boiling. Stir thoroughly. Cover and cook over medium-low heat until the broth is absorbed, about 15 minutes. Uncover and immediately stir the Parmesan cheese into the rice.

6. To serve, spoon the rice into the center of 4 dinner plates, dividing evenly. Top with the artichoke sauce, dividing all the ingredients evenly among the plates. Garnish each with a stem of fresh thyme.

SERVES 4

Anchovy Sauce over Rice and Cauliflower

This recipe is for anchovy lovers.

1 tablespoon unsalted butter

1 cup chopped onions

1 cup uncooked long-grain white rice or imported basmati or
American basmati-type white rice

1³/₄ cups water

1 bay leaf

¹/₂ teaspoon salt

1 head cauliflower (about 1¹/₂ pounds), rinsed and broken into
¹/₂-inch florets with stems attached (about 4 cups)

2 hard-boiled eggs, peeled

4 tablespoons finely chopped Italian (flat leaf) parsley

Anchovy Sauce

6 tablespoons unsalted butter

1 clove garlic, pressed

1 can (2 ounces) anchovy fillets, drained, rinsed, patted dry,
and coarsely chopped

1 tablespoon rinsed and drained capers

1 teaspoon fresh lemon juice

1. Select a large 10- or 12-inch skillet with a tight-fitting lid or a wide shallow saucepan. Heat the butter over medium heat until the foam subsides. Stir in the onion and sauté, stirring, until golden, about 5 minutes. Add the rice, stir to coat with the butter, and sauté until the rice is opaque, about 1 minute. Add the water, bay leaf, and salt, and heat to boiling. Stir once, cover, and cook over medium-low heat for 5 minutes. Uncover and add the cauliflower pieces, tucking them into the rice. Cover and cook for 12 to 15 minutes, or until the liquid is absorbed and the rice and cauliflower are both tender. Remove and discard the bay leaf.

2. Meanwhile, in a separate skillet make the anchovy sauce: Heat the butter over medium heat until the foam subsides. Stir in the garlic and anchovies and sauté over medium-low heat, stirring and mashing with the back of a spoon until the anchovies dissolve, about 10 minutes. Off the heat stir in the capers and lemon juice.

3. Separate the hard-boiled yolks from the whites. Discard the whites or reserve them for other use. Press the yolks through a fine sieve onto a piece of waxed paper and set aside.

4. Spoon the rice and cauliflower into a serving bowl. Drizzle the anchovy sauce over the top and sprinkle with parsley. Sprinkle the sieved egg yolks on top. Serve at once.

MAKES 4 SERVINGS

Rice Stir-fries

Stir-frying is a fuel-efficient cooking technique unique to Asian countries where so much of the terrain is a sea of rice paddies rather than forests that provide fuel. Stir-frying is also a quick, efficient, and healthy technique that is especially appealing to the busy contemporary cook. It is a good way to use refrigerated leftover cooked rice because the heat of stir-frying will soften the hard, dry texture associated with cold rice. The following recipes are Oriental in spirit but their ingredients are completely accessible to the home cook.

Freshly cooked rice for stir-fry recipes should be cooked according to package directions and then spread out on a dish towel to cool and to evaporate any excess moisture. Refrigerated rice should be stirred with chopsticks to separate the grains before using. Use a mixture of brown and white rices or all of one type.

Stir-fried Rice and Broccoli with Sesame Seeds and Garlic

The different flavors and textures of brown and white rice add visual and taste interests to this recipe. To make this all-vegetable dish just a little heartier, prepare the egg pancake from the next recipe (page 177) and add with the rice in step 4.

3 cups broccoli florets, cut into 2-inch-long pieces, rinsed, and
   drained
1/4 cup chicken broth
1 tablespoon Chinese wine or dry sherry
2 teaspoons soy sauce
1/2 teaspoon Oriental sesame oil
1 tablespoon sesame seeds
2 tablespoons peanut oil
1 tablespoon thinly slivered garlic
2 teaspoons minced fresh ginger
1 teaspoon minced garlic
1 1/2 cups each cooked white and brown rice

1. Blanch the broccoli in boiling salted water just until bright green, about 2 minutes, then drain well. In a small bowl stir together the broth, wine, soy sauce, and sesame oil, and then set aside.

2. Heat the sesame seeds in a dry wok or large, preferably nonstick, skillet over low heat, stirring, until toasted. Scrape onto a side dish and set aside.

3. Heat 1 tablespoon of the oil in the wok or skillet until hot enough to sizzle a piece of the garlic slivers. Add all the garlic slivers and stir-fry until golden, about 30 seconds. Quickly skim from the oil with a slotted spoon and drain on paper towels.

4. Add the remaining tablespoon of oil to the skillet. When hot enough to sizzle a piece of the ginger, add all the ginger and the minced garlic, and stir-fry for 30 seconds.

Add the broccoli and stir-fry about 1 minute more. Add the sauce and stir-fry just to coat. Add the rice and stir-fry until the ingredients are blended and the rice is hot, about 2 minutes.

5. Spoon into a serving dish and sprinkle with the toasted sesame seeds and crisp garlic slivers. Serve at once.

MAKES 4 SERVINGS

Stir-fried Glazed Chicken, Rice, and Cashews

1 teaspoon soy sauce
1 1/4 teaspoons Oriental sesame oil
2 1/2 teaspoons minced fresh ginger
1/2 teaspoon sugar
12 ounces boneless and skinless chicken breast, cut crosswise
    into thin slices
2 extra-large eggs
Pinch of salt and freshly ground black pepper
2 tablespoons plus 1 teaspoon peanut oil
1/2 cup coarsely chopped unsalted cashews
1 clove garlic, minced
1/2 cup slivered red bell pepper
3 scallions, trimmed and cut diagonally into thin slices
2 to 3 cups cooked short-grain brown rice or long-grain white
    or brown rice
Cilantro leaves (optional)

Brown Sauce
1 tablespoon oyster sauce
1 tablespoon water or chicken broth
1 tablespoon soy sauce
1 teaspoon Oriental sesame oil

1. Combine the soy sauce, 1 teaspoon of sesame oil, ¹/₂ teaspoon of minced ginger, and sugar in a small bowl. Add the chicken and let stand at room temperature for 30 minutes, or refrigerate, covered, for 1 hour or more.

2. Whisk the eggs, remaining ¹/₄ teaspoon of sesame oil, salt, and pepper until frothy. Heat 1 teaspoon of the peanut oil in a skillet or wok until hot. Add the eggs, tilt the pan so that a thin pancake forms, and cook until set. Transfer to a plate, cut up into thin strips, and set aside.

3. To make the brown sauce: Combine the oyster sauce, water or broth, soy sauce, and sesame oil in a small bowl. Set aside until ready to use.

4. Just before serving heat 1 tablespoon of the remaining peanut oil in a wok or large heavy, preferably nonstick, skillet until very hot. Add the cashews and stir-fry for 30 seconds. Remove with a slotted spoon to a side dish. Add the remaining tablespoon of oil and reheat. Add the remaining 2 teaspoons of minced ginger and the garlic, and stir-fry for 20 seconds. Add the marinated chicken and stir-fry until lightly browned, about 1 minute. Add the red pepper and scallions, and stir-fry 1 minute more.

5. Add the rice and egg strips, and pour the brown sauce over the top. Stir-fry until all the ingredients are blended and the rice is very hot, about 2 minutes. Serve at once sprinkled with the cashews and cilantro, if using.

MAKES 4 SERVINGS

Stir-fried Fiery Shrimp, Orange Rice, and Spinach

2 tablespoons plus 2 teaspoons soy sauce
2 tablespoons plus 1 teaspoon peanut oil
1 clove garlic, crushed, plus ¹/₂ teaspoon minced fresh garlic
2 teaspoons minced fresh ginger
¹/₂ teaspoon chili-flavored Oriental sesame oil
¹/₂ teaspoon crushed red pepper flakes
¹/₄ teaspoon freshly ground black pepper
1 pound medium-sized shrimp, shelled and deveined
2 strips (2 × ¹/₂ inch) orange zest, cut into very thin pieces
3 scallions, trimmed and cut lengthwise into thin pieces
4 cups (about 5 ounces) washed, trimmed, and torn spinach
   leaves
3 cups cooked long-grain white or brown rice

1. Combine 2 teaspoons of the soy sauce, 1 teaspoon of the peanut oil, crushed garlic clove, 1 teaspoon of the ginger, sesame oil, red pepper flakes, and black pepper in a large bowl. Add the shrimp and toss to coat. Cover and marinate for 30 minutes at room temperature, or 1 hour or longer in the refrigerator.

2. When ready to serve, heat a wok or large nonstick skillet over medium-high heat until hot enough to evaporate a drop of water on contact. Add 1 tablespoon of the remaining peanut oil and then the shrimp, a few at a time. Stir-fry just until lightly browned on both sides and remove to a side dish when they are cooked. Scrape any drippings over the shrimp. Wipe out the wok or skillet with paper towels.

3. Add the remaining tablespoon of oil to the wok or skillet. Heat until hot enough to sizzle a piece of the orange zest. Add all the orange zest and stir-fry for 1 minute. Add the remaining teaspoon of ginger and the ¹/₂ teaspoon of minced garlic, and stir-fry 30 seconds more. Add the scallions and stir once. Add the spinach and stir to coat with the ingredients.

4. Add the rice and reserved shrimp, and stir over high heat until blended with the other ingredients. Sprinkle with the remaining 2 tablespoons of soy sauce and stir-fry until heated through, about 2 minutes.

5. Spoon into a serving dish and serve at once.

MAKES 4 SERVINGS

RISOTTI AND PILAFS

Risotti

Spring Risotto
Clam Risotto
Fennel Risotto
Porcini Risotto
Apple Risotto
Sausage, Tomato, and Basil Risotto
Rice and Peas, *Risi e Bisi*

Pilafs

Pilaf with Curry, Raisins, and Almonds
Orzo and Pignoli Pilaf
Orange and Currant Pilaf
Bulgur and Rice Pilaf with Sautéed Walnuts and Dates
Lentil and Rice Pilaf with Dill and Mint
Potato and Rice Pilaf with Peas and Cumin
Tomato Pilaf

The major difference between risotto and pilaf is the type of rice used; also, pilaf cooks covered and undisturbed while risotto needs to be continuously stirred while cooking. Pilaf is indisputably the simpler dish of the two. Food historians claim that rice, indigenous to India, was introduced to the Mediterranean region from the East. It is entertaining to contemplate the notion that the pilafs of the exotic East might have become the risotti of Italy.

Plump medium grains of Italian rice (arborio and vialone nano are the most widely available in the United States) are essential for the unique consistency and texture of risotto. To make risotto the rice is first sautéed in butter or olive oil and then simmering broth is added slowly while the mixture is stirred. The rice expands as it absorbs the broth, and the friction of the stirring softens the outside (amylopectin) of the grain, forming a creamy, almost saucelike consistency. The center (pearl or core) of the rice remains firm to the bite, also popularly described as resistant or *al dente*. How and why the Italians decided to stir their rice constantly until it became a creamy mass is one of those culinary mysteries (and masterpieces) subject to discussion and conjecture.

American rice plant specialists are already experimenting with the idea of growing Italian rice here. This is exciting news considering the popularity of risotto and the expense of buying imported rice. It has not yet been determined if Italian rice can be grown successfully in the United States.

The word *pilaf* is from the Turkish word *pilau* or *pilaw,* but there are a variety of spellings, including *pilaou, pulav,* and *pulau.* A pilaf can be a simple dish of rice cooked with sautéed onion or an elaborate dish flavored with legumes, vegetables, and exotic seasonings. Imported basmati, with its long slender grains that cook dry and separate, is traditionally used in pilaf. Texmati, an aromatic American basmati-type rice (available as both brown and white), makes excellent pilaf. To substitute brown rice for white rice in any of the pilaf recipes, increase the liquid by $\frac{1}{2}$ cup and the cooking time to about 45 minutes.

MAKING RISOTTO

I have spent minutes enough to add up to hours, days—perhaps years—standing at the stove stirring risotto in anticipation of the moment when it is finally "ready." The time it takes to cook risotto depends on an assortment of variables, many of which cannot be controlled by the cook. For instance, I suspect that "older" rice (not rancid, but rice that has been stored for a while) takes a little longer to cook than "younger" rice. I suggest that you experiment with different varieties and brands until you find the one you prefer. The following recipes give a range for cooking times and the amount of broth needed. As friend and colleague Michele Scicolone advises, "Risotto is ready when it is ready!" Here are a few tips to get you started:

1. Buy Italian rice at a busy, reliable retailer concerned with quality. Rancidity can be detected by an off odor, broken or crumbled grains of rice, and dusty residue in the bottom of the bag or box.
2. To cook risotto use a heavy-bottomed, wide, and moderately shallow saucepan with ample space to allow plenty of room for thorough stirring.
3. Risotto should cook at a gentle, steady boil. Usually a medium to medium-low heat is adequate, but this is relative to the type of saucepan used and the heat source.
4. Use a ladle with about a $\frac{1}{2}$-cup capacity for adding consistent amounts of hot broth.
5. Taste the risotto frequently while stirring so you can keep tabs on the texture of the rice as the cooking progresses.
6. Serve immediately.

WHEN TO SERVE RISOTTO

In Italy risotto is served as the *primi piatti,* or first course, except for risotto alla Milanese, which is always served as a side dish with osso buco. The American palate, accustomed to a main course of pasta, also enjoys risotto as a main course. Usually one cup of rice will make enough risotto to serve two as a main course or four as a first course. The recipes can easily be doubled, and leftovers never go to waste (see recipe for *Risotto al Salto,* page 81).

Spring Risotto

It is in late winter that the first asparagus appears in the market, so I call this Spring Risotto, our culinary bridge from the dullness of winter to the anticipation of spring.

12 ounces tender fresh asparagus spears, trimmed, stems
    peeled, and soaked in cold water
4 to 5 cups unsalted chicken broth, preferably homemade
2 tablespoons unsalted butter or olive oil
¼ cup finely diced carrot
¼ cup diced sweet red onion
1 cup uncooked Italian medium-grain white rice
1 tablespoon fresh lemon juice
½ teaspoon finely shredded lemon zest
2 tablespoons freshly grated Parmigiano-Reggiano cheese, plus
    more to taste (see Basics, page 267)
2 tablespoons unsalted butter, cut into small pieces
Salt to taste

1. Drain the asparagus, and working with 2 or 3 at a time, cut diagonally into ¼-inch-thick slices and then set aside. There should be about 2 cups.

2. Heat the chicken broth in a small saucepan until boiling, then adjust the heat to maintain a steady simmer. Melt the butter in a heavy saucepan over low heat. Add the carrot and onion and sauté for 3 minutes. Add the rice and sauté, over low heat, stirring, 2 minutes more.

3. Add enough hot broth (about ½ cup) to just cover the rice. Adjust the heat to maintain a steady simmer and cook the rice, stirring constantly, until almost all the broth has been absorbed, about 3 to 4 minutes.

4. Add another ladle of broth (about ½ cup). Cook, stirring constantly, until all the broth has been absorbed. Continue adding the broth, about ½ cup at a time, and cooking and stirring. Add the next ladleful when the broth is absorbed and the rice begins to pull away from the sides of the pan as it is stirred. Cook until the rice is creamy and firm but not chalky in the center when it is tasted. The total cooking time is 25 to 35 minutes or more. (See the tips for making risotto on page 184.)

5. Stir in the asparagus, lemon juice, and lemon zest during the last 5 minutes of cooking. Remove from the heat and stir in the cheese, butter, and salt. Serve at once in soup plates. Serve extra cheese on the side.

MAKES 4 SERVINGS

Clam Risotto

The clams can be cooked a day ahead and reserved along with the strained broth for the next day.

Clams
1/4 cup extra-virgin olive oil
1 medium onion, cut vertically into thin slices
1 clove garlic, minced
1 cup dry white wine
1 cup water
1 stem basil
1 stem Italian (flat leaf) parsley
3 to 5 dozen Manila clams, soaked and scrubbed (see Basics, page 265)

Risotto
2 tablespoons unsalted butter or olive oil
1/2 cup diced sweet red onion
1/2 cup finely chopped celery
1 cup uncooked Italian medium-grain white rice
1/2 cup frozen tiny peas, thawed
Salt and freshly ground black pepper to taste

1. To prepare the clams and broth: Heat the oil in a large wide saucepan. Add the onion and sauté, stirring, until tender, about 10 minutes. Add the garlic and sauté for 1 minute. Add the wine, basil, and parsley, and heat to boiling. Boil for 5 minutes, add the water, and return to boiling.

2. Add the clams and cook, covered, over high heat until all the clams are open, about 5 minutes. Remove the open clams and continue to cook the unopened clams a few minutes longer until open. Cool the clams and remove from the shells. Set aside the clams and clam broth separately. Strain the clam broth left in the saucepan and the broth

from the open clams through a sieve. Measure the broth and add enough water to equal 4 to 5 cups. (This can be cooked up to 1 day ahead. Refrigerate the broth and the clams.)

3. When ready to cook the risotto: Heat the broth mixture in a small saucepan until boiling. Adjust the heat to maintain a steady simmer. Melt the butter in a separate heavy saucepan. Add the red onion and celery, and sauté, stirring, until tender, about 3 minutes. Add the rice and sauté, over low heat, stirring, for 2 minutes.

4. Add enough hot broth (about $1/2$ cup) to just cover the rice. Adjust the heat to maintain a steady simmer and cook the rice, stirring, until almost all the broth has been absorbed, about 3 to 4 minutes.

5. Add another ladle of broth (about $1/2$ cup) and cook, stirring constantly, until all the broth has been absorbed. Continue adding the broth, about $1/2$ cup at a time, cooking and stirring. Add the next ladleful when the broth is absorbed and the rice begins to pull away from the sides. Cook until the rice is creamy and firm but not chalky in the center when it is tasted, about 25 to 35 minutes or more. (See the tips for making risotto on page 184.)

6. Stir in the reserved clams and the peas during the last 5 minutes of cooking. Taste and add salt if needed. Grind fresh pepper over the top and serve at once.

MAKES 4 SERVINGS

Fennel Risotto

When I was a child I loved the finocchio *(fennel) that was served raw along with the celery and olives at holiday dinners. I still relish the crisp, clean anise taste of raw fennel, but the sweet flavor and silken texture of the cooked fennel now makes it one of my favorite vegetables. Here is a risotto with fennel.*

1 bulb fennel (about 12 ounces), quartered (bottom and
    blemishes pared off), plus 2 tablespoons chopped fernlike
    tops, reserved separately
4 to 5 cups unsalted chicken broth, preferably homemade
4 tablespoons unsalted butter
2 tablespoons olive oil
¹/₄ cup minced onion
1 cup uncooked Italian medium-grain white rice
2 tablespoons freshly grated Parmigiano-Reggiano cheese, or
    more to taste (see Basics, page 267)
Salt to taste

1. Soak the quartered fennel in ice water for 1 hour, then drain well and pat dry. Chop as uniformly (¹/₄-inch pieces) as possible and set aside.

2. Heat the chicken broth in a small saucepan until boiling. Adjust the heat to maintain a steady simmer. Heat 2 tablespoons of the butter and the oil in a heavy saucepan over low heat until the butter is melted. Add the onion and sauté until tender, about 5 minutes. Add the rice and chopped fennel bulb. Sauté over low heat, stirring, for 3 minutes.

3. Add enough hot broth (about ¹/₂ cup) to just cover the rice. Adjust the heat to maintain a steady simmer and cook, stirring constantly, until almost all the broth has been absorbed, about 3 to 4 minutes.

4. Add another ladle of broth (about ¹/₂ cup). Cook, stirring constantly, until all the broth has been absorbed. Continue adding the broth, about ¹/₂ cup at a time, and

cooking and stirring. Add the next ladleful when the broth is absorbed and the rice begins to pull away from the sides of the pan as it is stirred. Stir in the reserved fennel tops when the rice is almost cooked. Cook until the rice is creamy and firm but not chalky in the center when it is tasted. The total cooking time is 25 to 35 minutes or more. (See tips for making risotto on page 184.)

5. Remove from the heat. Cut the remaining 2 tablespoons of butter into small pieces and stir in with the grated cheese and salt. Spoon into bowls and serve at once with extra grated cheese on the side.

MAKES 4 SERVINGS

Porcini Risotto

There are certain foods that I associate very strongly with a particular season. Tomatoes and basil go with summer; asparagus suggests spring; apples and pumpkins evoke fall. When it is winter, I cook with porcini. These fragrant dried morsels go into soups, stuffing, potatoes, sauces, and, of course, risotto.

1 1/2 ounces dried porcini mushrooms
4 to 5 cups unsalted chicken or beef broth, preferably
    homemade
4 tablespoons unsalted butter
2 tablespoons olive oil
3 tablespoons finely chopped shallots
1 cup uncooked Italian medium-grain white rice
2 tablespoons freshly grated Parmigiano-Reggiano cheese, or
    more to taste (see Basics, page 267)
Salt and freshly ground black pepper to taste

1. Combine the porcini and broth in a small saucepan and heat to boiling. Cover and simmer over low heat for 10 minutes. Remove from heat and let stand, covered, for

20 minutes. Drain the porcini through a sieve lined with a dampened paper towel and set aside the broth separately. Rinse the mushrooms under running tap water and rub with your fingers; cut off and discard any gritty pieces. Drain well and pat dry. Finely chop and set aside. (There should be between $\frac{1}{2}$ and $\frac{3}{4}$ cup of reconstituted dried porcini.) Return the strained broth to the rinsed-out saucepan and heat to boiling. Adjust the heat to maintain a steady simmer.

2. Heat 2 tablespoons of the butter and the olive oil in a heavy saucepan over low heat until the butter is melted. Add the shallots and sauté, stirring, until tender, about 3 minutes. Add the rice and sauté over low heat, stirring, for 2 minutes.

3. Add enough of the hot broth (about $\frac{1}{2}$ cup) to just cover the rice. Adjust the heat to maintain a steady simmer and cook the rice, stirring constantly, until almost all the broth has been absorbed, about 3 to 4 minutes.

4. Add another ladle of broth (about $\frac{1}{2}$ cup). Cook, stirring constantly, until all the broth has been absorbed. Continue adding the broth, about $\frac{1}{2}$ cup at a time, and cooking and stirring. Add the next ladleful when the broth is absorbed and the rice begins to pull away from the sides of the pan as it is stirred. About halfway through the cooking time add the reserved chopped porcini. Cook until the rice is creamy and firm but not chalky in the center when it is tasted. The total cooking time is 25 to 35 minutes or more. (See tips for making risotto on page 184.)

5. Remove from the heat. Cut the remaining 2 tablespoons of butter into small pieces and stir in with the cheese and salt. Sprinkle generously with black pepper. Spoon into shallow bowls and serve at once with additional cheese on the side.

MAKES 4 SERVINGS

Apple Risotto

Years ago when I was working as a test chef for a culinary magazine, I made my first risotto—strawberry! Surprisingly, the flavor was excellent. Because I love the sweet-tart flavor of apples with the rich fat feel of Parmigiano-Reggiano, I decided to join the two in a risotto. The result is a unexpectedly happy marriage.

4 to 5 cups unsalted light chicken broth, preferably homemade

4 tablespoons unsalted butter

2 tablespoons minced onion

1 cup uncooked Italian medium-grain white rice

2 cups diced (about 1/4 inch) peeled sweet-tart apples (Golden Delicious are good)

1/3 cup dry white wine

2 tablespoons freshly grated Parmigiano-Reggiano cheese, plus more to taste (see Basics, page 267)

Salt to taste

Freshly grated nutmeg

1. Heat the chicken broth in a small saucepan until boiling. Adjust the heat to maintain a steady simmer.

2. Melt 2 tablespoons of the butter in a heavy saucepan over low heat. Add the onion and sauté for 3 minutes. Add the rice and 1 cup of the apple, and sauté, stirring, for 3 minutes. Stir in the wine and boil, stirring, until the wine is reduced by half.

3. Add enough hot broth (about 1/2 cup) to just cover the rice. Adjust the heat to maintain a steady simmer and cook, stirring constantly, until almost all the broth has been absorbed, about 3 to 4 minutes.

4. Add another ladle of broth (about 1/2 cup). Cook, stirring constantly, until all the broth has been absorbed. Continue adding the broth, about 1/2 cup at a time, and cooking and stirring. Add the next ladleful when the broth is absorbed and the rice begins to pull away from the sides of the pan as it is stirred. Add the remaining cup of

diced apple during the last 5 minutes of cooking. Cook until the rice is creamy and firm but not chalky in the center when it is tasted. The total cooking time is 25 to 35 minutes or more. (See the tips for making risotto on page 184.)

5. Remove from the heat. Cut the remaining 2 tablespoons of butter into small pieces and stir in with the cheese and salt. Spoon into bowls and serve at once; grate a little nutmeg on the top of each serving. Serve extra cheese on the side.

MAKES 4 SERVINGS

Sausage, Tomato, and Basil Risotto

Make this with the most flavorful sweet Italian sausage you can find. Use either fresh or canned peeled and chopped plum tomatoes, but be sure to use fresh basil.

1 pound sweet Italian sausage, with casings removed and
    crumbled
4 to 5 cups unsalted light chicken broth, preferably homemade
2 tablespoons olive oil
1/2 cup finely chopped onion
1 small clove garlic, minced
1 cup uncooked Italian medium-grain white rice
1/2 cup peeled, seeded, and chopped fresh or canned plum
    tomatoes, drained
1 tablespoon chopped fresh basil
2 tablespoons unsalted butter
1/4 cup freshly grated Parmigiano-Reggiano cheese, plus more
    to taste (see Basics, page 267)
Salt to taste
Freshly ground black pepper to taste
2 tablespoons packed torn fresh basil leaves

1. Brown the sausage in a heavy skillet, stirring and breaking up into small pieces with the side of a fork. Spoon out 1 tablespoon of the sausage fat and set aside. Drain and discard the remaining fat and set aside the browned sausage.

2. Heat the chicken broth in a small saucepan until boiling. Adjust the heat to maintain a steady simmer.

3. Combine the reserved sausage fat and olive oil in a heavy saucepan and heat over low heat. Add the onion and sauté, stirring, until golden, about 8 minutes. Add the garlic and sauté 1 minute more. Stir in the rice and sauté over low heat, stirring, about 2 minutes.

4. Add enough of the hot broth (about 1/2 cup) to just cover the rice. Adjust the heat to maintain a steady simmer and cook the rice, stirring constantly, until almost all the broth has been absorbed, about 3 to 4 minutes.

5. Add another ladle of broth (about 1/2 cup). Cook, stirring constantly, until all the broth has been absorbed. Continue adding the broth, about 1/2 cup at a time, and cooking and stirring. Add the next ladleful when the broth is absorbed and the rice begins to pull away from the sides of the pan as it is stirred. Add the tomatoes, chopped basil, and half of the reserved cooked sausage during the last 10 minutes of cooking. Cook until the rice is creamy and firm but not chalky in the center when it is tasted. The total cooking time is 25 to 35 minutes or more. (See tips for making risotto, page 184.)

6. Remove from the heat. Stir in the butter, cheese, and salt. Briefly reheat the reserved browned sausage. Spoon the risotto into shallow bowls and divide the warmed sausage evenly among the bowls. Sprinkle with the ground pepper and basil leaves. Serve with additional grated cheese on the side.

MAKES 4 SERVINGS

Rice and Peas,
Risi e Bisi

Risi e bisi, *or rice and peas, is served just a little soupier than a classic
risotto. Most experts agree that it should be thick enough to eat with a fork.
I add bits of prosciutto or a flavorful cooked ham to this dish, depending on
the season and my mood. It is wonderful with or without the ham. Leftovers
can be used to make croquettes (see recipe on page 89).*

2 tablespoons olive oil
2 tablespoons unsalted butter
¹/₂ cup finely chopped celery
¹/₂ cup finely chopped scallion (white parts only)
1 cup uncooked Italian medium-grain white rice
4 to 5 cups unsalted chicken broth, preferably homemade
¹/₂ teaspoon salt
2 cups sweet tiny peas
¹/₃ cup freshly grated Parmigiano-Reggiano cheese (see Basics,
    page 267)
¹/₄ cup slivered (about 1 × ¹/₈ inch) prosciutto (optional)
2 tablespoons finely chopped curly or Italian (flat leaf) parsley

1. Heat the oil and butter in a heavy saucepan. Add the celery and scallion, and
sauté over low heat, stirring, until the onion is golden, about 7 minutes. Stir in the rice
and sauté, stirring, for 2 minutes.

2. Meanwhile, heat the chicken broth in a separate saucepan until boiling. Adjust
the heat to maintain a steady simmer and season with the salt.

3. Add 1¹/₂ cups of hot broth to the rice. Simmer, uncovered, stirring frequently,
until almost all the liquid is absorbed, about 5 minutes. Add more stock (just enough to
barely cover the rice) and simmer, uncovered, stirring, until almost all the liquid is
absorbed. Continue with the remaining broth until all the broth is used. The total

cooking time will be about 25 minutes. Add the peas during the last 5 minutes of cooking.

4. Gently stir in the cheese, prosciutto, if using, and parsley. Let stand, covered, off the heat about 3 minutes before serving.

MAKES 4 TO 6 SERVINGS

Pilaf with Curry, Raisins, and Almonds

The sweetness of the raisins helps to balance the heat and spice of the curry in this pilaf. I like the monochromatic yellows in this dish—yellow rice, golden raisins, and toasted almonds—but if you choose dark raisins, the effect will be dramatic: black raisins against a background of vibrantly colored rice.

2 tablespoons unsalted butter

1/2 cup chopped onion

1 to 2 teaspoons curry powder

1 teaspoon ground turmeric

1 cup imported basmati or American basmati-type white rice

1/2 cup golden or dark raisins

1 3/4 cups unsalted chicken broth, preferably homemade

2 tablespoons slivered almonds

1. Melt the butter in a large wide saucepan over medium heat. When the foam subsides, add the onion and sauté over low heat, stirring, until golden, about 5 minutes. Stir in the curry, turmeric, rice, and raisins, and sauté 2 minutes more.

2. Add the chicken broth and heat to boiling, stirring once. Cook, covered, over medium-low heat until the broth is absorbed and the rice is tender, about 15 minutes. Let stand, uncovered, off the heat for 5 minutes before serving.

3. Meanwhile, toast the almonds in a 350°F. oven about 7 minutes. Sprinkle over the pilaf just before serving.

MAKES 4 SERVINGS

Orzo and Pignoli Pilaf

Orzo is the name of an oval pasta shape that looks just like a grain of rice; its name translates as barley. This is a pleasant side dish that quickly becomes a main dish with the addition of shredded cooked chicken and a topping of stir-fried broccoli.

2 tablespoons unsalted butter or olive oil
1/4 cup chopped onion
1 clove garlic, crushed
1/2 cup orzo
3/4 cup imported basmati or American basmati-type white rice
2 cups water
1 teaspoon salt
2 tablespoons pignoli (pine nuts)

1. Melt the butter in a large wide saucepan over medium heat. When the foam subsides, add the onion and sauté over low heat, stirring, until golden, about 5 minutes. Stir in the garlic and sauté 1 minute more.

2. Add the orzo and rice, and sauté, stirring constantly, for 3 minutes. Add the water and salt, and heat to boiling, stirring. Cook, covered, over medium-low heat for 15 minutes, or until the liquid is absorbed. Let stand, uncovered, off the heat for 5 minutes before serving.

3. Meanwhile, toast the pignoli in a small skillet over low heat, stirring constantly, until golden, about 2 minutes.

4. Add the pignoli to the cooked pilaf and toss to blend.

MAKES 4 SERVINGS

Orange and Currant Pilaf

The fresh, clean flavors in this dish are perfect with broiled or baked fish or shellfish.

1 tablespoon unsalted butter or olive oil
¼ cup finely chopped onion
1 cup imported basmati or American basmati-type white rice
1 tablespoon dried currants
1 teaspoon finely shredded orange zest
1 teaspoon finely chopped fresh ginger
1¾ cups water
½ teaspoon salt

1. Melt the butter in a large wide saucepan over medium heat. When the foam subsides, add the onion and sauté over low heat, stirring, until golden, about 5 minutes. Add the rice, currants, orange zest, and ginger, and sauté over medium heat, stirring, for 2 minutes.

2. Stir in the water and salt, and heat to boiling, stirring. Cover and cook over medium-low heat for 15 minutes, or until the water is absorbed. Let stand, uncovered, off the heat for 5 minutes before serving.

MAKES 4 SERVINGS

Bulgur and Rice Pilaf with Sautéed Walnuts and Dates

Bulgur and cracked wheat are often used interchangeably in recipes, although the actual milling process varies slightly. Cracked wheat is a wheat berry that has been finely cut up with a sharp blade; bulgur is cooked, dried, and then cut up. The flavors are slightly different. This nutritious grain has a delicious nutlike flavor that goes well with the addition of diced dates and sautéed walnuts.

4 tablespoons butter
¼ cup thinly sliced scallions
1 cup bulgur or cracked wheat, rinsed with cold water
1 cup imported basmati or American basmati-type white rice
2 cups unsalted chicken broth, preferably homemade
Salt
½ cup broken walnuts
1 clove garlic, crushed
¼ cup diced (⅛-inch pieces) dates

1. Heat 2 tablespoons of the butter in a large wide saucepan. Stir in the scallions and sauté, stirring, until tender, about 3 minutes. Add the bulgur or cracked wheat and rice. Sauté, stirring, until coated with butter, about 2 minutes.

2. Add the broth and 1 teaspoon of salt, and heat to boiling, stirring well. Cover and cook over medium-low heat for 15 minutes, or until the liquid is absorbed. Let stand, uncovered, off the heat for 5 minutes before serving.

3. Meanwhile, melt the remaining 2 tablespoons of butter in a small skillet. When the foam subsides, stir in the walnuts, garlic, and salt to taste. Sauté, stirring constantly, until the walnuts are golden and fragrant.

4. Spoon the pilaf into a serving dish and sprinkle the top with the dates and sautéed walnuts.

MAKES 4 SERVINGS

Lentil and Rice Pilaf with Dill and Mint

This recipe for pilaf was inspired by a delicious lentil and rice filling for stuffed grape leaves created by a good friend and wonderful Greek cook, Diane Kochilas. The dill, mint, and lemon juice give a fresh flavor to the lentil and rice mixture. Keeping with the Greek spirit, serve this with grilled lamb.

½ cup lentils, rinsed and sorted
3 tablespoons olive oil
½ cup chopped onion
1 clove garlic, minced
1 cup imported basmati or American basmati-type white rice
1¾ cups unsalted chicken broth, preferably homemade
1 teaspoon salt, or to taste
2 tablespoons chopped fresh dill
1 tablespoon chopped fresh mint
2 tablespoons fresh lemon juice

1. Stir the lentils into plenty of boiling water. Boil for 10 minutes or until almost tender. Drain and set aside.

2. Heat the olive oil in a large wide saucepan. Add the onion and sauté until tender, about 5 minutes. Add the garlic and sauté for 1 minute. Add the rice and reserved lentils, and sauté, stirring, until coated with oil. Add the broth and salt, and heat to boiling, stirring well.

3. Cover and cook over medium-low heat until the liquid is absorbed, about 15 minutes. Let stand, uncovered, off the heat for 5 minutes before serving.

4. Sprinkle the top with the dill and mint. Add the lemon juice and stir to blend. Spoon into a serving bowl.

MAKES 4 SERVINGS

Potato and Rice Pilaf with Peas and Cumin

Potatoes have a tendency to stick while they are being fried, so one has to stay with them, patiently turning and stirring, until they begin to turn golden. A saucepan with a nonstick coating is a help. This pilaf has a wonderful flavor and is a nice accompaniment with just about any meat, fish, or fowl. It is also tasty served solo as a light entree.

1/4 cup olive or vegetable oil
1 cup diced (1/4 inch) peeled potato (about 1 large potato)
1 teaspoon whole cumin seed
1/4 cup diced (1/4 inch) onion
1 clove garlic, minced
1 cup imported basmati or American basmati-type white rice
1 3/4 cups unsalted chicken broth, preferably homemade
1/2 teaspoon salt, or as needed
1/2 cup frozen peas, thawed

1. Heat the oil in a large wide saucepan, preferably nonstick, until hot enough to sizzle a piece of potato. Fry the potatoes, stirring and turning, until evenly golden, about 8 minutes.

2. Stir in the cumin and sauté for 1 minute. Add the onion and sauté until tender, about 3 minutes. Add the garlic and sauté for 1 minute. Stir in the rice and sauté 2 minutes more. Add the broth and salt, and heat to boiling, stirring well. Cover and cook over medium-low heat for 12 minutes. Sprinkle the peas over the top, cover, and cook for 3 minutes, or until the broth is absorbed.

3. Let stand, uncovered, off the heat for 5 minutes before serving.

MAKES 4 SERVINGS

Tomato Pilaf

This pilaf recipe is similar to the "red rice" recipes popular in the American South except that this has the Mediterranean flavors of fresh basil, olive oil, and black olives.

3 tablespoons extra-virgin olive oil
$\frac{1}{2}$ cup chopped onion
1 clove garlic, crushed
1 teaspoon grated orange zest
2 cups fresh or canned peeled tomatoes, pureed through a
    sieve or food mill, or in a food processor
$\frac{1}{2}$ cup water or unsalted chicken broth
1 teaspoon salt, or to taste
4 cups cooked long-grain white rice
$\frac{1}{4}$ cup torn fresh basil leaves
$\frac{1}{4}$ cup pitted and coarsely chopped brine-cured black olives
Fresh basil leaves (optional)

1. Heat the oil in a wide saucepan. Add the onion and sauté until tender, about 5 minutes. Add the garlic and orange zest, and sauté for 1 minute. Stir in the tomatoes and water or broth, and heat to boiling. Boil until slightly reduced, about 5 minutes. Season with salt.

2. Stir in the rice and fresh basil until blended with the tomatoes. Cover and cook over low heat for 15 minutes, or until the rice has absorbed all the tomato. Spoon into a serving dish and sprinkle with the olives and basil leaves.

MAKES 4 SERVINGS

WILD RICE

Soups and Appetizers

Butternut Squash, Apple, and Wild Rice Soup
Mushroom and Wild Rice Soup
Beef and Wild Rice Soup with Shiitake Mushrooms
Wild Rice and Whole Wheat Crepes with Sour Cream and Caviar

Main Dishes

Wild Rice and Smoked Turkey Salad
Red Peppers Stuffed with Italian Sausage and Wild Rice

Side Dishes

Wild Rice with Grapes, Raisins, and Toasted Almonds
Three-Mushroom Sauté with Wild Rice
Wild Rice, Brown Rice, and Bacon Stuffing

Baked Goods/Desserts

Wild Rice Buttermilk Biscuits
Apricot and Wild Rice Muffins
Wild Rice, Prune, and Walnut Molasses Bread
Wild Rice and Brown Rice Pudding

Wild rice is not a rice, nor is it as wild as it once was.

Botanically wild rice is *Zizania aquatica,* an aquatic grass totally unrelated to common rice and the only grain native to North America. Some say that the seventeenth-century French explorers and trappers first called it *folle avoine,* or crazy oats. Evidently this later became wild rice because of the similarity to rice.

Self-propagating in the lakes and rivers in the northern Great Lakes region, wild rice, like common rice, flourishes in water. Much of the "wild" rice produced today is cultivated in man-made paddies in Minnesota and California, where the industry has been developing for the last twenty-five years.

Original natural stands of wild rice continue to flourish in Minnesota and north into Canada, where it was once a staple food for the Indian tribes of the region. Traditionally the Indians gathered the grain as they glided their canoes quietly over the water and between the stands of wild rice. One person would bend the stands of rice with a 30-inch-long cedar pole called a knocking stick while thrashing it with a second pole, causing the ripe rice to shower the bottom of the canoe. Simultaneously a second person, called a puller, would navigate the boat much as a gondolier guiding his gondola through the canals of Venice. In the late 1800s, when the white traders had become established in the regions and had introduced their metal pots for cooking to the Indians, the traditional way of processing the wild rice began to change. Originally the rice had been slowly cured and toasted in the sun, but later the Indian women learned to quickly cure and toast the rice in the white traders' kettles set over wood fires. The rice was then emptied into a hole in the ground lined with deerskin. The men, their feet covered with moccasins, would dance or "jig" on the wild rice to loosen the hulls. Winnowing was accomplished by gently shaking the hulled rice in a birch bark tray or winnowing basket held aloft to allow the wind to blow away the light chaff as the wind-cleansed grains dropped to a blanket below. In the twentieth century this method of winnowing is still used in some of the more remote parts of the Far East. Today less than 6 percent of the approximately 6 million pounds of wild rice harvested in Minnesota and throughout the Canadian region is harvested in canoes. Removing the hulls by "jigging" is hardly ever done anymore, and the romance of winnowing has capitulated to the cold efficiency of a mechanized fanning device.

Since the development in the early 1960s of a cultivated "wild" rice seed (Uncle Ben's being the driving force in the research), the majority of the total 12 million pounds of wild rice sold each year is raised in man-made paddies and harvested and processed mechanically.

But legislation in the state of Minnesota early in the 1900s still upholds the ban on the use of mechanical harvesters in the lakes, rivers, and tributaries where the original natural stands of true wild rice grow, preserving, in part at least, the time-honored tradition of hand harvesting.

Buying Wild Rice

The difference in flavor or texture between hand-harvested true wild rice and mechanically harvested cultivated wild rice depends more on the quality of the processing—specifically how it is cured and roasted—than on the source of the grain. I have found that if the grains are long, slender, and uniformly shaped, the flavor and texture will be excellent whatever the source of the rice. The more perfect grains are the most expensive, whereas broken grains suitable for soups and stuffings cost less. The flavor and texture are so assertive that I often successfully mix cooked wild rice with brown or white rice.

Cooking Wild Rice

I always rinse wild rice in a sieve before cooking to remove tiny pieces of the hull that sometimes cling to the grain after processing. To cook wild rice use three cups of liquid to one cup of wild rice. The full nutty flavor of wild rice makes it possible to omit the salt without losing any flavor. It is wasteful to cook wild rice in enormous amounts of water and then throw away the excess since it is an extremely nutritious grain (much more so than common rice). Wild rice is cooked when most of the grains are cracked or open, revealing the fluffy white interior, and the texture (taste it!) is just slightly chewy. Depending on the rice this can take anywhere from thirty-five to sixty minutes, so it is best to let your eye and taste be the final judge. If there is just a small amount of water left in the pan, it usually is absorbed if you let the rice stand, covered, for ten minutes before serving. If preferred, cook over low heat, uncovered and stirring, until the water left in the bottom of the pan evaporates. One cup of raw wild rice will yield $3\frac{1}{2}$ to 4 cups of cooked rice, depending on the quality of the rice. (For Mail Order Sources, see page 271.)

Butternut Squash, Apple, and Wild Rice Soup

Squash, apple, and wild rice make this a perfect choice for a holiday menu. As an added convenience the soup can be prepared a day or two ahead and reheated just before serving. The fresh ginger gives the squash and apple— two old-fashioned favorites—a slightly contemporary twist. The soup can also be made with acorn squash or fresh pumpkin.

1 butternut squash (about 2¼ pounds), skin removed, quartered, seeded, and cut into 1-inch cubes (about 5 to 6 cups)

1 tablespoon plus 1 teaspoon unsalted butter

½ cup chopped onion

1 peeled, cored, and diced tart apple, such as Granny Smith (about 1 cup)

1 tablespoon peeled and minced fresh ginger

2 cups filtered unsweetened apple juice

1½ cups cooked wild rice

1½ to 2 cups milk or half-and-half, as needed to thin soup

Unsalted chicken broth (optional)

Salt

⅛ teaspoon freshly ground black pepper

½ cup chopped hazelnuts, natural (unblanched) almonds, or walnuts

Pinch of cinnamon

1 tablespoon finely chopped parsley

1. Steam the squash in a vegetable steamer set in a large covered saucepan over gently boiling water until very tender, about 15 minutes.

2. Meanwhile, melt 1 tablespoon of the butter in a saucepan. Add the onion and

apple, and sauté, stirring, until very tender, about 5 minutes. Stir in the ginger and sauté for 1 minute. Add the apple juice and steamed squash, and heat to boiling. Cover and cook over low heat for 10 minutes. Uncover and cool slightly, then puree, in batches if necessary, in a blender or food processor until smooth. Return to the saucepan. (The soup can be prepared up to 1 day or several hours ahead up to this point.)

3. Add the wild rice and milk or half-and-half, and season with 1 teaspoon of salt and the pepper. Add additional milk, half-and-half, or broth to thin to desired consistency. The thickness of the soup will vary with the amount of moisture in the squash. Reheat over low heat until steaming; do not boil. Correct the seasoning.

4. Melt the remaining teaspoon of butter in a small skillet, add the nuts, and sauté until golden. Sprinkle lightly with salt and cinnamon, add the parsley, and stir to blend. Remove from the heat.

5. At serving time ladle the hot soup into bowls and top each with a spoonful of the nut mixture.

MAKES ABOUT 8 CUPS OR 4 TO 6 SERVINGS

Mushroom and Wild Rice Soup

This soup is a real showpiece for dried porcini mushrooms. They have a deep, almost meaty aroma and a wonderful woodsy flavor. Although this soup is rich and elegant, it is easy to prepare.

1½ ounces dried porcini mushrooms
3 cups unsalted beef or chicken broth, preferably homemade
3 tablespoons unsalted butter
½ cup chopped onion
1 box (10 ounces) white button mushrooms, coarsely chopped
    (about 3 cups), plus 2 large mushrooms, cut into ¼-inch
    slices
1 tablespoon all-purpose flour
1½ to 2 cups half-and-half, at room temperature
¾ cup cooked wild rice
Salt and freshly ground black pepper to taste
1 tablespoon finely chopped red bell pepper
1 tablespoon finely chopped Italian (flat leaf) parsley
1 teaspoon fresh thyme leaves, stripped from stems

1. Combine the dried porcini mushrooms and broth in a saucepan, and heat to boiling. Lower the heat and cook, covered, for 15 minutes. Let stand off the heat for 15 minutes.

2. Meanwhile, heat 2 tablespoons of the butter in a large wide saucepan until the foam subsides. Stir in the onion and sauté over low heat, stirring, until the onion is golden, about 10 minutes. Stir in the coarsely chopped button mushrooms and sauté over medium-high heat, stirring, until the mushrooms are lightly browned. Cover and cook over very low heat for 10 minutes.

3. Strain the porcini mushrooms and broth through a fine sieve or a sieve lined with a piece of dampened paper towel. Set aside the rehydrated mushrooms and mushroom broth separately.

4. Uncover the mushroom and onion mixture, and stir in the flour until blended and cooked, about 2 minutes. Stir in the reserved mushroom broth and heat to boiling, stirring constantly. Cook, uncovered, over low heat for 10 minutes. Remove from the heat and let stand until slightly cooled.

5. Working in batches puree the mushroom and broth mixture in a food processor; the mixture should be as smooth as possible. Return to the saucepan and gradually stir in the half-and-half. Carefully rinse the rehydrated dried mushrooms and discard any sandy pieces. Finely chop and add to the soup. Stir in the wild rice and cook, uncovered, over very low heat for 20 minutes. Do not boil. Season with salt and pepper. (The dish can be prepared up to this point a day or several hours before serving.)

6. Heat the remaining tablespoon of butter in a skillet until the foam subsides. Stir in the sliced button mushrooms and red bell pepper, and sauté until the mushrooms are golden. Season with parsley, thyme, salt, and pepper.

7. Ladle the soup into bowls. Garnish each serving with a few sautéed mushroom slices, dividing evenly.

MAKES 6 CUPS OR 4 SERVINGS

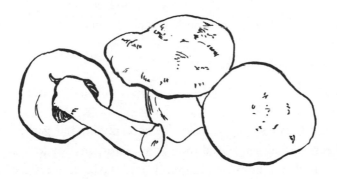

Beef and Wild Rice Soup with
Shiitake Mushrooms

This soup is a complete meal when served with a salad and a good loaf of crusty bread. Like other hearty soups the flavor of this one improves while standing. If the soup gets too thick, thin to a consistency you like with broth or water.

Spread the preparation time out over two days by preparing the stock one day and chilling overnight. The next day, remove the layer of fat on top, add the rice, and proceed with the recipe until finished.

1 tablespoon olive oil
1 or 2 pieces meaty beef shin, about 1 inch thick (about 1$\frac{1}{2}$ pounds)
$\frac{1}{2}$ onion, skin left on
1 clove garlic, skin left on and bruised with the side of a knife
3 quarts water
1 carrot, pared
1 bay leaf
5 medium-sized dried shiitake mushrooms (about $\frac{3}{4}$ ounce)
Salt to taste
$\frac{1}{2}$ cup uncooked wild rice, rinsed in warm water and drained
2 tablespoons tomato paste *or* $\frac{1}{2}$ cup peeled, seeded and chopped tomato (optional)
Freshly ground black pepper to taste
Finely chopped parsley

1. Heat the oil in a large heavy saucepan. Add the beef, onion, and garlic, and brown over medium-low heat, turning once. Add the water, carrot, and bay leaf. Cook over low heat (for a clear broth, do not boil) for 3 hours, or until the broth is reduced to 2 quarts and the meat is falling off the bone.

2. Lift the beef shin from the broth and set aside to cool. Strain the broth and set aside separately. Set aside the carrot and discard the other solids. Pull the meat from the bone and shred or finely chop; discard the gristle and fat. Push the marrow from the center of the bone and discard the bone. Dice the marrow and set aside with the meat. Slice the carrot and add to the meat. Carefully blot any fat from the surface of the broth with a double thickness of paper towels. (If making this part of the soup ahead, pour the broth into a bowl and place the meat, carrot, and marrow in a separate bowl. Cover and refrigerate. Remove the fat from the surface of the broth before using.)

3. Combine 2 cups of the broth and the dried shiitake mushrooms in a small saucepan. Heat to boiling, then remove from the heat, cover, and let stand for 30 minutes.

4. Meanwhile, in a large saucepan heat the remaining broth to boiling. Season with salt, stir in the wild rice, cover, and cook 40 to 45 minutes, or until almost tender.

5. Strain the shiitake mushrooms, setting aside the broth. Cut the stems from the soaked mushrooms and discard. Chop the caps into ⅛-inch pieces.

6. When the wild rice is cooked, add the reserved shredded beef, marrow, sliced carrot, chopped mushrooms, and soaking liquid to the rice and broth mixture. Stir in the tomato paste or chopped tomato, if using.

7. Cover and cook over low heat for 15 minutes. Season with salt and pepper. Ladle into bowls and sprinkle with chopped parsley.

MAKES ABOUT 10 CUPS OR 8 SERVINGS

Wild Rice and Whole Wheat Crepes with Sour Cream and Caviar

These crepes are fun when one feels like celebrating in an extravagant way. Crepes are usually folded smooth side out, but in this recipe the grains of wild rice sink to the under- or speckled side of the crepe, so I fold them inside out to show off the delicate morsels of rice. You can make these ahead; stack between sheets of waxed paper and refrigerate. Wrap in foil and reheat in a warm (not hot) oven before using.

1 large egg, at room temperature

1¾ cups milk

4 tablespoons unsalted butter, melted

1 teaspoon sugar

½ teaspoon salt

½ cup all-purpose flour

½ cup whole wheat flour

1 cup cooked wild rice

Vegetable oil, as needed

1 cup crème fraîche or sour cream

Minced fresh chives (optional)

1 jar (2 ounces) black caviar

Sprigs of watercress

Lemon wedges

1. Whisk the egg in a medium-sized bowl or a 1-quart measure until foamy. Whisk in the milk, 3 tablespoons of the butter, sugar, and salt. Sift the flour directly into the egg mixture. Add the whole wheat flour and rice. Stir gently with a whisk just until the dry ingredients are moistened. Do not overmix (the batter will be lumpy). Cover and refrigerate overnight or at least 1 hour.

2. Brush an 8-inch crepe pan or other small heavy skillet, preferably nonstick, with

a thin film of vegetable oil. Heat over medium-low heat until a small drop of water evaporates immediately on contact. Stir the batter before ladling a scant $1/4$ cup into the pan. Immediately tilt the pan to spread the batter evenly. Cook until the batter is set and the edges begin to brown, about 1 minute. Using a small flexible spatula turn the crepe and cook until the underside is speckled with brown spots. Transfer to a plate and cover loosely with a kitchen towel. Repeat with the remaining batter, brushing the skillet lightly with oil, if needed, and stacking the cooked crepes on the plate. (Cooked crepes can be kept warm in an oven set at the lowest setting.)

3. Brush each crepe lightly with the remaining tablespoon of melted butter. Spread about 1 tablespoon of crème fraîche or sour cream on half of the crepe, sprinkle with a pinch of chives, if using, and about 1 teaspoon of the caviar, and fold the crepe into a half circle. Repeat with the remaining crepes.

4. Serve on a large platter or on individual serving plates. Top with a spoonful of extra crème fraîche and a spoonful of the caviar. Garnish with watercress sprigs and lemon wedges.

MAKES 10 TO 12 CREPES OR 4 SERVINGS

Wild Rice and Smoked Turkey Salad

I love the idea of using fresh seedless red grapes and raisins in the same dish. The contrast of the flavors and textures is fun for the palate and the brain. A fully cooked corn- or apple-smoked ham could be used instead of the turkey. Another wonderful addition is diced smoked mozzarella cheese (about 1 cup), which is often available in Italian specialty stores. When chopping the parsley, don't forget to use the sweet and fragrant stems along with the leaves. I sometimes add 2 cups of cooked long-grain rice, double the remaining ingredients, and serve this as part of a summer salad buffet supper for eight guests.

1 cup uncooked wild rice, rinsed in warm water and drained
3 cups water
1 teaspoon salt
1/4 cup sliced natural (unblanched) almonds
1/2 cup olive oil
3 tablespoons fresh lemon juice
1 small clove garlic, crushed
Freshly ground black pepper to taste
6 ounces sliced smoked turkey, cut into thin (1 × 1/8 inch) slivers
1 cup small seedless red grapes, rinsed
1/4 cup finely chopped curly or Italian (flat leaf) parsley
2 scallions, trimmed and thinly sliced (about 1/4 cup)
1/4 cup raisins or dried currants

1. Combine the rice, water, and 1/2 teaspoon of the salt in a medium-sized saucepan and heat to boiling, stirring once. Cook, covered, over low heat until the rice is tender, about 45 minutes or more. Let stand, covered, until any water in the bottom of the pan is absorbed, or uncover and cook, stirring, until the liquid evaporates. Let stand, uncovered, off the heat until cooled.

2. Sprinkle the almonds in a small dry skillet set over low heat and stir frequently until lightly toasted, about 3 minutes; set aside.

3. Whisk the oil, lemon juice, garlic, remaining ½ teaspoon of salt, and a grinding of black pepper until blended; set aside.

4. Add the turkey, grapes, parsley, scallions, raisins or currants, toasted almonds, and oil and lemon juice dressing to the cooled rice. Toss gently to blend the ingredients.

MAKES 4 SERVINGS

Red Peppers Stuffed with Italian Sausage and Wild Rice

This recipe makes 6 stuffed red peppers, but you could forgo stuffing the peppers and simply bake the rice mixture in a casserole garnished with sautéed red pepper strips. Sometimes I use a mixture of long-grain white rice and wild rice for this stuffing, buying the premixed version but discarding the seasoning packet and adding my own flavors.

1 package (6 ounces) long-grain and wild rice mixture *or* 1 cup
    uncooked wild rice, rinsed with warm water and drained
8 ounces (about 4 links) Italian sweet sausage, removed from
    casings
2 tablespoons olive oil
1 cup chopped onions
2 cups (about 6 ounces) chopped white button mushrooms
1 clove garlic, minced or crushed
1/2 cup frozen green peas, thawed, or fresh peas, cooked
1/4 cup raisins *or* 2 tablespoons dried currants
1/2 teaspoon salt
1/8 teaspoon coarsely ground black pepper
1 cup (about 4 ounces) shredded smoked or plain mozzarella
    cheese
2 large red bell peppers, halved and with seeds and stems
    removed
Coarsely chopped fresh parsley

1. Cook the rice mixture according to the package directions and set aside at room temperature until ready to use. Or cook the wild rice in 3 cups of boiling water until almost tender, about 40 to 45 minutes. Let stand, covered, until any water in the bottom of the pan is absorbed, or uncover and cook, stirring, until the liquid evaporates. Set aside off the heat until ready to use.

2. Crumble the sausage into a skillet and sauté over medium-high heat until browned, stirring and breaking up the pieces. Drain in a sieve and discard the excess fat.

3. Wipe out the skillet and heat the olive oil. Add the onions and mushrooms, and sauté over medium-high heat, stirring, until the onion and mushrooms are tender and the edges are golden brown, about 8 minutes. Add the garlic and sauté for 1 minute.

4. Off the heat stir in the reserved rice, peas, and raisins or currants, and season with salt and pepper. Add the cheese and toss just to blend.

5. Heat the oven to 350°F. Use olive oil to lightly brush the outside of the peppers and a shallow baking dish just large enough to hold the peppers. Arrange the peppers in the baking dish and carefully spoon the rice mixture into the pepper halves, lightly pressing down on each spoonful. (Alternately, the rice can be spooned into a lightly oiled deep 2-quart casserole, covered with foil, and baked.)

6. Cover with foil and bake for 45 minutes. Sprinkle with chopped fresh parsley before serving.

MAKES 4 SERVINGS

Wild Rice with Grapes, Raisins, and Toasted Almonds

This is a great side dish with roasted chicken, broiled duck breasts, or roast beef. It is easy to make but sophisticated enough for a special dinner.

1 cup uncooked wild rice, rinsed with warm water and drained
3 cups water or chicken broth
Salt (optional)
1/4 cup sliced natural (unblanched) almonds
4 tablespoons unsalted butter or half butter and half olive oil
1/2 cup chopped sweet red onion
1 to 2 cups small seedless red grapes, stripped from stems and
    rinsed
1/2 cup raisins or currants
Freshly ground black pepper to taste

1. Combine the wild rice, water or broth, and 1 teaspoon of salt, if needed. Heat to boiling, stirring, and cook, covered, over low heat until the rice is tender, about 45 minutes. Let stand, covered, until any water in the bottom of the pan is absorbed, or uncover and cook, stirring, until the liquid evaporates. Let stand, uncovered, until ready to use.

2. Meanwhile, heat a large dry skillet over medium heat until hot. Add the almonds and heat, stirring constantly, until lightly browned, then transfer to a side dish. Melt the butter in the skillet. Add the onion and sauté, stirring, until tender, about 5 minutes. Add the grapes and raisins or currants, and sauté, stirring, until coated with butter and hot. Add the cooked rice and cook, stirring, until heated through. Season with salt, if needed, and pepper.

3. Spoon into a serving dish and sprinkle with the toasted almonds.

MAKES 4 TO 6 SERVINGS

Three-Mushroom Sauté with Wild Rice

The flavors of wild rice and mushrooms complement each other. Depending on your mood, budget, and the availability of raw mushrooms, make this dish with one or three different types. Mushrooms shrink when cooked so use a ratio of at least 4 cups of raw mushrooms to 3 cups of cooked wild rice. The smoked ham, pancetta, or prosciutto, although not essential, adds a pleasant touch. This dish is delicious served with lamb, game, or Italian sweet sausage.

1 cup uncooked wild rice, rinsed with warm water and drained

3 cups water or broth

Salt

4 tablespoons unsalted butter or half butter and half olive oil

2 tablespoons minced onion

2 tablespoons minced smoked ham, pancetta, or prosciutto (optional)

2 cups (about 6 ounces) coarsely cut up white button mushrooms

1 cup (about 4 ounces) diced (¼ inch) shiitake mushroom caps, with stems discarded

1 cup (about 4 ounces) diced chanterelle mushrooms (optional)

Freshly ground black pepper

1 clove garlic, crushed or minced

2 tablespoons finely chopped fresh Italian (flat leaf) parsley

½ teaspoon fresh thyme, stripped from stems, *or* pinch of dried thyme

2 tablespoons chopped toasted hazelnuts or pignoli (optional)

1. Combine the rice, water or broth, and ½ teaspoon of salt, if needed. Heat to boiling, stirring, and cook, covered, over low heat until the rice is tender, about 45 minutes. Let stand, covered, until any water in the bottom of the pan is absorbed, or

uncover and cook, stirring, until the liquid evaporates. Set aside, uncovered, until ready to use.

2. Heat the butter or butter and oil in a large heavy skillet until the foam subsides. Add the onion and ham, if using, and sauté for 2 minutes. Add the white and shiitake mushrooms, and sauté over medium-high heat, stirring, until the mushrooms begin to brown, about 5 minutes. Add the garlic and sauté for 1 minute. Stir in the chanterelle mushrooms, if using, and sauté just until tender, about 2 minutes. Season the mushrooms with salt and pepper to taste. Add the reserved wild rice, garlic, parsley, and thyme, and sauté, stirring, until heated through, about 3 minutes.

3. Correct the seasoning and spoon into a serving dish. Sprinkle with toasted nuts, if using.

MAKES 4 TO 6 SERVINGS

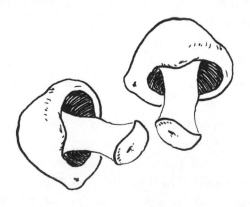

Wild Rice, Brown Rice, and Bacon Stuffing

This recipe can be cooked in a casserole as a side dish or as a stuffing for turkey, chicken, or Cornish hens.

1 cup uncooked wild rice, rinsed with warm water and drained
1 cup uncooked long- or short-grain brown rice
6 thick slices (about 6 ounces) slab bacon, diced
2 tablespoons olive oil
2 cups chopped sweet yellow onions
1 cup chopped celery plus some leaves
1 cup pared and diced (¼ inch) carrots
2 cups (about 6 ounces) sliced white button mushrooms
½ cup slivered red bell pepper
½ cup chopped natural (unblanched) almonds
1 tablespoon finely chopped garlic
½ cup diced (¼ inch) dried apple slices
½ cup golden raisins
¼ cup finely chopped Italian (flat leaf) parsley
1 tablespoon fresh thyme leaves, stripped from stems
1 teaspoon minced fresh sage leaves, stripped from stems
1 teaspoon salt, or to taste
Freshly ground black pepper to taste

Glazed Pearl Onions (optional garnish)
1 tablespoon olive oil
1 pint basket (about 2 cups) red or white pearl onions,
    blanched and peeled
1 teaspoon granulated sugar

1. Cook the wild rice and brown rice together in 4 cups of boiling salted water until both rices are almost tender, about 45 to 50 minutes. Let stand, covered, until any water

in the bottom of the pan is absorbed, or uncover and cook, stirring, until the liquid evaporates. Let stand, uncovered and off the heat, until slightly cooled.

2. Meanwhile, sauté the bacon in the olive oil in a large deep skillet or wide saucepan until crisp and browned, about 10 minutes. Add the onions, celery, and carrot, and sauté over medium-low heat, stirring frequently, until the vegetables are golden and tender, about 15 minutes. Stir in the mushrooms, red pepper, almonds, and garlic, and sauté until the mushrooms are golden, about 10 minutes.

3. Add the cooked wild and brown rice, apple, raisins, parsley, thyme, sage, salt, and pepper. Cook, stirring, until the ingredients are thoroughly blended and heated through. Cool slightly before using to stuff the poultry.

4. If preparing the glazed pearl onions as a garnish: Heat the oven to 350°F. Heat the olive oil in a large skillet, add the pearl onions, sprinkle with the sugar, and sauté, stirring, until the onions are glazed.

5. Spoon the stuffing into a 3-quart casserole and top with the onions. Cover and bake for 30 minutes, or until heated through.

6. If using as a stuffing, spoon into the cavity (or cavities) of the poultry. Bake any leftovers in a casserole as in step 5, with or without the pearl onion garnish.

MAKES 10 CUPS OF STUFFING OR 10 SERVINGS AS A SIDE DISH

Wild Rice Buttermilk Biscuits

These delicious morsels were inspired by some leftover cooked wild rice. Now I cook wild rice just so I can use the leftovers in these biscuits.

1 1/2 cups all-purpose flour
1/2 cup whole wheat flour
1 tablespoon baking powder
1/2 teaspoon baking soda
1/2 teaspoon salt
8 tablespoons (1 stick) cold unsalted butter, cut into 1/4-inch
    cubes, plus 2 tablespoons unsalted butter, melted
1/2 to 2/3 cup cooked wild rice
1/2 cup buttermilk

1. Heat the oven to 450°F.

2. In a large bowl stir together the all-purpose and whole wheat flours, baking powder, baking soda, and salt. Add the butter and, using a pastry blender, cut it in until well blended. Stir in the wild rice.

3. Drizzle the buttermilk over the dry ingredients and mix lightly with a fork just until the mixture begins to pull away from the sides of the bowl. Lightly gather the dough with floured hands and transfer to a lightly floured work surface.

4. Pat or roll the dough into a circle about 1/2 inch thick. Cut out the biscuits with a round cutter about 2 1/2 inches in diameter. Press the scraps together to make another biscuit.

5. Lightly brush a baking sheet with some of the melted butter. Place the biscuits on the baking sheet and generously brush the tops with the remaining melted butter.

6. Bake for 10 minutes or until the edges are golden. Serve hot or warm.

MAKES APPROXIMATELY NINE 2 1/2-INCH BISCUITS

Apricot and Wild Rice Muffins

^{1}/₂ cup chopped pecans
6 ounces dried apricots, diced (^{1}/₄-inch pieces) (about 1 cup)
^{1}/₂ cup vegetable oil
^{1}/₂ cup packed light brown sugar
1 extra-large egg
^{1}/₂ teaspoon vanilla extract
2 cups all-purpose flour
2 teaspoons baking powder
^{1}/₂ teaspoon ground cinnamon
^{1}/₂ teaspoon baking soda
^{1}/₂ cup cooked wild rice

1. Heat the oven to 350°F. Butter and flour a 12-cup muffin pan. Spread the pecans in a baking pan and heat in the oven until toasted, about 10 minutes; set aside.

2. Combine the apricots and 1 cup of boiling water in a bowl. Let stand, covered, for 30 minutes, then drain and set aside the liquid (about ^{1}/₂ cup).

3. Combine the vegetable oil, reserved apricot liquid, sugar, egg, and vanilla in the bowl of a food processor, and process until well blended. Meanwhile, stir together the flour, baking powder, cinnamon, and baking soda in a large bowl. Pat the apricots and wild rice dry with paper towels. Add to the dry ingredients along with the pecans, stirring just to blend.

4. Pour the liquid ingredients over the dry and stir just to moisten the dry ingredients.

5. Spoon into the prepared muffin cups, dividing evenly. Bake until golden and the edges begin to pull away from the sides, about 25 to 30 minutes. Cool slightly on racks before turning out of the pans.

MAKES 12 MUFFINS

Wild Rice, Prune, and Walnut
Molasses Bread

This part-whole-wheat and part-white-flour bread is rich with wild rice, prunes, and walnuts. Serve in thick slices, toasted in a toaster oven or under the broiler and spread with sweet butter. Perfect with a cup of tea.

$\frac{1}{2}$ cup water
$\frac{1}{2}$ cup milk
1 teaspoon sugar
3 tablespoons unsalted butter, melted and cooled
1 envelope active dry yeast
2 tablespoons dark molasses
1 cup whole wheat flour
1$\frac{1}{2}$ cups all-purpose flour, or more as needed
1 teaspoon salt
$\frac{1}{2}$ cup cooked wild rice
$\frac{1}{2}$ cup pitted and cut up ($\frac{1}{4}$-inch pieces) prunes
$\frac{1}{2}$ cup coarsely chopped walnuts

1. Heat the water, milk, and sugar in a small saucepan until lukewarm (105°F. to 115°F.). Add 2 tablespoons of the butter, transfer to a large bowl, and stir in the yeast. Cover with plastic wrap and let stand in a warm place for 5 minutes, or until foam forms on the surface of the mixture.

2. Stir in the molasses. Add the whole wheat flour, 1 cup of the all-purpose flour, and salt. Stir until blended and the mixture forms a soft dough. Knead the dough on a lightly floured board using the remaining $\frac{1}{2}$ cup of flour, plus more as needed, until the dough is smooth and springs back when pressed lightly with a finger, about 8 minutes. Brush the surface of the dough with a little vegetable oil and place in a clean bowl. Cover with plastic wrap and let the dough rise until double in bulk, about 1$\frac{1}{2}$ to 2 hours.

3. Punch the dough down and turn out onto a lightly floured board. Roll the dough out into a large rectangle. Sprinkle the wild rice, prunes, and walnuts on the dough. Roll

the dough up and knead with lightly floured hands until the ingredients are thoroughly blended with the dough. Roll again into a small rectangle (about 6 × 9 inches) and roll loosely into a loaf shape. Place in a lightly buttered loaf pan. Brush the top with the remaining tablespoon of melted butter, cover loosely with plastic wrap, and let rise in a warm place until the bread fills the pan, about 1 to 1½ hours.

4. Heat the oven to 350°F. Bake the bread until golden and the loaf sounds hollow when it is tapped with a knuckle, about 30 to 35 minutes. Turn out on a wire rack to cool before slicing.

MAKES 1 LARGE LOAF

Wild Rice and Brown Rice Pudding

Eat this wonderful mixture of soft cooked brown rice and slightly crunchy wild rice for dessert with heavy cream, a garnish of sliced fresh peaches, and a dusting of freshly ground nutmeg. Or for a nutritious breakfast eat it plain out of a cereal bowl; it's great with a few raisins and broken walnuts sprinkled on top. It is good with or without the currants soaked in brandy.

½ cup raisins or dried currants (optional)

2 tablespoons brandy (optional)

½ cup uncooked wild rice, rinsed with warm water and
    drained

½ cup uncooked short-grain brown rice

½ teaspoon salt

1 quart milk

½ cup packed light brown sugar

1 teaspoon vanilla extract

1 cup heavy cream, whipped (optional)

Sliced fresh peaches or nectarines (optional)

Grated nutmeg or ground cinnamon to taste

1. If using the raisins or currants, combine with the brandy and 2 tablespoons of water in a small saucepan. Heat to boiling, then set aside, covered, until the dried fruit has absorbed the moisture, about 30 minutes.

2. Meanwhile, combine the wild rice, brown rice, 3 cups of water, and salt in a large saucepan, and heat to boiling. Cover and cook over medium-low heat until the rices are almost tender, about 40 to 45 minutes.

3. Stir in the milk and heat to boiling. Cook, stirring and adjusting the heat to prevent sticking, until the mixture is very thick, about 30 minutes. Stir in the brown sugar and cook, stirring, for 5 minutes, or until the sugar is dissolved.

4. Let cool slightly at room temperature, then stir in the vanilla. Serve the pudding warm with heavy cream, sliced peaches or nectarines, if available, and a sprinkling of grated nutmeg or cinnamon. Or refrigerate and serve cold. For a more elaborate dessert fold in a cup of heavy cream, stiffly beaten, before spooning into a stemmed glass and sprinkle the top with nutmeg or cinnamon.

MAKES 8 SERVINGS

SWEETS

Breads and Muffins

Maple and Fig Rice Bran Muffins
Raisin and Rice Bran Scones
Double Corn and Rice Bread
New Orleans Rice Fritters, *Calas*

Cakes

Pecan Carrot Cake
Orange and Rice Torte with Grand Marnier

Puddings

Creamy Rice Pudding with Summer Berries
Old-fashioned Rice Pudding
Banana Rice Pudding
Lemon Custard Rice Pudding
Brown Rice Pudding with Maple Syrup
Rice Pudding Retro
Creamy Rice Pudding with Mangoes and Pistachios
Quick Chocolate Rice Pudding
Vanilla Rice Pudding Ice Cream
Caramel Syrup
Orange and Rice Crème Caramel

Cookies

Molasses Rice Bran Fig Bars
Mixed Dried Fruit and Nut Squares

Breakfast Dishes

Hot Rice with Fruit and Honey
Brown Rice with Walnuts, Raisins, and Maple Syrup
Hot Oatmeal and Rice Cereal

The major rice-consuming countries in the world all include sweets among their popular rice dishes. During a recent visit to Japan I was impressed by the numerous rice sweetmeats and confections—a favorite being a ravioli-type dumpling called *mochi* filled with a red bean paste that varied in quality from delicate and delicious to leaden and revolting. Throughout Southeast Asia and Indonesia, confections, snacks, and desserts based on finely ground rice are extremely popular. Puddings using whole grains of rice are familiar to American, French, Swedish, and British cooks, while rice flour–thickened puddings are more common in Indian, Arabic, Greek, and Turkish cooking. The Italians make wonderfully elaborate *torta, bomba, gelati,* and other *dolci* with rice.

It is not surprising, considering their popularity and versatility, that puddings are the core of this chapter.

We all remember A. A. Milne's famous poem

> *What is the matter with Mary Jane?*
> *She's perfectly well and she hasn't a pain,*
> *And it's lovely rice pudding for dinner again—*
> *What is the matter with Mary Jane?*

Some good and interesting breads are also appealing in their use of small amounts of leftover cooked rice. Be forewarned, though, that nonchalantly folding leftover cooked rice into just any cake, muffin, or bread batter can yield some dismal results due in part to retrogradation (see page 4).

I have successfully used rice bran in muffins, cookies, and scones, primarily because

I enjoy the nutty flavor of bran in general, with its healthful properties being a nice extra bonus. And to round out the chapter there are three breakfast cereals—all family secrets gone public.

Maple and Fig Rice Bran Muffins

The maple syrup and dried figs add just the right level of sweetness to these moist muffins, and the figs contribute a nice crunchy texture as well. The muffins freeze very well; by sealing them in heavy-duty plastic bags, you can easily remove one or two at a time. You can heat cold or semithawed and halved muffins in a toaster oven or wrapped in foil in a preheated oven. You can substitute diced dried apricots or prunes for the figs. To read all about rice bran turn to page 7.

1 1/2 cups all-purpose flour
1/2 cup rice bran
2 teaspoons baking powder
1 teaspoon ground cinnamon
Pinch of salt
1/2 cup diced dried figs, discarding the stem end
1/2 cup broken pecans
1/2 cup low-fat yogurt
1/2 cup maple syrup
1/3 cup vegetable oil
1 large egg

1. Heat the oven to 400°F. Lightly butter 8 cups of a muffin pan (or spray with nonstick spray).

2. In a large bowl stir the flour, rice bran, baking powder, cinnamon, and salt until blended. Add the figs and pecans, and toss to coat with flour.

3. Combine the yogurt, maple syrup, vegetable oil, and egg in a separate bowl, and whisk to blend.

4. Pour over the dry ingredients and stir gently just until blended. Do not overmix.

5. Spoon into the prepared muffin cups. Bake until the tops are golden and the edges have pulled away from the sides of the pan, about 15 to 20 minutes. Cool on a rack for 5 minutes before turning out of the pan.

MAKES 8 MUFFINS

Raisin and Rice Bran Scones

Here is a simple twist for a classic tea scone. Rice bran, the nutritious outer layer of a kernel of rice, has an intensely nutty flavor. These scones can be made with as little as $1/4$ cup or as much as $1/2$ cup.

2 cups all-purpose flour
$1/4$ to $1/2$ cup rice bran
$1/2$ cup granulated sugar
4 teaspoons baking powder
$1/2$ teaspoon salt
8 tablespoons (1 stick) cold unsalted butter, cut into $1/4$-inch
   pieces, plus 2 tablespoons unsalted butter, melted
$1/3$ cup raisins or dried currants
1 cup buttermilk (plus 1 to 2 tablespoons if using $1/2$ cup rice
   bran)
1 large egg

1. Heat the oven to 400°F. and lightly butter a baking sheet. In a large bowl combine the flour, rice bran, sugar, baking powder, and salt. Using a pastry blender cut in the cold butter pieces until the mixture resembles coarse meal. Add the raisins or currants and toss to blend.

2. In a small bowl beat the buttermilk and egg together until blended. Gradually add to the dry ingredients while tossing the mixture lightly with a fork just to moisten. If using a full $1/2$ cup of rice bran, sprinkle the mixture with 1 or 2 more tablespoons of buttermilk, or as needed.

3. Turn the dough out (it will be wet) onto a lightly floured board and with floured hands lightly pat into a disk about 8 inches in diameter. Using a large sharp knife cut into 6 or 8 evenly sized pie-shaped wedges.

4. Place on a baking sheet and lightly brush the surface of each scone with a thin film of melted butter. Bake the scones until lightly browned, about 25 minutes. Serve warm with jam.

MAKES 6 TO 8 LARGE SCONES

Double Corn and Rice Bread

I like the texture of cornmeal and rice mixed together. Adding cooked rice to a batter only works when the batter is wet enough to accommodate the constantly expanding rice kernels. This delicious corn bread is moist and tangy from the yogurt. For a pleasant jolt add pieces of minced fresh green chili peppers.

5 tablespoons unsalted butter, melted
1 cup regular yellow cornmeal
1 cup all-purpose flour
3 tablespoons granulated sugar
4 teaspoons baking powder
$^1/_2$ teaspoon salt
1 cup cooked long- or medium-grain white rice or Italian
    arborio rice
$^3/_4$ cup corn kernels, preferably fresh, or frozen or canned
$1^1/_2$ cups plain yogurt
2 large eggs, beaten

1. Heat the oven to 400°F. and brush a 9- or 10-inch round or square cake pan generously with 1 tablespoon of the melted butter.

2. In a large bowl stir together the cornmeal, flour, sugar, baking powder, and salt until blended. Stir in the rice and corn.

3. Whisk together the yogurt, eggs, and remaining 4 tablespoons of butter. Pour over the dry ingredients and fold just until blended. Spoon into the prepared pan.

4. Bake until the edges of the bread begin to pull away from the sides and the bread is springy when touched in the center, about 25 to 30 minutes. Cool slightly, then cut into wedges and serve warm with butter or jam.

MAKES ONE 9- OR 10-INCH BREAD OR 6 TO 8 SERVINGS

New Orleans Rice Fritters, Calas

"Belles calas tout chaud" *was a familiar cry on the back streets of the New Orleans French Quarter. Sold from carts by street vendors,* calas *were a popular breakfast food and a practical way to use leftover cooked rice from the night before. This two-day recipe from Terry Thompson is made with a yeast dough and produces a light, airy fritter that is hard to resist.*

½ cup warm water (105°F. to 115°F.)
2 tablespoons granulated sugar
1 package active dry yeast
1½ cups cooked long-grain white rice
3 large eggs, beaten
1½ cups all-purpose flour
½ teaspoon salt
½ teaspoon vanilla extract
¼ teaspoon freshly grated nutmeg
Vegetable oil for deep frying
Confectioner's sugar (optional)
Warm honey (optional)

1. Combine the warm water and 1 teaspoon of the sugar in a large bowl. Sprinkle the yeast over the water, cover with plastic wrap, and let stand until the yeast is foamy and dissolved, about 10 minutes. Stir in the rice and let stand, covered, in a warm place overnight.

2. The next day the rice will be swollen. Stir just to blend. Add the eggs, flour, salt, vanilla, nutmeg, and remaining tablespoon and 2 teaspoons of sugar. Beat with a wooden spoon just until smooth. Cover and let stand in a warm place until the dough is doubled in bulk, about 1 hour.

3. Heat 3 inches of oil in a heavy deep saucepan or a deep-fat fryer and heat until the oil temperature reaches 350°F. to 375°F. Drop the rice dough by rounded table-spoonfuls, stirring the dough gently to blend. Fry 3 or 4 at a time, tapping the frying *calas* with the back of a spoon, until golden, about 4 minutes. Drain on paper towels. Serve hot, sprinkled with confectioner's sugar or drizzled with warm honey.

MAKES ABOUT 24 FRITTERS

Pecan Carrot Cake

This carrot cake recipe is indestructible. I have been playing around with the ingredients for years—mostly with great success. Sometimes I add wheat germ and use whole wheat flour, sometimes I use all brown sugar, sometimes half brown and half granulated sugar; and sometimes I use rice flour (available in health-food stores) and fold in leftover cooked rice. I have not tampered with the recipe's heart, which I believe to be the holy trinity of carrot cake: 1¹/₄ cups vegetable oil, 4 whole eggs, and 3 cups of sliced carrots (a very efficient 1-pound bag)—all conveniently pureed in the food processor. This version is a family and neighborhood bake sale favorite.

1 cup pecans (walnuts and almonds are also good)
1¹/₂ cups all-purpose flour
1 cup brown rice flour *or* ¹/₂ cup whole wheat flour
2 teaspoons baking powder
1 teaspoon baking soda
2 teaspoons ground cinnamon
¹/₂ teaspoon salt (optional)
1 cup cooked long- or short-grain brown rice
¹/₂ cup raisins
1¹/₄ cups vegetable oil
4 extra-large eggs
¹/₂ cup honey
¹/₂ cup packed light brown sugar
2 teaspoons vanilla extract
3 cups trimmed, pared, and thinly sliced carrots (about 1 pound)

1. Heat the oven to 350°F. Lightly butter (or spray with nonstick spray) a 10-inch tube pan. Line the bottom with a circle of waxed paper cut to fit; butter or spray the paper. Sprinkle the pan lightly with flour, shaking out the excess.

2. Finely chop the nuts in the bowl of a food processor and transfer to a large bowl. Add the all-purpose and rice or whole wheat flours, baking powder, baking soda, cinnamon, and salt, if using, to the nuts, and stir well to blend. Add the rice and raisins, toss until evenly coated with the dry mixture, and set aside.

3. Combine the vegetable oil, eggs, honey, brown sugar, and vanilla in the bowl of a food processor. With the motor running gradually add the carrots through the feed tube until coarsely ground. (If your food processor does not have a large bowl, this might have to be accomplished in two batches.)

4. Pour over the dry ingredients and stir gently until thoroughly mixed. Pour into the prepared cake pan and bake until the edges of the cake begin to pull away from the sides and a thin wooden skewer inserted in the center of the cake comes out clean, about 1 hour. Cool on a wire rack. Loosen the sides and around the center tube of the cake pan with a narrow spatula and invert the cake onto a rack. Turn the cake right side up onto a serving plate. Serve cut in thin slices.

MAKES ONE 10-INCH TUBE CAKE OR ABOUT 12 SERVINGS

Orange and Rice Torte with Grand Marnier

In Bologna, Italy, the rice torte or **torta di riso** *is a regional specialty. Inspired by a recipe from Biba Caggiano, a wonderful cook, restaurateur, and cookbook author, I developed this delicious torte with the texture of a cheesecake and the flavors of a pudding. The quality of the candied orange peel is critical to the success of this torte. If you must rely on the supermarket brand, be sure it is a fresh supply (usually available around the holidays), or buy in bulk at a specialty food shop. For Mail Order Sources see page 271.*

¾ cup uncooked medium-grain white rice or Italian arborio
   rice
   4 cups milk
1½ cups granulated sugar
1 tablespoon grated orange zest
1 cup finely ground natural (unblanched) almonds
1 tablespoon unsalted butter, melted
5 large eggs
½ cup finely chopped candied orange peel
4 tablespoons Grand Marnier
¼ teaspoon almond extract
Confectioner's sugar
1 pint raspberries or strawberries (optional)
1 cup heavy cream, stiffly beaten (optional)
Additional minced candied orange peel (optional)

1. Several hours before baking the torte: Stir the rice into plenty of boiling salted water. Cover and cook over medium-low heat for 10 minutes, or until it is partially cooked, then drain well. Combine the precooked rice with the milk and sugar in a large (4-quart) wide saucepan, and heat to boiling. Simmer, uncovered, over medium-low heat, stirring frequently, until the mixture is thickened and the rice is very tender, about 30 minutes. Remove from the heat, cool to room temperature, and stir in the orange zest.

2. Heat the oven to 350°F. Spread the almonds in a baking pan and heat until toasted, about 10 minutes, then cool. Brush the bottom and sides of a 10-inch springform pan with the melted butter. (Make sure the seal is tight so that the cake batter will not seep out during baking.) Coat the bottom and sides of the buttered pan with approximately 1/4 cup of the ground almonds. Set aside the remaining almonds for the torte.

3. Beat the eggs in an electric mixer until light in color. Stir in the cooled rice mixture, candied orange peel, remaining ground almonds, 2 tablespoons of the Grand Marnier, and the almond extract until thoroughly blended. Pour into the prepared pan and smooth the top.

4. Bake for 45 to 50 minutes, or until the cake is well browned and the sides begin to pull away from the pan. While the cake is still warm, make holes in the surface with a wooden toothpick and drizzle with the remaining Grand Marnier. When the cake is cool, run a thin spatula around the edges and remove the outer rim of the pan. Serve sprinkled with confectioner's sugar and with a few fresh raspberries or sliced strawberries on the side, or cover the surface of the torte with tiny rosettes of stiffly whipped cream pushed through a fluted tip on a pastry bag. Sprinkle the cream with finely chopped candied orange peel.

MAKES 10 TO 12 SERVINGS

Creamy Rice Pudding with Summer Berries

I've never met a rice pudding I didn't like, but this one is one of my favorites. The basic mixture of cooked rice, milk, and sugar can be the basis of many flavor combinations. Copying two favorite desserts, Fruit Fool and Summer Pudding, I fold cream into the rice and then gently fold sweetened berries into the cream and rice mixture. The results are grand. Save this recipe for the summer berry season or adapt it for winter by using a puree of sweetened persimmons, rehydrated dried apricots, or even quince cooked with honey.

1 cup uncooked long-grain white rice

2 teaspoons salt

3 cups milk

1 cup sugar

1 teaspoon vanilla extract

1 pint small ripe strawberries, stems removed and halved

$1/2$ pint raspberries, rinsed and sorted

$1/2$ pint black raspberries, rinsed and sorted

1 cup blueberries, rinsed and sorted

1 cup heavy cream

1. Combine the rice, 8 cups of water, and salt in a large heavy saucepan, and heat to boiling, stirring frequently so the rice doesn't stick. Simmer the rice, uncovered, until the grains are split and very soft, about 20 minutes. Drain off the water and rinse out the pan so you can use it again.

2. Combine the cooked rice, milk, and $3/4$ cup of the sugar in the same pan. Cook over low heat, stirring frequently, until the mixture is creamy, about 20 minutes. Stir in the vanilla. Cool to room temperature, about 30 minutes, stirring occasionally.

3. Meanwhile, combine the strawberries, raspberries, black raspberries, and blueberries in a large bowl. Sprinkle with the remaining $1/4$ cup of sugar, gently fold to blend, and set aside.

4. At serving time whip the cream until stiff peaks form, then fold into the rice mixture. Using a slotted spoon add $3/4$ of the sweetened fruit and gently fold, forming streaks of the fruit throughout the rice mixture. Spoon into stemmed glasses and garnish each with a spoonful of the reserved sweetened fruit and a spoonful of the sweetened berry juices.

MAKES 6 TO 8 SERVINGS

Old-fashioned Rice Pudding

A collection of rice puddings would not be complete without the old-fashioned, slowly baked, stir-and-wait type of pudding. This is the type my grandmother—probably everyone's grandmother—made. It is wonderful with or without a little grated orange or lemon zest, ground cinnamon or grated nutmeg, raisins, even white or brown rice. If you use brown rice, increase the baking time by about 1 hour.

½ cup uncooked long-grain white rice
½ cup sugar
½ teaspoon salt
½ teaspoon ground nutmeg or cinnamon
2 quarts milk
¾ cup raisins
Heavy cream (optional)

1. Heat the oven to 325°F. Combine the rice, sugar, salt, and nutmeg or cinnamon in a large shallow 2½-quart baking dish. Stir in 1 quart of the milk until thoroughly blended.

2. Place the baking dish on the center rack of the oven. Gradually stir in the remaining quart of milk and bake for 2½ hours, stirring once after the first 30 minutes. After 1 hour of baking stir the browned edges into the pudding once or twice. Stir the raisins in after 2 hours, and then bake undisturbed for the final 30 minutes so that a top crust can form.

3. Remove to a wire rack and cool slightly. Serve warm or cold with cream, if desired.

MAKES 8 TO 10 SERVINGS

Banana Rice Pudding

If you are a banana fan, then this recipe is for you. Surprisingly, the cut bananas don't darken when leftover pudding is refrigerated for serving the next day. The already intense banana flavor actually grows stronger when standing. If you are a coconut fan, sprinkle the top of the pudding with a halo of toasted coconut.

4 extra-large egg yolks
1/2 cup sugar
2 cups milk
2 cups cooked long-grain white rice or imported basmati or
    American basmati-type white rice
1/4 cup heavy cream
1 teaspoon vanilla extract
1/2 cup mashed medium-ripe banana
1 cup sliced medium-ripe banana
Ground cinnamon
Toasted coconut (optional)

1. In a large bowl whisk the egg yolks and sugar until light in color. Meanwhile, heat the milk in a medium-sized saucepan until scalded or small bubbles appear around the edge. Gradually whisk the hot milk into the egg yolks until thoroughly blended.

2. Pour the mixture back into the saucepan. Cook over low heat, stirring constantly, until the mixture thickens and begins to coat a metal spoon, about 10 minutes. Stir in the rice and cook over low heat, stirring, until very thick, about 5 minutes. Stir in the heavy cream. Let stand off the heat, stirring frequently, for 5 minutes, then stir in the vanilla.

3. Pour into a bowl and refrigerate until very cold. Just before serving prepare the bananas. First stir the mashed banana in until well blended, then fold in the sliced banana.

4. Spoon into small bowls and serve lightly sprinkled with ground cinnamon and garnished with toasted coconut.

MAKES 6 SERVINGS

Lemon Custard Rice Pudding

This delicate custard is lightly flavored with grated lemon zest enveloping plump grains of rice. Use as little as 1 1/2 cups of cooked long-grain white rice for a greater custard-rice ratio and as much as 3 cups of cooked rice for a stiffer pudding. I eat this for breakfast.

1 1/2 to 3 cups cooked long-grain white rice (see headnote)
1/2 cup dark or golden raisins (optional)
6 cups milk
1 vanilla bean *or* 2 teaspoons vanilla extract
6 extra-large eggs, at room temperature
1 cup granulated sugar
1 tablespoon grated lemon zest
Freshly grated nutmeg

1. Heat the oven to 325°F. Generously butter a 13 × 9-inch baking dish. Select a baking pan large enough to hold the baking dish. Heat a kettle of water to boiling for the hot water bath.

2. Spread the rice and raisins, if using, in the buttered baking dish. Pour the milk in a large saucepan and add the vanilla bean, if using. Heat the milk until scalded or small bubbles appear around the edges.

3. Meanwhile, beat the eggs and sugar in a large bowl until foamy. If using the vanilla bean, remove from the scalded milk, carefully split the bean, and scrape the soft center into the milk; discard the outside of the bean. Gradually whisk the milk into the beaten eggs until blended. Add the lemon zest and vanilla extract, if using instead of the vanilla bean.

4. Place the baking dish inside the baking pan. Carefully pour half of the custard

mixture over the raisins and rice, and carefully stir to distribute evenly. Transfer the baking pan to the cénter rack of the oven. Pour the remaining custard mixture into the baking dish. Sprinkle the top evenly with the nutmeg.

5. Carefully pour enough of the boiling water from the kettle into the baking pan until it comes halfway up the sides of the baking dish. Bake 1 hour and 15 minutes, or until the custard is almost set and the edges are golden. Cool the pudding in the water bath. Cut into squares and serve at room temperature or chilled.

MAKES ABOUT 8 SERVINGS

Brown Rice Pudding with Maple Syrup

Sure to please the most discriminating rice pudding aficionado, this heavenly dessert serves at least eight people. It is a rather hearty dessert to serve after a meal, so instead I enjoy it with an afternoon cup of tea or an espresso.

1/3 cup golden raisins
2 1/2 cups cooked short-grain brown rice
1 quart milk
Pinch of salt
1/2 cup maple syrup
1 teaspoon vanilla extract
3/4 cup heavy cream
Ground cinnamon or freshly grated nutmeg

1. Place the raisins in a small heat-proof bowl. Add boiling water to cover and let stand 10 minutes. Drain.

2. In a medium-sized saucepan combine the rice, milk, and salt. Heat to boiling over medium heat. Cook over low heat, stirring, for 30 minutes, or until the mixture is very thick. Stir in the maple syrup and cook, stirring, for 15 minutes. Let stand off the heat for 15 minutes, then stir in the vanilla and raisins.

3. Heat the oven to 350°F. Select a shallow 1 1/2-quart baking dish or deep

10-inch pie plate and butter it generously. Spoon the rice mixture into the dish and smooth with the back of a spoon. Pour the heavy cream evenly over the top.

4. Bake until the cream is browned and bubbly, about 30 minutes. Cool slightly, sprinkle the top evenly with the cinnamon or nutmeg, and serve warm or chilled.

MAKES 6 SERVINGS

Rice Pudding Retro

I developed this rice pudding in response to the remorse I felt (mostly about the waist) after eating more than my share of the previous puddings. I fed it to my husband without an ounce (or grain) of guilt.

1 quart skim milk
1 1/2 cups cooked long-grain white rice
1/2 cup maple syrup
1/4 cup golden raisins
1/2 teaspoon vanilla extract
Ground cinnamon (optional)

1. Combine the milk and rice in a large (4-quart) wide saucepan. Heat to boiling over medium heat, stirring. Lower the heat and simmer, stirring frequently, until the mixture is thickened and the rice is tender, about 30 minutes. Stir in the maple syrup and cook 15 minutes more.

2. Meanwhile, place the raisins in a heat-proof bowl and add boiling water to cover. Let stand for 10 minutes, or until the raisins are plumped, then drain. Stir into the hot rice. Cool at room temperature, then stir in the vanilla until blended. Sprinkle with cinnamon, if desired, and serve warm or chilled.

MAKES 6 SERVINGS

Creamy Rice Pudding with Mangoes and Pistachios

Mango is delicious in this pudding, but if it is unavailable, you can use sweet ripe peaches or nectarines. Garnish the pudding with finely chopped toasted pistachios or sliced unblanched almonds. The addition of toasted coconut adds crunch, sweetness, and that addictive coconut flavor.

1 cup uncooked long-grain white rice

2½ cups water

½ teaspoon salt

1 cup whole milk plain yogurt (as opposed to low-fat or nonfat), plus additional yogurt, thinned with a small amount of milk (optional)

½ cup heavy cream

⅓ cup sugar (or more or less)

1 teaspoon vanilla extract

⅛ teaspoon almond extract

½ cup flaked coconut (optional)

¼ cup shelled and peeled pistachios or sliced natural (unblanched) almonds

2 cups peeled, pitted, and diced ripe mangoes, peaches, or nectarines

1. Combine the rice, water, and salt in a medium-sized saucepan. Heat to boiling over high heat, stirring once. Turn the heat to low, cover, and cook until very soft and tender but still moist, about 25 minutes. Let stand, covered, off the heat for 5 minutes.

2. While the rice is cooking, whisk the yogurt, cream, sugar, vanilla, and almond extract in a bowl and let stand at room temperature, stirring occasionally to dissolve the sugar.

3. Heat the oven to 350°F. Spread the coconut, if using, at one end of a baking sheet and the pistachios or almonds at the other. Bake until lightly toasted, about 5 minutes. Cool before using.

4. Add the hot rice to the room-temperature yogurt mixture. Add additional yogurt thinned with a little milk if the mixture gets too stiff while standing. Fold in the fruit. Sprinkle with the toasted coconut and/or pistachios or almonds, and serve warm or at room temperature.

MAKES 6 SERVINGS

Quick Chocolate Rice Pudding

The basis for this recipe is a favorite quick but soul-satisfyingly rich chocolate pudding. The secret is a good-quality imported semi- or bittersweet chocolate. I like this pudding best served at room temperature without chilling. Warm chocolate pudding is the only way to go.

1/4 cup sugar

1 tablespoon cornstarch

2 cups milk, scalded

3 ounces semisweet or bittersweet chocolate, preferably imported, coarsely chopped

1 cup cooked medium- or long-grain white rice or Italian arborio rice

1 teaspoon vanilla extract

1. Stir the sugar and cornstarch together in a medium-sized saucepan until thoroughly blended. Gradually stir in the scalded milk. Heat, stirring frequently, until the sugar is dissolved. Add the chocolate and rice.

2. Cook over medium-low heat, stirring frequently, until the chocolate is melted and the mixture boils and is very thick, about 10 minutes. Let stand off the heat for 5 minutes.

3. Stir in the vanilla and pour into four 4-ounce custard cups. Serve warm or at room temperature.

MAKES 4 SERVINGS

Vanilla Rice Pudding Ice Cream

This is actually a frozen rice pudding. The trick here is to cook the rice until it is very soft and each kernel is split. I usually make this not more than two to three hours before serving so that the ice cream is still soft and smooth. The caramel syrup is a nice touch, but a simple raspberry or strawberry sauce is also good.

3 cups milk
1 cup heavy cream
1 vanilla bean, split
2 large eggs
3/4 cup granulated sugar
Pinch of salt
2 cups very well cooked long- or medium-grain
     white rice or Italian arborio rice

1. Combine the milk, cream, and vanilla bean in a medium-sized saucepan and scald. Remove the vanilla bean and cool slightly.

2. Whisk the eggs, sugar, and salt until light. Gradually whisk in the hot milk mixture. Return to the saucepan. Scrape the tiny vanilla seeds from inside the bean into the custard. Add the cooked rice and cook over low heat, stirring constantly, until thick enough to coat the back of a spoon, about 15 minutes. Cool the custard at room

temperature, stirring often. Press the custard through a food mill to break up the grains of rice. (The custard can be made ahead and refrigerated until ready to freeze in an ice-cream maker.)

3. Freeze the custard in an ice-cream maker according to the manufacturer's directions. Serve with caramel syrup (see recipe that follows) or other favorite sauce.

MAKES 1 (GENEROUS) QUART

Caramel Syrup

1 ½ cups granulated sugar
¼ cup lemon juice
¼ cup cold water
½ cup boiling water
2 tablespoons unsalted butter

1. Combine the sugar, lemon juice, and cold water in a heavy medium-sized saucepan or skillet. Heat to boiling, stirring, until the sugar dissolves.

2. Cook the syrup gently over medium-low heat, stirring occasionally, until the syrup turns a golden brown. Remove the saucepan from the heat.

3. Protecting your hand with a mitt and using a long-handled spoon, stir in the boiling water and butter until blended. Serve warm or at room temperature, thinning the sauce with a little more boiling water if necessary. (It will thicken while standing.)

MAKES ABOUT 1 ½ CUPS

Orange and Rice Crème Caramel

As these little gems bake, the rice settles to the bottom and absorbs the caramelized sugar. The result is a crown of golden caramel-soaked rice grains on the top of each unmolded pudding. The inspiration for orange-laced custard is from a recipe by Jane Helsel, an old friend and colleague from my Cuisine *magazine days.*

1 1/2 cups granulated sugar
1 cup half-and-half
1 cup milk
2 pieces (2 × 1/2 inch) orange zest
2 whole eggs
2 egg yolks
1 cup cooked medium- or long-grain white rice, imported
  basmati or American basmati-type white rice, or Italian
  arborio rice
1 tablespoon Grand Marnier or other orange-flavored liqueur
1 teaspoon vanilla extract

1. Heat the oven to 325°F. Have ready six 4-ounce ovenproof ceramic or glass custard cups and a baking pan large enough to use for the water bath. Heat a kettle of water to boiling for the water bath.

2. Over medium-low heat warm 1 cup of the sugar in a heavy skillet (about 10 inches in diameter) until the sugar begins to dissolve. Brush any granules down from the side of the skillet with a pastry brush dipped in a cup of water. Cook the syrup without stirring until it turns a golden caramel color. Pour a thin layer of the caramel in the bottom of the custard cups, dividing evenly, and set aside.

3. Scald the half-and-half, milk, and orange zest in a medium-sized saucepan. Remove from the heat.

4. Whisk the whole eggs, egg yolks, and remaining 1/2 cup of sugar in a bowl until light in color. Gradually whisk in half of the scalded milk. Add the remaining milk in a

slow steady stream. Strain the mixture back into the saucepan, discarding the orange zest.

5. Add the rice and cook over low heat, stirring constantly, until the rice is heated through and the mixture thickens just a little, about 3 minutes. Remove from the heat and let stand for 10 minutes. Stir in the Grand Marnier and vanilla.

6. With a slotted spoon divide the rice mixture evenly among the prepared custard cups. Fill the cups with the custard, dividing evenly. Place the baking pan with the custard cups on the middle rack of the oven. Add enough boiling water to the baking pan to come halfway up the sides of the custard cups. Bake for 35 minutes, or until the custard is set. Carefully lift the custard cups from the hot water and cool on a wire rack.

7. Refrigerate the custard cups until thoroughly chilled. To serve loosen the edges with a sharp knife and invert on individual dessert plates. (Note: To soften caramelized sugar that remains stuck to the bottom of the cups, heat in the microwave for 1 minute, or until the sugar melts, and pour over the inverted custards.)

MAKES 6 SERVINGS

Molasses and Rice Bran Fig Bars

I have a weakness for figs—fresh figs in the summer, the new crop of dried California figs in the early winter, and any kind of figs whenever I can get them. These fig bars are made with a layer of cooked-down dried figs sandwiched between a rich cookie dough that is fortified with a healthy dose of rice bran. The flavors are excellent, moist and chewy, so they are good keepers—that is, if you hide them from hungry snackers.

12 ounces figs, preferably a moist-packed California variety
1½ cups water
2 tablespoons dark molasses
½ cup natural (unblanched) almonds
1½ cups all-purpose flour
½ cup rice bran
½ cup packed light brown sugar
½ teaspoon baking powder
Pinch of salt
12 tablespoons (1½ sticks) cold unsalted butter, cut into small
    pieces
1 extra-large egg, beaten
½ teaspoon vanilla extract
Confectioner's sugar (optional)

1. Using kitchen shears cut off and discard the stem end from the figs, then cut the figs into ½-inch dice. Combine in a saucepan with the water and heat to boiling. Cook, covered, over medium-low heat, stirring occasionally and adjusting the heat to maintain a gentle simmer, until the figs are very soft and have absorbed most of the liquid, about 45 minutes. Cool slightly at room temperature. Place the figs, remaining cooking liquid, and molasses in the bowl of a food processor and puree until smooth. Spread on a large plate and refrigerate until cooled and stiff.

2. Meanwhile, grind the almonds in the food processor or with a Mouli hand

grater. Combine the nuts with the flour, rice bran, light brown sugar, baking powder, and salt in the bowl of a food processor and process until well blended.

3. With the motor running add the pieces of butter until the mixture is crumbly. Beat the egg and vanilla together in a cup. Add through the feed tube with the processor running and process just until a dough begins to form. Turn the dough out onto a work surface and divide into 2 even pieces. Flatten with floured hands, wrap in foil, and refrigerate until firm enough to handle, about 1 hour. (The dough will be soft before refrigerating.)

4. Heat the oven to 350°F. Lightly butter a 7 × 11-inch or 10-inch square baking pan.

5. Remove the dough from the refrigerator. Roll one piece with a lightly floured rolling pin into a shape just large enough to fit into the bottom of the prepared pan. Press the dough to the edges and into the corners of the pan with your fingertips. Mend any tears in the dough with your fingertips. Spread the fig mixture in an even layer, completely covering the dough. Prepare the top layer of dough and arrange on top of the fig mixture. Press very lightly to the edges and corners and repair any tears.

6. Bake until the edges of the dough begin to brown, about 25 to 30 minutes. Cool in the pan before cutting into bars and sprinkle with confectioner's sugar, if desired.

MAKES ABOUT 24 SMALL RECTANGULAR BARS

Mixed Dried Fruit and Nut Squares

The flavors in this snack can vary with whatever dried fruits you might have on hand. Use golden or dark raisins, muscat raisins, or dried cranberries (sometimes called crasins); or use diced dates, pitted prunes, or cut-up dried apples, apricots, or peaches in any configuration. I like the soft but chewy consistency of chopped walnuts here, but pecans would also be good. The rice bran adds a rich nutty flavor and lots of goodness.

1 cup all-purpose flour
1/2 cup rice bran
1/2 teaspoon ground cinnamon
1/2 teaspoon baking powder
1/4 teaspoon salt
8 tablespoons (1 stick) unsalted butter, melted
3 extra-large eggs
1 cup packed light brown sugar
1 teaspoon vanilla extract
2 cups diced (1/4-inch pieces) mixed dried fruit
2 cups chopped walnuts or pecans

1. Heat the oven to 350°F. Lightly butter a 13 × 9-inch baking pan and dust with flour, shaking out the excess.

2. In a large bowl stir together the flour, rice bran, cinnamon, baking powder, and salt. In a second bowl whisk the melted butter, eggs, brown sugar, and vanilla until blended.

3. Add the dried fruit and nuts to the dry ingredients and stir to coat. Add the butter mixture and stir until well blended.

4. Spread the batter in the prepared baking pan. Bake for 25 to 30 minutes, or until the batter is set and the edges begin to pull away from the sides of the pan. Cool on a rack before cutting into squares.

MAKES 20 SQUARES

Hot Rice with Fruit and Honey

Rice for breakfast is not such a far-flung idea when you consider the hundreds of rice-based cold cereals lining the shelves in supermarkets. To start with a pot of plain cooked rice and turn it into breakfast food is what I call real food. This begins with uncooked rice and will serve four for a hearty breakfast. As a variation omit the dried fruit and spoon sliced fresh strawberries, peaches, raspberries, or blueberries over the cereal before serving.

1 cup uncooked long-grain white rice
2¼ cups water
¼ cup diced dried pear, apricot, or apple (optional)
1 tablespoon unsalted butter
½ teaspoon salt
1 to 1½ cups milk or half-and-half
Honey to taste
Ground cinnamon (optional)
Thin slices of butter to taste (optional)
Sliced fresh fruit (optional)

1. Combine the rice, water, dried fruit, if using, butter, and salt in a medium-sized saucepan. Heat to boiling, stirring well, and cook, covered, over low heat until the rice is tender and the water is absorbed, about 15 to 20 minutes.

2. Add the milk or half-and-half and cook over low heat, stirring, until the rice is thick and creamy, about 5 minutes.

3. Spoon into bowls and drizzle with a spiral of honey. Sprinkle with cinnamon and add thin slivers of butter to melt on top of the cereal, if desired. Top with fresh fruit, if desired.

MAKES 4 SERVINGS

Brown Rice with Walnuts, Raisins, and Maple Syrup

Use either warm, freshly cooked brown rice or leftover brown rice for this recipe. A quick-cooking variety is also good here.

2 cups cooked short- or long-grain brown rice
2 cups milk
1/4 cup raisins
2 tablespoons broken walnuts, or to taste
1 tablespoon light brown sugar, or to taste
1 tablespoon unsalted butter (optional)
Warm maple syrup to taste

1. Combine the rice and milk in a medium-sized saucepan and heat to boiling. Cook over medium heat, stirring, until the mixture thickens, about 10 minutes. Stir in the raisins and cook for 5 minutes.

2. Spoon into bowls and sprinkle with walnuts and sugar, dividing evenly. Add a piece of cold butter, if desired, and drizzle with maple syrup. Serve warm.

MAKES 4 SERVINGS

Hot Oatmeal and Rice Cereal

My daughter, Stephanie, created this recipe.

1 cup water
½ cup regular cut oatmeal
½ cup leftover cooked white or brown rice
1 tablespoon raisins (optional)
Honey or maple syrup

1. In a small saucepan heat the water to boiling. Stir in the oatmeal and cook, stirring, for 3 minutes. Add the rice and cook, stirring, until the mixture is thickened. Stir in the raisins, if using.

2. Spoon into a bowl and drizzle with honey or maple syrup.

MAKES 1 SERVING

BASICS

Chicken Broth
Cooked Chicken
Chilies
Dried Beans
Herbs, Fresh and Dried
Manila Clams
Mussels
Mushrooms
Nuts
Olive Oil
Parmigiano-Reggiano
Red Bell Peppers
Saffron
Tomatoes
Tomato Sauce
Sautéed Tomatoes and Red Onions

Here are some basic recipes and bits of practical knowledge gleaned after many hours of cooking and thinking about food.

Chicken Broth

I prefer the subtle flavor of homemade chicken broth, although in a pinch unsalted and defatted canned broth will do. Add salt to taste to the finished dish.

How to Make Chicken Broth Collect the wing tips, backs, and necks from uncooked chicken and freeze in a heavy-duty zippered plastic bag until there are enough saved to make a pot of broth. Alternately, buy necks, backs, and wings to make broth as needed.

> 2 pounds chicken wings, backs, and/or necks
> Salt
> 1 small onion, halved
> 1 leafy inside rib of celery
> 1 small carrot or piece of a large carrot, trimmed and pared
> 1 clove garlic, bruised with the side of a knife
> 1 bay leaf

1. Rinse the chicken with cold running water and place in a large bowl. Add a generous pinch of salt and water to cover. Let stand for 10 minutes, then remove any fat or clumps of blood from the backs, if using. Drain well.

2. Combine the chicken, 3 quarts of water, onion, celery, carrot, garlic, and bay leaf in a large saucepan or stockpot. Heat over medium heat just until foam forms on the surface of the water; skim the foam with a slotted spoon.

3. Cook the broth over medium-low heat—do not boil—for 3 hours, or until the broth is fragrant. Set aside to cool. Set a large strainer over a bowl and carefully transfer the pieces of chicken and vegetable to the strainer and drain. Reserve the carrot for soup and discard the remaining solids or reserve them for other use. Pour the broth through the strainer and cool at room temperature.

4. Refrigerate until cold, preferably overnight. Lift the solid fat off the surface and discard. Do not stir the broth but ladle it into plastic containers. Discard the cloudy broth on the bottom of the bowl. Mark the amounts on the outside of the containers and freeze for future use. Freshly made broth will keep in the refrigerator up to 3 days.

MAKES ABOUT 8 CUPS

Cooked Chicken

Use the above recipe for chicken broth, substituting one 2¹/₂-pound whole chicken for the backs, necks, and wings and using 2 quarts of water. Simmer over medium-low heat for 1 hour, or until the juices run clear when the chicken is pierced with a fork. Carefully lift the chicken from the broth and cool at room temperature. Strain the broth as directed in the recipe above. The chicken will yield approximately 3 cups of boneless, skinless, and diced, shredded, or cubed cooked chicken for salad.

Chilies

There are many different types of chilies available. The three I use most frequently, from the smallest to the largest, are serrano, jalapeño, and poblano.

Although poblano chilies are mildly hot, they are not for those with a timid palate. All chili peppers—or at least those found in markets where I live—tend to vary in heat just like humans vary in temperament. Sometimes the same variety of pepper from the same box is very hot, mildly hot, or not hot at all. Since there is never a guarantee and the only way to find out is by taking a tiny taste, I usually buy three or four extra just so I can pick and choose after tasting. (Warning: Do not take a big bite. I usually place a tiny piece of chili on the tip of a finger and then gingerly taste with the tip of my tongue.)

How to Roast and Peel Poblano Chilies Roasting and peeling the poblano chilies is labor-intensive but not difficult. They can be prepared up to one day before using. Warning: I always protect my hands with rubber gloves or small plastic sandwich bags when working with chilies. The oils can take days to wash off your hands.

Preheat the broiler. Line a baking sheet with a large piece of foil, folding the ends under the baking sheet. Arrange the chilies on the baking sheet and broil 2 inches from the heat, turning the peppers often as they become charred and blackened. Remove from the oven, pull the foil up around the peppers to seal, and let stand until cool enough to handle. Peel off the loosened charred skins (remember to protect your hands with rubber gloves or plastic bags). Lay the skinned chilies out on a work surface and carefully make a cut (through one layer of chili) from stem to pointed end. Using the tip of a teaspoon carefully lift out the seeds. Don't be discouraged if the chilies tear or the stem end comes out of a few chiles. When they are stuffed and covered with sauce, no one will even know.

Dried Beans

Dried beans are becoming more and more popular as people rediscover how good they really are. The dryness and consequently the cooking time of the beans can vary. Actually, tasting the beans is the best way to determine if they are cooked. The suggested cooking time in the recipes is a guide; cook the beans longer, if necessary, adding more liquid as needed. Canned beans are excellent for salads, but I find the texture and flavor lacking when they are adapted to any of the slow-cooked bean dishes in this collection.

How to Soak Dried Beans Rinse the beans in a colander under running water, drain, and pick out any stones. Place the beans in a large bowl and cover generously with cold water. Soak overnight and drain before cooking. To speed up the process place the beans in a large saucepan and add plenty of water to cover. Heat to a rolling boil and boil for 1 minute. Let stand off the heat, covered, for 1 hour, then drain before cooking.

Herbs, Fresh and Dried

Fresh herbs, often available in supermarkets in convenient small packages, play an important part in my cooking. To keep herbs perky stand them in a small glass or jar filled with water and drape a plastic bag over the top before refrigerating. Change the water every few days, and the herbs will keep for at least a week, often longer. Fresh herbs make a wonderful garnish, so keep extras on hand and use them liberally. In the summer buy plants and grow them in pots.

The *dried herbs* I find acceptable are rosemary, thyme, and oregano. When substituting dried herbs for fresh, use about 1/2 teaspoon of thyme or oregano and 1 teaspoon of rosemary for 1 tablespoon of the fresh herb. To capture the most flavor from dried herbs chop them together with some fresh parsley. The parsley juice will help rehydrate the dried herbs before they are added to the dish. I love fresh basil so much that I would rather substitute another dried herb than use the bland, uninteresting dried version.

Manila Clams

Indigenous to the Orient, Manila clams, also known as the Japanese littleneck, are farm-raised throughout the Pacific Northwest and are sometimes available in the Northeast. They are small, anywhere from ³/₄ to 1¹/₂ inches in diameter, with pale orange, very sweet, tender meat. They are often used in Italian restaurants as a substitute for the tiny Mediterranean clam called *vongole*. I use them when littleneck clams are scarce and expensive. Usually free of sand, they only need to be rinsed in a couple of changes of cold water before cooking.

Mussels

Farm-raised mussels are raised in waters frequently tested for pollutants. They are almost always free of sand and grit, and are a favorite among mussel lovers. There are twenty to thirty mussels to a pound depending on their size; often sold in 2-pound bags, a bag is usually enough for four servings.

How to Store and Clean Mussels Remove the mussels from the plastic bag and refrigerate lightly covered with a damp paper towel if not using immediately. Just before cooking sort the mussels, tapping any slightly opened mussels with your finger until they begin to close. Discard any mussels that have cracked shells or that refuse to close up. Using your fingers pull off the threads (called beards). Wash thoroughly, rubbing any rough spots with a coarse brush. Soak in very cold fresh tap water for 5 to 10 minutes before cooking.

Mushrooms

Along with plain white button mushrooms, I also like to use the more exotic cultivated mushrooms now available in many supermarkets. Among my favorites are the shiitake, also called Golden Oak and Black Forest, with their almost meaty flavor, and the cremini, a cultivated Italian mushroom with a dark brown cap and an intense mushroom flavor. I never wash mushrooms but prefer brushing them lightly with a soft brush or wiping them with a dampened paper towel. Porcini are Italian wild mushrooms with a deep earthy flavor and robust aroma. Although fresh porcini are rarely available, we can compensate by substituting dried porcini, available in specialty shops and some supermarkets.

Nuts

Toasted nuts have a more intense nut flavor. Toast 1 to 2 tablespoons of pignoli (pine nuts), chopped walnuts, or sliced almonds by stirring in a dry skillet over low heat until golden and fragrant. For larger amounts of almonds, walnuts, pecans, or hazelnuts, spread in a baking pan and toast in a 350° F. oven, stirring once or twice, for 10 to 15 minutes, or until golden. To peel toasted hazelnuts, wrap them in a roughly textured kitchen towel and let stand until cooled. Briskly rub the hazelnuts to remove as much of the skin as possible. Nuts can be roasted and stored in an air-tight container at room temperature until needed.

Olive Oil

I am passionate on the subject of olive oil and use it almost exclusively in my cooking except for rare recipes where I want the sweet milky flavor of butter. Today consumers can find a wide selection on their supermarket shelves of both the more expensive extra-virgin olive oils and the less expensive pure olive oils. When buying extra-virgin olive oil, buy for taste, not price. I like the full rich flavor of Italian olive oils, although many excellent oils from Spain are also widely available. I use extra-virgin oil in salads, as a seasoning or condiment, or whenever the fruity flavor of the olive is important to the finished dish. I sometimes use the lighter-tasting pure olive oil for cooking, especially when the flavor of the oil is not essential to the recipe or when I think the robust olive flavor of an extra-virgin oil will be intrusive. A product called light olive oil is pure olive oil with all the flavor removed; it was invented for the American consumer who wants the monounsaturated benefits of olive oil but does not want the olive flavor. I never use it.

Parmigiano-Reggiano

Cheese made exclusively from milk produced in a legally defined region including Parma, Reggio Emilia and Modena, and parts of Mantua and Bologna is called Parmigiano-Reggiano. It is a hard cheese that seems to melt in your mouth and has a flavor that is full and rich without being strong. It is a staple in my kitchen. Buy wedges of Parmigiano-Reggiano—look for the name stamped on the rind—and wrap them in plastic wrap; grate the cheese as needed. When a wedge of the cheese has been consumed, I wipe the outside of the rind with a damp cloth and then freeze it in a heavy-duty zippered plastic bag until needed. Small pieces of the rind (the air-hardened outside of the cheese) cook up soft and chewy in slowly simmering soups and stews.

Red Bell Peppers

Red bell peppers are among the top ten of my favorite ingredients. I usually indulge lavishly when locally grown or California red peppers are in season, so I don't have to pay air freight from Holland.

How to Roast, Peel, and Marinate Red Bell Peppers Preheat the broiler. Arrange a large sheet of aluminum foil in a baking pan just large enough to hold the peppers. Broil the peppers about 2 inches from the heat, turning as they become charred, until they are evenly blackened. Remove from the broiler. Fold the foil around the peppers and let them stand until cool enough to handle, about 30 minutes. Working over the foil to save the pepper juices, carefully peel off the charred skin and quarter the peppers, discarding the stems, seeds, and any thick inside ribs. Do not rinse the peppers (it rinses off the flavor), but carefully remove any stubborn seeds with the tip of a knife. Strain the juice left in the foil and use to keep the peppers moist. Peppers can also be roasted over a charcoal or gas grill. In a pinch you can use jarred red peppers: Drain off the liquid, rinse them, and add extra-virgin olive oil for flavor.

To marinate roasted peppers, sprinkle with salt, a grinding of black pepper, and fresh thyme, oregano, or basil leaves removed from the stem. Coat generously with olive oil. Marinate at room temperature for one hour before serving. When refrigerated and tightly covered, marinated roasted red peppers will keep for up to two weeks.

Saffron

This orange-colored stigma of the crocus flower is best known for the color and aroma it imparts to the paella of Spain and the classic risotto alla Milanese of northern Italy. The harvesting and processing is so labor-intensive that it is reputed to be the most expensive spice in the world. Fortunately a few threads of saffron go a long way. I use a pinch, which to my eye means about five or six threads. Saffron is also available powdered, but someone once told me that saffron in its powdered form is sometimes diluted with other spices by unscrupulous merchants. This may or may not be the case, and I would certainly trust the powdered form purchased from any of the large domestic spice companies. To extract the ultimate flavor from the delicate threads of saffron, they should first be heated. One of the simplest ways to do this is to steep the threads in a small amount of boiling water or broth.

Tomatoes

Where I live, beautiful, lush, ripe tomatoes are available only two or three months of the year. Rather than struggle with less flavorful specimens the rest of the year, I use canned Italian-style plum tomatoes. The imported Italian tomatoes grown and packed in the San Marzano region of Italy have an excellent flavor, but if I can't find them, I experiment with other brands until I find firm red tomatoes with good flavor. Canned tomatoes are mostly available in 14- and 14½-ounce, 16-ounce, and 28-ounce cans. Tomatoes packed in juice rather than puree have a lighter, fresher tomato flavor. I often puree canned tomatoes in a food mill to pulverize them and to remove the stem ends and seeds. If you don't have a food mill, you can puree the tomatoes in batches in a food processor or blender and then press through a sieve.

Tomato Sauce

This is a good, basic, and multi-useful quick tomato sauce. I use this sauce seasoned with fresh parsley and basil, with a spoonful of finely chopped sun-dried tomatoes with 1 cup of sautéed fresh mushrooms, with 2 tablespoons of minced prosciutto or pancetta, or with minced reconstituted dried porcini mushrooms with their soaking liquid. The recipe can easily be doubled or tripled. Make extra and store in the freezer.

2 tablespoons olive oil
¼ cup chopped sweet red onion
1 small clove garlic, crushed
2 cups peeled and coarsely chopped tomatoes *or* 1 can (14½
    ounces) Italian-style plum tomatoes with juice
Salt and freshly ground black pepper to taste
2 tablespoons chopped fresh basil or parsley or other fresh
    herbs to taste

1. Heat the oil in a large skillet. Add the onion and sauté for 5 minutes. Add the garlic and sauté for 1 minute.

2. Stir in the tomatoes and heat to boiling. Cook over low heat, stirring frequently and breaking up the tomatoes with the side of a spoon, until the mixture is thickened, about 15 minutes. Season with salt, pepper, and basil or parsley. Set aside. (This can be made up to 2 days ahead.)

MAKES ABOUT 1½ CUPS

Sautéed Tomatoes and Red Onions

Serve this fresh-tasting sauté with a frittata or on freshly cooked rice.

1 tablespoon olive oil
$\frac{1}{2}$ medium-sized red onion, cut into $\frac{1}{4}$-inch-thick wedges
   (about $\frac{1}{2}$ cup)
1 small clove garlic, crushed or finely chopped
6 to 8 ripe plum tomatoes, cut into $\frac{1}{4}$-inch-thick wedges
Salt and freshly ground black pepper to taste
Torn fresh basil leaves

1. Heat the oil in a small skillet. Add the onion and garlic, and sauté, stirring occasionally, until crisp-tender, about 2 minutes.

2. Add the tomatoes, cover, and cook over low heat until the tomatoes are soft, about 5 minutes. Season with salt and pepper. Add the basil to taste. Serve spooned over wedges of frittata.

MAKES ABOUT 2 CUPS

MAIL ORDER SOURCES

Dried Fruit and Nuts

American Spoon Foods, Inc.
1015 East Mitchell
Petosky, MI 49770
Tel.: (616) 347-9030

Timber Crest Farms
4791 Dry Creek Road
Healdsburg, CA 95448
Tel.: (707) 433-8251
Fax: (707) 433-8255

Wild Rice

Gibbs Wild Rice
P.O. Box 387
Live Oak, CA 95953
Tel.: (800) 344-6378 *or*
(800) 824-4932

Rice Bran, Rice Flour, and Other
Rice Products

Ener-G Foods
P.O. Box 84487
Seattle, WA 98108
Tel.: (800) 331-5222

Aromatic Rices

Texmati (American basmati-type rice)
P. O. Box 1305
Alvin, TX 77512
Tel.: (713) 393-3502 *or*
(800) 232-7423

Douget-Dishman Rice Company
(jasmine rice)
795 S. Major Drive
Beaumont, TX 77707
Tel.: (409) 866-2297

Lundberg Family Farms (American
basmati-type and Wehani)
Box 369
Richvale, CA 95974-0369
Tel.: (916) 882-4551

Gourmet Rice
Ellis Stansel
P. O. Box 206
Gueydan, LA 70542
Tel.: (318) 536-6140

BIBLIOGRAPHY

Anderson, Jean. *The Food of Portugal*. New York: William Morrow and Company, Inc., 1986.

Andoh, Elizabeth. *At Home with Japanese Cooking*. New York: Alfred A. Knopf, 1980.

Bastianich, Lidia, and Jacobs, Jay. *La Cucina di Lidia*. New York: Doubleday, 1990.

Bhumichitr, Vatcharin. *The Taste of Thailand*. New York: Atheneum, 1988.

De' Medici, Lorenza. *The Renaissance of Italian Cooking*. New York: Fawcett Columbine, 1989.

Dethloff, Henry C. *A History of the American Rice Industry 1685–1985*. College Station, Texas: Texas A & M University Press, 1988.

Fabricant, Florence. "Reaping Wild Rice by Machine or Hand," *The New York Times*, October 30, 1985.

Fehr, Walter R. *Principles of Cultivar Development*. New York: Macmillan Publishing, 1987.

Grist, D. H. *Rice*. Third Edition. London: Longmans, Green and Company, Ltd., 1959.

Jones, Evan. *American Food: The Gastronomic Story*. New York: Random House, 1975.

Juliano, B. O. *Rice Chemistry and Technology*. Second Edition. St. Paul: American Association of Cereal Chemists, 1985.

Law, Ruth. *Southeast Asia Cookbook*. New York: Donald I. Fine, Inc., 1990.

Luard, Elisabeth. *The Old World Kitchen: The Rich Tradition of European Peasant Cooking*. New York: Bantam Books, 1987.

McGee, Harold. *On Food and Cooking—the Science and Lore of the Kitchen*. New York: Charles Scribner's Sons, 1984.

Paul, Pauline C., and Palmer, Helen H. *Food Theory and Applications*. New York: John Wiley & Sons, 1972.

Root, Waverley, and de Rochemont, Richard. *Eating in America: A History*. New York: William Morrow and Company, Inc., 1976.

Sahni, Julie. *Classic Indian Vegetarian and Grain Cooking*. New York: William Morrow and Company, Inc., 1985.

Simeti, Mary Taylor. *Pomp and Sustenance*. New York: Alfred A. Knopf, 1989.

Smith, Julia Floyd. *Slavery and Rice Culture in Low Country Georgia, Seventeen Fifty to Eighteen Sixty*. Knoxville: University of Tennessee Press, 1985.

Sokolov, Raymond. *Fading Feast*. New York: Farrar, Straus & Giroux, 1981.

Sokolov, Raymond. "A Small World in a Cooking Pot," *Natural History*, December, 1988.

Tannahill, Reay. *Food in History*. New York: Stein and Day Publishers, 1973.

Taylor, John Martin. "Carolina Gold: A Rare Harvest," *The New York Times*, December 28, 1988.

Visser, Margaret. *Much Depends on Dinner*. New York: Grove, 1986.

Willson, Jack H., *Rice in California*. Richvale, California: Butte County Rice Growers Association, 1979.

Yin-Fei Lo, Eileen. *New Cantonese Cooking*. New York: Viking, 1988.

INDEX